Confederate Exceptionalism

CULTUREAMERICA

Erika Doss
Philip J. Deloria
Series Editors

Karal Ann Marling
Editor Emerita

Confederate Exceptionalism

Civil War Myth and Memory
in the Twenty-First Century

Nicole Maurantonio

University Press of Kansas

Published by the University Press of Kansas (Lawrence, Kansas 66045),
which was organized by the Kansas Board of Regents and is operated and
funded by Emporia State University, Fort Hays State University, Kansas
State University, Pittsburg State University, the University of Kansas, and
Wichita State University.

Library of Congress Cataloging-in-Publication Data

Names: Maurantonio, Nicole, author.
Title: Confederate exceptionalism : Civil War myth and memory in the
    twenty-first century / Nicole Maurantonio.
Description: Lawrence : University Press of Kansas, [2019] | Series:
    CultureAmerica | Includes bibliographic references and index.
Identifiers: LCCN 2019019338
    ISBN 9780700628698 (cloth)
    ISBN 9780700628704 (ebook)
Subjects: LCSH: Exceptionalism–Confederate States of America. | Collective
    memory–Confederate States of America. | Material culture–Confederate
    States of America. | White supremacy movements–United States. |
    Racism–United States. | United States–History–Civil War,
    1861–1865–Influence.
Classification: LCC E489 .M38 2019 | DDC 973.7–dc23
LC record available at https://lccn.loc.gov/2019019338.

British Library Cataloguing-in-Publication Data is available.

Printed in the United States of America

10 9 8 7 6 5 4 3 2 1

The paper used in this publication is recycled and contains 30 percent
postconsumer waste. It is acid free and meets the minimum requirements of
the American National Standard for Permanence of Paper for Printed Library
Materials Z39.48–1992.

To my parents
and Justin, with love

Contents

Acknowledgments

This book has an origin story about which you will soon read, tethered to my experiences over the past eight years in Richmond, Virginia. During this time, countless people have supported, encouraged, and motivated me as the project moved to completion. It is with tremendous gratitude that I acknowledge them here.

While this book did not begin as my doctoral dissertation, it nonetheless owes a great debt to my PhD advisor, Barbie Zelizer. I first met Barbie when I was a University of Virginia (UVA) undergraduate visiting the University of Pennsylvania as a prospective student in the history graduate program. Little did I know, that chance meeting would dramatically shape my academic life and career. I am extraordinarily thankful for her generosity as a scholar and mentor.

This book was most immediately prompted by experiences following an afternoon spent with colleagues at the University of Richmond (UR) on a faculty excursion coordinated through the Bonner Center for Civic Engagement. Led by Jeannine Keefer and Erling Sjovold, our travel to various sites throughout the city, meditating on architecture, nature, and art followed by dinner, prompted a series of questions about my surroundings. Few work-related experiences have had such a profound effect. I extend sincere thanks to Terry Dolson and Sylvia Gale for not only this opportunity but also continued chances to connect and learn with and in the city of Richmond.

Since beginning my job at UR, I have had the opportunity to teach courses on public memory in Richmond, enabling me to share this research as it has evolved with phenomenal students. A special thank-you to Meghan Benner, Emily Bradford, Victoria Charles, Ayele d'Almeida, Dom Harrington, Madeleine Jordan-Lord, Alyssa Joyce, Elizabeth Mejía-Ricart, Kristi Mukk, Jennifer Munnings, Claire Noppenberger, Mysia Perry, Benjamin Pomerantz, Destiny Riley, Jacob Roberson, Cory Schutter, Molly Silvia, and Shira Smillie.

Working on the Race & Racism at the University of Richmond Project has been one of the most rewarding teaching experiences I have had, leading to a series of collaborations both within and outside UR. Project archivist Irina Rogova shared relevant articles and links to help me grow my own archive of source materials. Free Egunfemi and Kelley Libby reminded me what it means to be a good listener and true community partner. Chelsea Higgs Wise and Ryan Rinn have been more recent Richmond partners with whom I have shared this project and from whom, I have no doubt, I will continue to learn.

Over the years this book has benefited from the support of numerous colleagues who have encouraged different stages of this project, provided me with readings, and celebrated when various deadlines were met. It is an honor to work with Bert Ashe, Tim Barney, Alexandra Byrum, Jordana Cox, Monti Datta, Alicia Díaz, Joanna Drell, Jan French, Eva Hageman, Julian Hayter, Glyn Hughes, Atiya Husain, Lynda Kachurek, Lauranett Lee, Martha Merritt, Mari Lee Mifsud, Derek Miller, Rob Nelson, Melissa Ooten, Nicole Sackley, Nabeel Siddiqui, Monika Siebert, Andrea Simpson, Lauren Tilton, Armond Towns, Helen Williams, Doug Winiarski, and Eric Yellin.

A very special thanks to Eric Grollman, Bedelia Richards, and Sojourna Cunningham, who provided helpful advice and indispensable citations as I navigated language usage choices. Sam Schuth in Interlibrary Loan and Ryan Brazell in the Center for Teaching, Learning, and Technology helped me secure valuable source materials as well as answer technical and technological questions. Patricia Herrera offered feedback on some of this book's earliest and draftiest versions. Amy Howard has been not only a keen reader of this manuscript but a kind listener and thought partner. Laura Browder has read more drafts of this book than is probably good for anyone. Our writing group was crucial to moving me to the finish line. Simply put, I am privileged to have brilliant colleagues whom I have come to call friends.

Outside UR, I am grateful for a group of dear friends who, while I don't see them as often as I would like, have been there for important milestones to cheer me on. Thank you to René Alvarez, Anne Casey, Mike Fix, Laura Keenan Spero, and Pat Spero.

Over the past several years, I have participated in a number of seminars and institutes that have been critical to my thinking about the Confederacy and the contemporary moment. In June 2015, as news broke of the Charleston massacre, I sat in Patricia Williams's "Racial Formations and Justice Today" seminar at the New School's Institute for Critical Social Inquiry. That week has remained a powerful backdrop for this project. The NEH Summer Institute, "Recognizing an Imperfect Past: History, Memory, and the American Public," convened by Stan Deaton at the Georgia Historical Society in June 2017, provided an auspicious start to my sabbatical year. The Arc of Racial Justice Institute, Faculty Humanities

Seminar, and International Faculty Seminar to South Africa were formative experiences supported by the University of Richmond.

This project has developed in important ways due to feedback received
at various conferences and symposia, including the "Troubling Histories:
Public Art and Prejudice" symposium at the University of Johannesburg,
the "Falling Monuments, Reluctant Ruins" conference sponsored by the
History Workshop at the University of Witwatersrand, and the "Confederate Memorials: Considering Ways Forward" forum at Wofford College,
as well as meetings of the National Communication Association, International Communication Association (ICA), and Organization of American
Historians. Conversations with Trina Jones, Karen Goodchild, and Ron
Robinson at Wofford College helped me further refine my thinking on
the topic of sacred relics, while impromptu meals with Carolyn Kitch and
Carolyn Marvin in Prague at ICA provided additional insights, which I
have sought to incorporate. A public presentation at Virginia Humanities
on Little Sorrel and taxidermy led to a later conversation with my UR
colleague Ed Ayers for a segment of *BackStory*. I thank Ed for this opportunity.

Much of my writing took place during a yearlong sabbatical. This time
would not have been possible without the financial assistance of Virginia
Humanities and the University of Richmond. I thank Patrice Rankine,
dean of the School of Arts and Sciences at UR, and the Board of Trustees
for granting me leave to work on this book as well as the Faculty Research
Committee for providing summer funding. A generous subvention from
the School of Arts and Sciences and Department of Rhetoric and Communication Studies at UR supported this book. I am grateful to Virginia
Humanities Senior Fellow William W. Freehling for supporting my work
through the Edna and Normal Freehling Fellowship in South Atlantic
Studies. At Virginia Humanities, Jeanne Siler was a source of constant
energy, sending me articles and news of events in Charlottesville. During
my fellowship year, I had the privilege of being part of a vibrant cohort
of fellows, including Alison Bell, Keith Clark, Lulu Miller, and Earl Swift.

While housed at the Library of Virginia (LVA) in Richmond during my
fellowship, I not only had access to extraordinary resources but also the
opportunity to work with a cadre of wonderful historians, archivists, and
librarians. Weekly lunches with John Deal, Mari Julienne, Matt Gottlieb,
Brent Tarter, and my fellow Fellow Kristen Green included lively conversation and food for thought. I owe special thanks to Brent for bringing his
knowledge of Virginia and Virginia history to earlier drafts of this book,
and to Kristen for reminding me that the research and writing process
need not be a solitary endeavor. In special collections at the LVA, Dale

Neighbors and Audrey McElhinney shared their expertise and indulged my sometimes unusual archival requests. Bill Gilliam provided me with important context as I ventured into the history of picture postcards. Steve Rogers, collection manager for the Section of Birds at the Carnegie Museum of Natural History, shared expertise on the history of taxidermy in the United States.

This book would not have been possible without the help of many of the people referenced in the following pages. Thank you Teresa Roane, Sgt. Maj. James Haymes, Karen Cooper, Barry Isenhour, Susan Hathaway, Keith Gibson, and Goad Gatsby, along with many more people with whom I spoke or had the opportunity to observe.

In Johannesburg at the "Troubling Histories" symposium I met Erika Doss, who took an interest in this project and encouraged me to share more of my work. I am extraordinarily grateful to her and Phil Deloria for their faith in this book. I am humbled to be part of this series, whose books have long lined my shelves. Kim Hogeland at the University Press of Kansas graciously helped me navigate this process, offering welcome suggestions and (less welcome but no less necessary) deadlines. Kelly Chrisman Jacques, Lori Rider, and Michael Kehoe have each helped shepherd this project along in different ways. Matthew Mace Barbee and Robert Cook offered incisive feedback and suggestions on earlier versions of this manuscript. I am especially grateful to Sonya Clark for allowing me to use *Black Hair Flag* for the cover of this book. Her works continue to be an inspiration.

I am extremely fortunate to have a most dedicated family and supportive friends. My parents, Nicholas and Jacqueline Maurantonio, asked difficult questions as I worked on this project, helping me shape this book with them in mind. Our family trips taken in our minivan form some of my fondest and most poignant childhood memories, instilling in me not only a love for history but also an appreciation for the power of storytelling. I am proud to share this book with them. Rosie Maurantonio, Ben Malowski, Laura Maurantonio, and Bryan Forst have responded to the different stages of this process with welcome distractions and corresponding bitmojis. Ed and Judy Alexander have not only welcomed me into their family but also encouraged me and this project, particularly as it moved toward completion. Joseph Schwartz has talked through every methodological challenge, question, and complication this project has wrought. He has listened and, as always, helped me troubleshoot with characteristic humor. Crisotomo Gouveia shared sources as he happened upon them—sources that I came to incorporate in this book—reminding me that history can be bizarre. My companion on my first tour of the White House of the Confederacy, Kyle Roberts, has seen this project both in person and on the printed page. He has read drafts, offered feedback, and encouraged me to keep plugging away, as only the best of friends do.

Finally, my husband, Justin Alexander, has seen this project through its many ups and downs yet remains its (and my) greatest fan. He has come to my office with pizza and our beloved dog, Boo, to give me the chance to write. He has made me laugh when I most needed it. He has even joined me on some of my research trips throughout the state, despite his own dizzying schedule. Most significantly, he has believed in me and this project even when I had my doubts. I am grateful to have such a loving and caring partner, whose many talents far exceed my own. I share this book with him, with love.

A Note on Language Usage

Given this book's focus on the ways in which the Confederacy and its attendant discourses have become normalized in public culture, I have made a series of choices in this text about which I aim to be transparent.

First, I capitalize "Black" in order to reference "a culture, ethnicity or group of people."[1] However, I capitalize the term in neither printed quotations nor the interviews from which I draw. Contrary to some style manuals, I do not capitalize "white." As historian Martha Biondi notes, the term "white" has been "deployed as a signifier of social domination and privilege, rather than as an indicator of ethnic or national origin."[2] While the decision to keep "white" lowercase may lead to a "typographical inequality,"[3] it is a move I nonetheless embrace in an effort to work toward dismantling white supremacy culture.

Also, throughout the book, I reference "enslaved people" rather than "slaves" as a reminder that being enslaved was a condition imposed on men, women, and children rather than an innate characteristic of their existence. I use the term "enslaver" rather than "master" to similarly connote individual agency. Persons enslaved others. This practice needs to be named.[4] In cases where I have used the terms "slave" or "master," I place them in quotes to reference the "faithful slave" or "loyal slave" narrative that constitutes a defining feature of Lost Cause mythology, along with the "benevolent master."

Finally, I reference "Black people," "Black men," "Black women," "Black children," or other Black individuals rather than employ the phrases "African Americans" or "blacks" in text, unless I am citing a direct quote.[5] My decision to do so stems from an effort to be more inclusive, recognizing the complexity surrounding individual and collective identities as well as the ethnic and cultural diversity among Black people around the world.

While I have sought advice from scholars across the disciplines as I made these choices, any errors in the text are mine alone.

Racism doesn't start, nor will it end, because of some statues on a tree-lined street—it resides in hearts and minds.

And the way to change hearts is to educate minds.

—Richmond mayor Levar Stoney announcing the appointment of the Monument Avenue Commission, June 22, 2017

Preface: Confederates on My Corner

When I arrived in Richmond, Virginia, in August 2010, I had in mind a particular image of the city I was to call my new home. I imagined a city steeped in the past—celebrated in places I had read about like the hallowed Monument Avenue and witnessed firsthand on family vacations south of the Mason-Dixon Line. I recalled fondly the bucolic southern landscape I had witnessed—the Blue Ridge Mountains, Monticello, the Biltmore House—on trips that led my family down the I-95 corridor in our blue minivan from the pothole-laden Belt Parkway leaving Long Island. A far cry from the trafficked highways of the North, the South was more deliberate, less frenetic. There was a peacefulness, a calm that sharply contrasted with my experiences in the suburbs of New York City.

These family trips south were enchanting, if a bit disarming. I was not used to strangers smiling at me. As a middle school student, I assumed what I witnessed was what many referred to as "southern hospitality." It surprised me nearly as much as references to "Mr. [Thomas] Jefferson" in Charlottesville, as if the third president of the United States were a friendly, albeit revered, neighbor whom you might run into on a quiet walk. That sense of history, of tradition, was captivating. It was part of what drew me to the University of Virginia (UVA) in the late 1990s as an undergraduate. Of course, in high school I had read Margaret Mitchell's epic *Gone with the Wind*, and later I watched popular Hollywood movies set in southern towns, such as *Sweet Home Alabama* starring Reese Witherspoon—films that only reinforced a sense of the South's quaint contrast to the urban centers of the North that I had come to know so well.

When I stepped on Grounds as a first-year student at UVA in August 1998, that mythology had already begun to unravel for me.[1] My college years hastened the process. I read Thomas Jefferson's *Notes on the State of Virginia*, which divulged the venerated president's views on the inferiority of Africans, and later Dr. Martin Luther King Jr.'s "Letter from Birmingham Jail." I learned about massive resistance, a Virginia policy adopted to block public school desegregation mandated by the landmark Supreme Court decision *Brown v. Board of Education of Topeka, Kansas*.[2] I watched the PBS documentary *Eyes on the Prize* about the civil rights movement, with its haunting images of southern violence—the still of Emmett Till's mutilated corpse and the video of the smug white perpetrators of the Black teenager's murder.

The intervening years in graduate school at the University of Pennsylvania further expanded my understandings of slavery and its legacies. The latter seemed to come to life as I rode the SEPTA regional rail along the Northeast Corridor to visit my family in New York. Passing through Trenton and Newark, once thriving urban centers, I witnessed the aftershocks of competing historic forces: white flight, immigration, segregation, and dwindling employment opportunities. It had been Philadelphia's story as well.

Thus, while I knew I would not be met with Scarlett O'Hara's romanticized antebellum Tara on my arrival in Richmond, the city I confronted on stepping off the plane from Boston on that hot and humid August day was even more familiar than I anticipated. As I drove my economy rental car down Broad Street, Richmond's once-bustling commercial thoroughfare, I was met with a series of empty storefronts, lines of chain restaurants, and strip malls. Hardly mirroring the fields of green and elegant estates I had pictured in my mind, Broad Street bore all the markers of the quintessential postindustrial city. I was met with the reality that the South I had imagined was more than a mosaic of family vacations, popular culture, and nostalgic college memories. It was in fact the product of a well-curated set of messages packaged predominantly, though not exclusively, for white, middle-class northerners like myself[3]—messages that had been circulating and internalized for more than a century.[4]

The greatest culture shock I experienced as a recent transplant from Boston, however, occurred just months after my arrival. Across the street from my apartment in Richmond's historic Fan district, in front of the Virginia Museum of Fine Arts (VMFA), a small gathering of men and women waved Confederate battle flags, carrying signs proclaiming "Heritage Not Hate." They were mostly, but not exclusively, older (60+) and white. The group, known as the Virginia Flaggers, became a more permanent fixture of the landscape I observed—never "normalized" but ever present. I would come to think of them as the "Confederates on my corner," drawing from the work of Pulitzer Prize–winning journalist Tony Horwitz.[5] The Flaggers define their members as those who will "stand with our flags against those in opposition in a peaceful, yet forceful manner, to educate and inform the general public, and in open and visible protest against those who attacked us, our flags, our ancestors, or our Heritage."[6] The Flaggers appeared like clockwork on Thursday and Saturday afternoons to protest the VMFA's 2010 decision to remove the Confederate battle flag from the front of Pelham Memorial Chapel, the Confederate chapel on museum grounds. At the turn of the twentieth century, the grounds had been home to the Lee Camp No. 1, an organization for Confederate veterans. It remained as such until the last local veteran died in 1941, at which point the grounds became property of the state.

The Flaggers sought the reinstatement of the Confederate battle flag in an effort to "restore" history. Their commitment to this endeavor reminded me of a scene I had witnessed more than a decade earlier at UVA where Charlottesville residents passionately denied that "Mr. Jefferson" had fathered children with an enslaved woman, Sally Hemings, despite overwhelming DNA and textual evidence proving the contrary.[7] The Flaggers, like those enraged Charlottesville residents, were not protesting for a more accurate rendering of history. Rather, they were enmeshed in a complex struggle over memory.

One Saturday morning while walking my dog in April 2014, I broke my pattern of avoidance of the Virginia Flaggers and struck up a conversation with a white man, who I would estimate was in his sixties, wearing jeans and a shirt printed with a Confederate battle flag. The man handed me a flyer and proceeded to explain why he was wearing that battle flag. When given the opportunity to introduce myself, I shared that I was a professor of rhetoric and communication studies at the University of Richmond, and that I studied memory cultures. I gave Barry Isenhour, the Flagger in question, my contact information and told him he could "friend" me on Facebook.

Before returning to my house, I stopped to speak with another protester mere feet from the Flaggers, this one an "anti-Flagger." A white rapper/DJ in the Richmond music scene, Goad Gatsby is a hipster with a trucker cap, handlebar mustache, red plaid flannel shirt, and cutoff black denim shorts.[8] Carrying a sign reading "Not My Flag," while standing next to the amp he brought to the site on his bicycle, Gatsby explained his rationale for standing next to the Flaggers: disruption. They could not think straight with the lyrics of rapper Kanye West blaring in their ears, he said. This was, of course, years before West would announce his belief that slavery was a choice—an irony I could not have recognized then.[9] I gave Gatsby my Facebook information as well.

Days later, I received a message from Gatsby informing me that a photograph had been posted to the Virginia Flaggers Facebook group by Flagger photographer Judy Smith. The photograph, taken without my knowledge while I was speaking with Isenhour, was captioned "Changing Hearts and Minds . . ." When Gatsby sent me the note, the photograph had fifty-five "likes" and two comments. The first was "History 101 taught by Barry Isenhour." The second was "She looks like an Obummerite spoiling for a fight?"

What I had thought of as a set of innocent questions posed to Isenhour had been received, at least by members of the Facebook group, as a hostile attack. What had I done to communicate hostility? Was it the fact that my hand was on my hip? Was it my dog's disinterested stance? While it seemed that "Obummerite" was a pejorative reference to an Obama supporter, what had led the commenters to that assumption? I certainly had shared nothing of my politics. I presumed that such assumptions stemmed from my association with the University of Richmond, hardly a liberal bastion, but nonetheless made up of academics, more than a few of whom had drawn the Flaggers' ire.

I had been implicated in a moment of "Confederate conversion" without my consent. Through the production and circulation of that photograph with its caption, my interaction with Isenhour had been imbued with meaning that ran counter to my understanding of the exchange. The photograph had been reanimated as a battle between knowledge (Isenhour) and ignorance (me), conservatism and liberalism, South and North.[10] The photograph was a frieze of a battle that I had, at the time, seen as an exemplar of a common assumption that southerners are "still fighting" the Civil War. It seemed to provide evidence of yet another cliché.

These early experiences in Richmond compelled me to confront the extent to which I had internalized a series of at times competing messages cultivated about the South and the Confederacy. I was intimately familiar with the so-called moonlight and magnolias tradition, romanticizing "Dixie" as the consummate exemplar of rural pastoralism. At the same time, I was familiar with the history that undergirded what legal historian Michelle Alexander famously labeled "the New Jim Crow," its legacies evidenced in the carceral state in America.[11] I had seen D. W. Griffith's (1915) *Birth of a Nation,* and I had read Langston Hughes's 1949 poem "One-Way Ticket," in which he expresses his fear of cruel people and his frustration with Jim Crow and with lynching, proclaiming "Any place that is North and East—And not Dixie."[12] While I knew racism persisted in the North and West, woven into the fabric of the nation's educational system, housing codes, and criminal justice system, to name just a few institutions, my initial readings of the photograph of Barry and me, with its particular caption, crystallized precisely how what many have dubbed "the myth of southern exceptionalism" had been embedded in my own imagination.

Cast as "an epic showdown," historians Matthew Lassiter and Joseph

Crespino note, between "the retrograde South and a progressive na-tion,"[13] the myth of southern exceptionalism holds, following historian C. Vann Woodward, that the South's experience of "poverty, failure, defeat, and . . . skepticism about 'progress'" led to the formation of a uniquely backward and racist South.[14] What became increasingly clear to me, how-ever, was that the myth propagated a false dichotomy. The "American Dilemma" to which Gunnar Myrdal famously referred in the 1940s, iden-tifying persistent racial inequality in the United States, was not a uniquely southern phenomenon.[15] While performed regionally, what I was in fact observing was a discourse that transcended its locale. Standing outside the VMFA on that Saturday in April 2014, the Flaggers could just as easily be found in my home state, where the United Daughters of the Confed-eracy (UDC), surprisingly, has "deep roots."[16] My exchange with Isenhour was less about the South per se than it was about the Confederacy and the mythology surrounding this historical, mediated, and consumable entity.

That chance meeting outside the VMFA turned out to be the first of many conversations with Isenhour. On receiving a copy of the Facebook photograph from Gatsby, I decided to pursue Isenhour and the Flaggers further in an attempt to better understand the processes by and circum-stances under which the stories they told of the Confederacy had taken shape. This move led me to follow a number of individuals and groups throughout the state of Virginia who advocate on behalf of Confederate memory at a moment when so-called Confederate culture[17] has become an even more contested and visible part of the landscape. This book is my effort to make sense of what I observed. My approach has been interdis-ciplinary in its method and in its selection of case studies. Throughout, I have sought to accord my subjects with respect, despite at times being the object of mockery myself.

Contrary to my initial, dismissive impulse, what I had witnessed in that Facebook photograph of Isenhour and me was not a frieze of a trite bat-tle—an attempt to relive the Civil War. While I had indeed been standing on contested ground when I first met Isenhour outside the VMFA and the Confederate chapel, what I had witnessed in that Facebook photograph was a complex rhetorical move: a strategic poaching of my body in an at-tempt to narrate a past that never took place—at least not as indicated by the photo's caption and comments. The photograph, frozen, had been di-vorced from its immediate context, a contemporary diorama whose mean-ing had been determined by its captioner. I had been rendered a strategic stand-in for an imagined enemy, implicated in what this book argues is the myth of Confederate exceptionalism. Drawing on elements of late nineteenth-century Lost Cause mythology and American exceptionalism, the myth of Confederate exceptionalism updates these historic frames by rendering them through the lens of racial neoliberalism. Attempting to correct the so-called politically correct historiography of "progressives," the myth of Confederate exceptionalism presents the Confederacy, and by extension the neo-Confederacy, as a model form of Americanism by "bracket[ing] race and nam[ing] any explicit focus on race as *racism*."[18]

When I reexamined that Facebook photograph, I recognized it was not my Yankee roots that had betrayed me. Rather, my presumed politics had identified me as in need of an education. My silence during the exchange with Isenhour had made me an ideal potential convert. His silence around issues of race and racism were equally suggestive. Making meaning of those silences, I realized, would become every bit as important as dissecting neo-Confederate speech.

Often viewed as the absence of speech, its antithesis, silence, in fact, speaks.[19] Over the past five years, I have traveled throughout the state of Virginia, driving from my home in Richmond, "ground zero" for the Confederacy and subsequently the Lost Cause,[20] to cemeteries in Warrenton, museums in Appomattox, monuments in Lexington, and community conversations in Charlottesville—to name just a few stops. At most of these sites, while the artifacts on display in an exhibit case or in a public park do not speak in the traditional sense, their voice is not silent—quite the contrary. They are often shouting loudly, whether to paying museum goers or to passersby. This book listens to the different registers of voice, considering the ways in which, when taken together, a coherent mythical narrative surrounding the Confederacy emerges—a narrative that lays anchored in the American cultural consciousness.

Confederate Exceptionalism

Introduction
History, the Museum, and Confederate Exceptionalism

On October 7, 2006, Richmond, Virginia's American Civil War Center at Historic Tredegar became home to *In the Cause of Liberty*, the first museum exhibit aimed at telling the story of the Civil War from the perspectives of three central stakeholders: Unionists, Confederates, and African Americans.[1] The exhibit's opening was publicly lauded by Richmond's newspaper of record, dubbed "a fresh telling of the story of the war" and a "truly inclusive story."[2] An effort to frame the divisive American Civil War as "a shared national heritage,"[3] the American Civil War Center was praised as having "the potential to become one of the foremost destinations for patriots eager to understand a beloved homeland's past."[4]

Little more than a decade later, in the hours following the announcement of Donald J. Trump's election to the US presidency, the words "Your Vote Was a Hate Crime" were emblazoned in red spray-painted letters on Richmond's monuments to Jefferson Davis and Matthew Fontaine Maury on the famed Monument Avenue, located in the heart of the city's historic Fan district. Ten months after the graffiti in Richmond had been cleaned—erased from the landscape—a gathering of white nationalists, including hate groups such as the Ku Klux Klan and the neo-Nazi movement—convened in nearby Charlottesville to protest the removal of the city's Lee monument specifically and Confederate monuments across the country more broadly. The violence culminated in the death of one counterprotester, Heather Heyer, who was mowed down by white supremacist James Alex Fields in an act of terrorism, and the wounding of several others. Fields, an Ohio native, was known for idolizing Adolf Hitler and, on the day of the Unite the Right rally, was photographed holding a shield bearing the emblem of Vanguard America, a hate group identified by the Southern Poverty Law Center (SPLC).[5]

At first glance, these dramatic, historic flashpoints might seem to offer a contemporary declension narrative—evidence of a shift from celebrated attempts at reconciliation to violent racial division. In several ways, this declension story is not an inaccurate one. Once lurking in the shadows, white supremacists are now in plain view. As Matt Thompson wrote for the *Atlantic* in the wake of the August 2017 violence in Charlottesville, "*We used to whisper these thoughts,* the new white supremacists suggest. *But now we can say them out loud.*"[6] Neo-Nazis need no longer hide their faces. They proudly embrace the Confederate battle flag, much like Dylann Roof had in photographs uncovered following the June 17, 2015, massacre at Emanuel AME Church in Charleston, South Carolina.

The visibility of white supremacists in twenty-first-century America owes much to a climate fostered by a president who, instead of openly condemning acts of terrorism as occurred in Charlottesville, called for the necessity of placing blame on "many sides." Yet it does not wholly explain the complicated relationship between members of Confederate heritage groups and discourses surrounding race and racism in the United States. How is it that so-called neo-Confederates can distance themselves from the actions of Roof and other white supremacists, dubbed "horrific" and "cold-hearted" by leaders of the Sons of Confederate Veterans,[7] while also clinging to the symbols and narratives that tether the Confederacy to histories of racism and oppression in the United States?

This book answers this question through an exploration of the varied objects, rituals, and people who have contributed to the central myth that has fostered and facilitated this distancing: the myth of Confederate exceptionalism.[8] Fusing elements of Lost Cause ideology and American exceptionalism, the myth of Confederate exceptionalism nostalgically remembers "the South" through an amalgam of embodied and textual practices that alternately embrace and revise the Confederacy's racial history. Rather than simply invoking the Lost Cause's casting of the "faithful slave" as evidence of the benign nature of the institution of slavery[9] or American exceptionalism's concept of the "melting pot"as evidence of the triumph of multicultural assimilation, the myth of Confederate exceptionalism appropriates these historic ideologies in the twenty-first century, rearticulating them through discourses of racial neoliberalism. By attempting to "suppress . . . 'race' as a legitimate topic or term of public discourse and public policy,"[10] the myth of Confederate exceptionalism enables contemporary neo-Confederates to deny charges of the Confederacy's racism by clinging, as communication scholars Lisa Flores and Christy-Dale Sims summarize, to "frames of neutrality, objectivity, and distance that associate inappropriate emotional intensity with raced bodies and race consciousness."[11] Such a move renders race a "threat," as critical race theorist David Theo Goldberg has argued, giving way to antiracialism.[12]

If race or racialism, as Goldberg notes, "is about the manufacture of homogeneities" and racism about the policing of their boundaries, antiracialism "is to take a stand, instrumental or institutional, against a concept, a name, a category, a categorizing. It does not itself involve standing (up) against (a set of) conditions of being or living, as it is not clear what those conditions might in fact be for which race is considered to stand as a sort of shorthand." Antiracialism, in sum, "suggests forgetting, getting over, moving on, wiping away the terms of reference, [and] at best (or worst) a commercial memorializing rather than a recounting and redressing of the terms of humiliation and devaluation." This forgetting, largely manifested in the substitution of a romanticized antebellum (pre-Confederate) South for the Confederacy's history, affords neo-Confederates the space to reduce racism to the mere invocation of race, forsaking its historical and structural roots. The myth of Confederate exceptionalism thus, like antiracialism, "is whiteness by another name, by other means, with recruitment of people of color to act as public spokespersons for the cause."[13]

While, as scholars Euan Hague, Edward Sebesta, and Heidi Beirich note, "It may be a truism to say that neo-Confederacy is practiced differently by different people in different places in different times,"[14] the designation "neo-Confederate" deserves further clarification. With roots dating back to the 1890s, neo-Confederacy "is best viewed as a spectrum," defined by the SPLC as "a reactionary, revisionist predilection for symbols of the Confederate States of America (CSA), typically paired with a strong belief in the validity of the failed doctrines of nullification and secession—in the specific context of the antebellum South—which rose to prominence in the late 20th and early 21st centuries."[15] Tethered to the recent past, "neo-Confederacy" is something of an umbrella term, used to encompass heritage groups such as the Sons of Confederate Veterans (SCV) and United Daughters of the Confederacy (UDC) as well as far-right hate groups such as the League of the South (LOS).

The first mainstream articulation of this most recent strand of neo-Confederate ideology is traced to Michael Hill and Thomas Fleming's "The New Dixie Manifesto: States' Rights Shall Rise Again,"[16] published in the *Washington Post* in October 1995. Hill and Fleming's opinion piece, speaking on behalf of "a new group of Southerners," professes to call "for nothing more revolutionary than home rule for the states established by the U.S. Constitution." The "manifesto" holds that southerners are "maligned as 'racist' and 'anti-immigrant' by hypocritical, prejudicial Northerners," that race relations were better in the South than the North, and that "the United States is a 'multicultural, continental empire' run by elites." The "manifesto" calls for an end to "the war that is being waged against Southern identity and its traditional symbols," citing pressure to rename streets and remove monuments dedicated to Confederate soldiers as well as to remove the Confederate battle flag from public spaces.[17]

Hill and Fleming's invocation of Confederate symbols as icons of "Southern identity" highlights a key feature of Confederate exceptionalism: its exploitation of the slippages between the "South" and the "Confederacy." This book examines this "latest version" of neo-Confederacy, focusing further on individuals belonging to heritage groups such as the SCV, UDC, and Virginia Flaggers. While these Confederate heritage groups hold many neo-Confederate principles and celebrate the "darker parts of our history,"[18] they are not characterized as hate groups by the SPLC. This book contends, however, that the stories, rituals, and practices performed by these individuals have fanned the culture wars,[19] enabling the myth of Confederate exceptionalism to be an increasingly visible part of the American landscape.

Intimately tied to right-wing, Tea Party politics, the myth of Confederate exceptionalism seeks to offer a corrective to the so-called political correctness of liberals and to promote the former Confederacy as a twenty-first-century archetype. Stitching together nostalgic stories of "the South's" nonracist "heritage" and attempting to normalize the Confederacy through everyday practice, the myth of Confederate exceptionalism seeks to make the Confederacy, drawing on the work of Michael Billig, banal.[20] It is a narrative, this book argues, that slyly substitutes a series of constructed historical memories for history.

This book makes a careful distinction between history and memory, two terms whose relationship has been historically fraught, if not at times downright antagonistic.[21] For historian David Blight, "History is what trained historians do, a reasoned reconstruction of the past rooted in research; it tends to be critical and skeptical of motive and action, and therefore more secular than what people commonly call memory. If history is shared and secular, memory is often treated as a sacred set of absolute meanings and stories, possessed as the heritage or identity of a community."[22] History attends to the lived experience of the past, memory the presentation of it. History explains the past; memory offers a guide to how the past is molded to serve the needs and interests of the present.

This book is concerned with a particular subset of memory—*public memory*—as it pertains to the Confederacy. While scholars have spilled considerable ink attempting to delineate the conceptual terrain of memory studies, differentiating terms such as *collective memory, social memory, popular memory*, and *individual memory*,[23] I use *public memory*, following communication scholar Carolyn Kitch, to invoke the necessity of place as setting and a stage for interaction.[24] Philosopher Edward Casey writes, "Public memory in turn gathers place, people, and topics in its encompassing embrace by acting as the external horizon that encircles the situation—the human situation, the human condition, the place we are always at when we are not merely standing by others or with family and friends." Public memory constitutes identities, national and regional, as well as social and individual. Its power, Casey notes, "resides in its capacity to be for the most part located to the edge of our lives, hovering, ready to be invoked or revised, acted upon or merely contemplated, inspiring us or boring us."[25] It is the contention of this book that public memory of the Confederacy, molded in the exceptionalist cast, hovers around us, whether located in the South or across the United States, poised for its strategic use by so-called protectors of Confederate heritage.

The Myth of Confederate Exceptionalism

A legendary narrative whose power stems from its ability to be told and retold, "myth,"[26] within this book, connotes not a falsehood per se but rather a recognizable story that wields the potential to transcend its immediate context. Myths pervade public culture, offering, according to communication scholar Jack Lule, "sacred, societal narratives with shared values and beliefs, with lessons and themes, and with exemplary models that instruct and inform."[27] Like all mythical narratives, the myth of Confederate exceptionalism serves a common purpose: the translation of the unfamiliar into the familiar. Among the most recognizable enduring myths in American culture are the myths of the hero, the victim, and the scapegoat.[28]

Drawing liberally from each of these archetypes, the myth of Confederate exceptionalism brings together elements of two of the most prominent ideological traditions in American history: the Lost Cause and American exceptionalism. The former, traced to Edward Pollard's *The Lost Cause: A New Southern History of the War of the Confederates* (1866), is summarized as a "white, patrician, and self-justifying narrative"[29] that argues that the American Civil War was fought over states' rights rather than the preservation of slavery, for the protection of "beautiful and virtuous women and children"[30] rather than the supremacy of whiteness. As historian Gary Gallagher summarizes, Lost Cause advocates "blamed sectional tensions on abolitionists, celebrated antebellum Southern slaveholding society, portrayed Confederates as united in waging their war for their independence, extolled the gallantry of Confederate soldiers, and attributed Northern victory to sheer weight of numbers and resources."[31] Anchored to the image of the "loyal slave," dubbed by Blight as "one of the most hackneyed clichés in American history,"[32] Lost Cause mythology presents slavery as an ultimately benign institution with the men who fought on the Confederacy's behalf, the likes of Robert E. Lee and Thomas "Stonewall" Jackson most famously, cast as heroes, worthy of collective respect and admiration.

Emphasis on the soldiers' valor, coupled with "women's bravery, slave fidelity, and Southern innocence regarding slavery," gave way to a particular twisting of the historical record by Lost Cause adherents.[33] This distortion, Blight notes, was captured in an April 1911 speech delivered by Robert E. Lee, grandson of the famous Confederate leader. Lee declared that had the South "been heeded, slavery would have been eliminated years before it was. It was the votes of the southern states which finally freed the slaves."[34] Lost Cause mythology, Blight summarizes, thus "not only absolved Southerners of responsibility for slavery, but made them the truest abolitionists."[35] The Lost Cause materialized in the late nineteenth and early twentieth centuries with the proliferation of monuments and memorials across the United States, many of which were funded through the steadfast efforts of the United Daughters of the Confederacy.[36] Extending beyond the South, Lost Cause mythology became a part of "popular American understanding."[37] It continues to circulate today, although in updated form.

While the origins of American exceptionalism are typically dated much earlier—to the late seventeenth century, commonly with reference to John Winthrop's "City Upon a Hill" speech—the phrase did not find purchase and more explicit articulation until the 1920s. As American studies scholar Donald Pease writes, American exceptionalism "includes a complex assemblage of theological and secular assumptions out of which Americans have developed the lasting belief in America as the fulfillment of the national ideal to which other nations aspire."[38] It is "an academic discourse, a political doctrine, and a regulatory ideal assigned responsibility for defining, supporting, and developing the U.S. national identity." This identity was deemed "not merely different from, but also qualitatively better than, the European nation-states whose social orders were described as having been devastated by Marxism."[39] Among those qualities that distinguished America were the absence of class conflict and hierarchies, "tolerance for diversity, [and] liberal individualism." Perhaps unsurprisingly, it was the threat of alternatives to capitalism and democracy, most powerfully during the Cold War, that made American exceptionalism most alluring.[40]

American exceptionalism's appeal is invariably tethered to the concept's malleability and adaptability. For Pease, "American exceptionalism operates less like a collection of discrete, potentially falsifiable descriptions of American society than as a fantasy through which U.S. citizens bring these contradictory political and cultural descriptions into correlation with one another."[41] It has historically deployed "trans-historical themes (assimilation, political liberation, cultural rebirth, and social mobility) to the national myths through which they were idealized (the melting pot, the endless frontier, American Adam, Virgin Land)." Such themes largely fostered the casting of "a hardworking unified national monoculture" where difference was underplayed and, in some instances, imagined as downright antithetical to the nation.[42] When elements no longer align with the demands of the rhetorical situation, American exceptionalism is reconfigured to meet presentist ends, which Pease suggests is the "fantasy" that guided the United States through the War on Terror.[43]

Confederate exceptionalism, this book suggests, functions much like its national counterpart, serving as a fantasy for its adherents. Drawing on elements of the Lost Cause and American exceptionalism while attempting to combat, at least to some extent, the residues of southern exceptionalism, the myth of Confederate exceptionalism functions as critical geographers David Roberts and Minelle Mahtani describe racial neoliberalism, "camouflag[ing] practices anchored in apparent meritocracy, making possible a utopic vision of society that is non-racialized."[44] Refuting the belief that the region "possessed a separate and unique identity . . . which appeared to be out of the mainstream of American experience,"[45] Confederate exceptionalism rests on the claim that the defunct entity is not only relevant in the contemporary landscape but mainstream and accessible to all.

Southern exceptionalist writers such as W. J. Cash, author of *The Mind of the South* (1941), characterized the "Old" South as "a sort of stage piece out of the eighteenth century. . . . Its social pattern was manorial, its civilization that of the Cavalier, its ruling class an aristocracy coextensive with the planter group."[46] Such description stands in stark contrast to the lurid melodrama of Erskine Caldwell's *Tobacco Road*, which tells the story of the Lesters, "the poorest, whitest, trashiest, horniest family in rural Georgia."[47] This is the South pictured in Margaret Bourke-White's *You Have Seen Their Faces* (1937)—a Depression-era South that resembled South Africa.[48] It was this version of the South that led President Franklin D. Roosevelt to refer to the region as "the Nation's number one economic problem."[49]

Once used to bolster the case for southern studies, southern exceptionalism had the unintended consequence of reducing the South to a backward, agrarian region defined by white supremacy, patriarchy, and intolerance. In so stigmatizing the South, the image of a morally superior North was cultivated. Poet and novelist Robert Penn Warren crystallized this sentiment when he wrote, "the War gave the South the Great Alibi and gave the North the Treasury of Virtue."[50] The result of this and other such characterizations is a bifurcated view, with the nation, as Peter Applebome wrote, "Ping-Pong[ing] between views of the South as a hellhole of poverty, torment, and depravity and as an American Eden of tradition, strength, and grace."[51] It is the former image that neo-Confederates fight so fervently against. It is the premise of a book Virginia Flagger spokesman Barry Isenhour gifted me during one of our exchanges. Titled *Give This Book to a Yankee: A Southern Guide to the Civil War for Northerners* (2014), Lochlainn Seabrook's "Jefferson Davis Historical Gold Medal Winner" seeks to inculcate among the "unenlightened Yank or reconstructed Southerner . . . a sense of courteousness, good will, and deference toward Dixie and her gallant, gracious, and fiercely independent people."[52] Seabrook's treatise captures the essence of Confederate exceptionalism's attempts to rehabilitate the image of the South with its championing of small government and the amenities the region affords. *Give This Book to a Yankee* states proudly, "our women are prettier, our men are politer, our children are nicer . . . our land is grander . . . our food is tastier, our society is more diverse, and our history is more interesting than what you find up North."[53] While placing emphasis on region—the South—the slim book's content focuses on "righting" the "wrongs" of Civil War historiography. A condensed version of Seabrook's *Everything You Were Taught About the Civil War Is Wrong, Ask a Southerner* (2010), *Give This Book to a Yankee* is, fundamentally, a book seeking to exonerate the Confederacy, distancing it from the institution of slavery and the racism with which it is associated. Packaging an imagined Confederacy as an educational product to be consumed, literally and figuratively, the myth of Confederate exceptionalism declares war not on "the North" per se but on "liberalism (with socialist leanings)," a phrase Seabrook used to describe President Abraham Lincoln.[54]

Recent debates surrounding Confederate monuments and the battle flag across the United States,[55] not simply the South, remind us that Confederate exceptionalism has become widespread, even if the backlash has been most acute in the South.[56] Confederate exceptionalism is not specific to a particular place, emphasizing that Richmond, the former capital of the Confederacy, while vital to the story, is not anomalous.

Remembering the Confederacy

While, as historian Barbara Gannon notes, "There is no one way Americans remember their Civil War,"[57] historians have approached the question of how the Civil War is remembered from a variety of entry points. A number of studies have identified and critiqued the Lost Cause and the material artifacts reflecting this ideology emerging in tandem with Jim Crow.[58] Others have emphasized, as historian Caroline Janney argues, that the categories of Unionist, Emancipationist, Lost Cause, or Reconciliationist memories "were never clear cut, nor did they remain static."[59] Historians have also explored various artifacts of popular Civil War commemoration throughout the twentieth century, from anniversary celebrations to films to textbooks, demonstrating how political ideologies have been fortified and circulated, as well as their longer-term implications.[60]

Contributing to the expanding corpus of excellent and important studies of Civil War memory, this book takes a series of artifacts, objects, and rituals circulating in the twenty-first century as its point of departure, exploring the strategic appropriations of historical narratives and their updating to formulate the myth of Confederate exceptionalism. While this book began with an attempt to explain how neo-Confederates, an admittedly motley cast of characters ranging fairly widely along the (predominantly) ideological right, could dissociate Confederate symbols from the racist histories to which they are intimately connected, I quickly realized that Confederate exceptionalism suffuses even the most seemingly benign displays of "history." While the deadly violence in Charlottesville is perhaps one of its most dramatic consequences, the myth of Confederate exceptionalism pervades public culture, often operating in subtle and arguably nuanced ways. This book uncovers the rhetorical moves that have enabled the myth of Confederate exceptionalism to fan the culture wars.

Despite the passage of more than 150 years since the Confederacy's defeat by Union forces, immortalized in Tom Lovell's painting "Surrender at Appomattox," memory of the defunct entity has never fully receded from American historical consciousness. The dedication of more than 1,700 monuments, memorials, and other public symbols commemorating the Confederacy stands as testament to the durability of Confederate memory.[61] As the SPLC reminds us, the mantle of the Confederacy and, by extension, Confederate memory was taken up with the greatest zeal during two specific eras in American history: the eras of Jim Crow (1890–1930) and the civil rights movement of the 1950s and 1960s, coinciding with the centennial of the American Civil War. It was during the latter era that schools in particular began to assume the names of Confederate leaders, signaling the educational legacies of the Lost Cause as well as massive resistance.[62]

Since the 2015 Charleston massacre, such symbols of Lost Cause memory have been revisited with renewed vigor. Following Dylann Roof's deadly rampage, political activist Bree Newsome scaled the thirty-foot South Carolina State House pole and removed the Confederate battle flag, which had flown since 1961. Little more than a week later, South Carolina's Republican governor Nikki Haley, in a dramatic reversal from earlier public statements, claimed the flag "should have never been there."[63] The Memphis city council voted to remove a statue commemorating the life of Nathan Bedford Forrest, first grand wizard of the Ku Klux Klan. In May 2017 Mayor Mitch Landrieu of New Orleans announced the removal of four Confederate monuments in a dramatic public speech, proclaiming the statues "symbols of white supremacy,"[64] spurring cities across the United States, not just the South, to publicly debate and in many cases remove Confederate monuments, including New York City and Baltimore.[65] Since the massacre at the historically Black Emanuel AME Church, more than a hundred monuments and other symbols of the Confederacy have been removed. Within the past two years, close to forty school names have been changed, yet many more remain.[66] However, if the political tides seem to be turning against icons of the Confederacy, popular culture remains littered with examples of individuals and institutions doubling down on the claim that the Confederacy represents "heritage not hate."[67]

In 2004 a Kentucky teenager sued her school district for prohibiting her from wearing a dress styled after a large Confederate battle flag.[68] She reached a settlement with Greenup County school officials two years later, the terms of which were not publicly disclosed.[69] In 2010 Texas school officials advocated that Abraham Lincoln's and Jefferson Davis's inaugural addresses be given equal weight in the state's social studies curriculum. Little more than a year later, a group of Colorado high schoolers caught national attention after posing for their prom photograph with a large Confederate flag. Two girls in the photo held guns, while three others posed using their fingers to imitate a gun, *Charlie's Angels* style.[70]

In August 2017 HBO announced a program in process called *Confederate*, a fictional series premised on the question, "What would have happened had the South won the Civil War?" The announcement of the series, initially set to premiere in 2019, sparked a strong negative reaction and the Twitter hashtag #NoConfederate.[71] The fate of the program remains to be seen.[72]

Why Richmond?

While these debates continue to swirl around the United States, this book takes as its focus the city of Richmond and the larger state of Virginia.

The former capital of the Confederacy, Richmond bears the distinction of occupying center stage where memory of the Confederacy is concerned. On April 3, 1865, under orders from Confederate and municipal authorities, Confederate soldiers set fire to the city's waterside warehouses. High winds during the night spread the flames, which destroyed much of Richmond's business district. Although its smoldering ruins might have signaled defeat, Richmond sought to be defined by its resilience, seeking to evolve, as urban studies scholar John Moeser would later write, from "Old Virginny" to the "New Dominion."[73]

This transition, while romanticized in popular tourism brochures attempting to lure visitors south, was hardly smooth or peaceful. In March 1987 the *Los Angeles Times* noted with some surprise,

> Richmond is a city where blacks and whites have few disputes over the Confederate legacy. That harmony is all the more remarkable because Richmond is the former capital of the Confederacy and boasts a wealth of Confederate shrines, including the White House of the Confederacy, the Museum of the Confederacy, the South's largest Confederate museum, and, along Monument Avenue, the grandest display of statues of Confederate heroes below the Mason-Dixon Line.[74]

Despite this affirming portrayal of an enlightened city that seemed to have worked through its divisive legacy, the reality for Richmond's Black communities bore little resemblance to life as described by the newspaper.

Indeed, as urban studies scholars Christopher Silver and John Moeser note, Richmond did not experience the "level of racial enmity found in Memphis."[75] Richmond's racism, however, was of a different sort. As political scientists Lewis Randolph and Gayle Tate summarize, "Richmond boasts a benign racism, a reality that offered few opportunities for black incorporation into city politics until the adoption of a nine-seat single-member district system in 1977."[76] Richmond is thus, fundamentally, a city that is "very much a part of the hegemonist Old South."[77]

Despite the persistence of Old South hegemony, the latter decades of the nineteenth century were defined by Black mobilization, displayed in organized protests against the "pass system," which required Black people to carry passes while moving around as well as sit-ins to end discriminatory practices in public spaces. This period also saw a flourishing of Black enterprises in the neighborhood of Jackson Ward, known as the "Black Wall Street" and the "Harlem of the South." From the Hippodrome Theater, which drew performers including Billie Holiday and Louis Armstrong, to the Saint Luke Penny Savings Bank, opened by Maggie Lena Walker, the first Black woman bank president in the United States, Richmond's Black business thrived in the late nineteenth and early twentieth centuries, as did Black activism.[78] Leading the charge was John Mitchell, editor of the *Richmond Planet*. Mitchell's antilynching editorials, like his 1904 editorials calling for Black people to boycott the city's streetcars after attempts to enforce racial segregation, stirred readers.

With these expressions of resistance and Black self-determination, however, came white backlash. As Richmond underwent significant political, social, and economic change in the wake of the American Civil War, the city assumed the mantle of inscribing Lost Cause memory on the landscape. The unveiling of the Robert E. Lee Monument in 1890 before a crowd of more than 100,000 in an area that would later become one of the most elite and white neighborhoods in the city ensured the livelihood and viability of the Lost Cause, with monuments to Confederate president Jefferson Davis (1907), generals J. E. B. Stuart (1907) and Stonewall Jackson (1919), and naval commander Matthew Fontaine Maury (1929) following in concert with the instantiation of Jim Crow.

White supremacy, as historian J. Douglas Smith has argued, manifested in a form of "genteel paternalism" that became known popularly as "the Virginia Way."[79] This "kinder, gentler" white supremacy, captured by the political machine of Democrat Harry Byrd, dominated Virginia politics through Byrd's death in the mid-1960s.

In Richmond, newspaper editor and Pulitzer Prize–winning historian Douglas Southall Freeman saluted Lee's statue each day as he drove to work at the *Richmond News Leader*. The *Daily Press* would later report of a "headwaiter at the Commonwealth Club, [who] cited Lee's moving farewell at Appomattox incessantly to diners at the club. Writer Joe Bryan III provided readers with poignant accounts of the ex-Confederates who used to trade war stories at the bar of the old Westmoreland Club."[80]

The latter half of the twentieth century showed that Richmond was by no means the tranquil city that the *Los Angeles Times* described in 1987. The Civil War centennial, the boycott of department stores such as Thalhimer's in the city center, and attempts to dilute the power of the Black vote that eventually led to a shift to a majority Black city council in 1977, revealed the residues of centuries of white supremacy culture. The heated debate surrounding efforts to "integrate" Monument Avenue with a statue to Arthur Ashe in the mid-1990s only reinforced how deeply rooted this culture was.[81]

Richmond continues to be a powerful site of Civil War memory and history. While sesquicentennial programming titled "The Future of Richmond's Past" displayed an effort to encourage an honest reckoning with histories of oppression,[82] Richmond is also home to the headquarters of the United Daughters of the Confederacy, located in between the city's Virginia Museum of Fine Arts, the former home to the Confederate Soldier's Camp, a group for local veterans, and what is now known as the Virginia Museum of History and Culture (formerly the Virginia Historical Society). In June 2017 Mayor Levar Stoney appointed a Monument Avenue Commission tasked with making recommendations for the fate of the historic and controversial thoroughfare, entertaining options from statue removal to the addition of "context."[83] As the public hearings of the commission demonstrated, however, reckoning is neither easy nor immediate.[84]

Over the past thirty years, four Virginia governors have issued proclamations attempting to recognize Richmond's Confederate history. Douglas Wilder (Democrat), the grandchild of formerly enslaved people and the first elected Black governor in the United States, declared a week in April 1990 "Last Chapter of the Civil War Days." The week was dedicated to honoring Robert E. Lee, Ulysses Grant, and Abraham Lincoln. Wilder's successor, George Allen (Republican), the son of a former Washington Redskins coach, declared April "Confederate Heritage Month" (1995–1997), narrativizing the Civil War as a war "fought for noble purposes on both sides."[85] Republican James Gilmore, in an attempt to learn from Allen's mistakes, issued his own Confederate History Month proclamation in 1998, which sought to "include everyone," "reflect the complete society," and "denounce slavery."[86] Finally, in April 2010 Robert F. McDonnell (Republican) issued a proclamation recognizing Confederate History Month. The proclamation posted online stated, "It is important for all Virginians to reflect upon our commonwealth's shared history, to understand the sacrifices of the Confederate leaders, soldiers and citizens during the period of the Civil War, and to recognize how our history has led to our present."[87] The statement drew almost immediate criticism for failing to make any reference to the institution of slavery.[88]

Throughout this thirty-year period, Virginians witnessed leadership that shifted between a recognition of the racism embedded in the Confederate past and one in which Black people were conspicuously excluded from the narrative. While the debate surrounding Confederate Heritage Month has, at least temporarily, stalled, there remain many for whom the city's continued celebration of Lee-Jackson Day—the Friday before Martin Luther King Jr. Day in January—is an affront. The holiday, which closes city offices, celebrates the birthdays of Robert E. Lee and Stonewall Jackson. Formerly combined with Martin Luther King Jr. Day, a tradition started in 1984, Lee-Jackson Day was rendered a separate holiday in 2000.[89]

Lost Cause education has been found to persist across the state of

Virginia as well.[90] The University of Richmond's own mascot, the spider, could be seen donning the Confederate uniform as late as the 1970s, with "Dixie" the unofficial anthem of the university until close to 1980.[91] In 2011 Virginia schools adopted a fourth-grade textbook claiming that thousands of Black people fought on behalf of the Confederacy.[92] While the myth of Black Confederates is a subject of intense debate today,[93] historians have shown that the number of Black men who fought on behalf of the Confederacy was strikingly low—insignificant enough to counter claims of large-scale support for the Confederacy on the part of enslaved people.[94]

Virginia may be for lovers according to its contemporary tourism slogan, but, as historian Marie Tyler-McGraw has claimed, Richmond's efforts to mobilize under the aegis of heritage tourism have forced it to confront "the painful lessons of trying to make *unum* out of *pluribus* on the historic landscape as well as in narratives."[95] Despite efforts at a more inclusive rendering of the Civil War by developing a narrative that offers multiple histories, coupled with Mayor Stoney's call for citywide reconciliation through reconsidering Monument Avenue, Richmond is a city where visitors can purchase Confederate battle flags as bumper stickers and as souvenirs to lay at the grave of Jefferson Davis in Hollywood Cemetery. Driving around my neighborhood recently, I sat next to a pickup truck at a stoplight with a bumper sticker announcing, "John Wilkes Booth Day on April 14th, a True Southern Hero." The image of a Confederate battle flag was positioned next to the text. This is to say nothing of the T-shirts sporting the Confederate battle flag that are worn proudly by those who maintain "heritage not hate." Tensions between official efforts to reckon with history and more popular, unofficial modes of remembrance define the cityscape.

Nowhere was this tension between the official and the popular placed into sharper relief than in 2011 when Hollywood descended on Richmond for the filming of Steven Spielberg's epic *Lincoln*. Open calls for extras spoke to a city of bearded men who might be interested in gaining their fifteen minutes of fame by being cast as soldiers. There was a buzz throughout the city, as the likes of Daniel Day-Lewis and Sally Field could be seen frequenting local establishments, along with Bill O'Reilly, whose *Killing Lincoln* also found a home in Richmond. Lincoln film tours conducted via Segway rolled through the streets. Public interest prompted the city's Valentine Museum to curate a "Beard Wars" exhibit, featuring photographs of members of the Richmond Beard League, whose facial hair was styled to imitate the facial hair of Union and Confederate generals.[96]

While local news reiterated Spielberg's (and the lead actors') high praise for Richmond's restaurant scene and the hospitality of its residents, Spielberg was quoted sharing a particular surprise: "We did have some young people who turned down work because they did not want to put on the Union uniform." To backtrack a bit, Spielberg clarified, "But those were isolated moments, and they only come to mind because I wasn't accustomed to that because I live in Los Angeles. Those were very isolated moments and did not dominate our incredible experience of cooperation in making this movie in Richmond."[97] Although Spielberg was careful to emphasize that this was the anomalous behavior of a few, the fact that there were young people who refused to don the Union uniform suggests a deep-seated loyalty to the Confederacy and a generational commitment to preserving its memory. The body was a site of contest over memory, and young men were not eager to have their bodies marked as fighting on behalf of the Union. If the filming of *Lincoln* reminded Richmonders of anything, it was that memory of the Confederacy has been passed down for generations. Confederate memory would not simply "die out" when veterans of the "War Between the States," as it is often called by Confederate heritage advocates, died.

Spielberg's reflection on his time in Richmond pointed to an underlying reality: the Civil War, while distant temporally, is narratively and experientially proximate. And Richmond is a critical canvas, as both a historic and contemporary center, for exploring its meaning.

The Civil War and the Confederacy in particular are connected to the lived experience of Richmonders. The past is unmistakably present in debates surrounding license plates acknowledging membership in the Sons of Confederate Veterans; the past is visible to commuters to Washington, DC, who regularly pass a large Confederate battle flag as it flies off I-95.[98] In this present, Civil War museums in Richmond attempt to narrate the causes and history of the "War between the States." The result has been mixed. While attempting to present a bold narrative of slavery as *the* central cause of the Civil War, the American Civil War Center at Tredegar, for instance, undercut its powerful message with populist appeals celebrating alternating visions of "liberty" and "freedom," attempting to unite through claims of liberty's polysemy.[99] In this way, Richmond has enabled the myth of Confederate exceptionalism to flourish.

The Neo-Confederate Museum

This book uses the museum, a particular site of public memory—*lieu de memoire* following the work of Pierre Nora—as its organizing framework.[100]

As an institution whose value has been historically linked to its ability to educate, the museum is a space encountered through architecture and design, in curated exhibitions, and in the objects it sells in gift shops. It is a site most school-age children are required to visit, like it or not, with the hope that some novel insight into a historical period, person, or organization, depending on the museum, might be offered. The museum guides visitors regarding "what is important," or, for the more discerning observer, what is most important to the individuals responsible for collecting and curating the objects on display.

While there is a sense, admittedly flawed, that the museum's role is to "educate" objectively—to communicate facts and stories rooted in historical "truths"—there is a more personal dimension to the museum experience. As historian Susan Crane notes, "We go to museums to learn about ourselves, to witness what has been identified as significant art or history or science, and to come away with a stronger sense of ourselves as implicated in a vast web of tradition and knowledge."[101] Museums are places that anchor identities to objects, stories, and people. Functioning on multiple planes of experience, the museum is a powerful arbiter between history and memory, as visitors share experiences that draw groups together.

Although we are socialized to engage with museums as sites to be revered—to remain quiet, to keep our hands to ourselves, to not eat or drink anything in the presence of "history" or "art," the museum has not been an uncontested space.[102] As historic controversies surrounding the Smithsonian's *Enola Gay* exhibit and the Holocaust Museum in Washington, DC, recall,[103] while the museum's objects may be revered, its rhetorical tactics are hardly neutral. The museum, like memory more generally, is political.

While scholars such as Crane and others have acknowledged the inherent politics of museums, others have been less sanguine. Rather, following Michel Foucault, many have argued that the museum is a site crafted to "discipline and punish" the bodies who enter.[104] Historian Steven Conn has critiqued such a view, noting that "treating museums as part of the same institutional constellation as prisons, asylums, and hospitals simply begs the question of why people would ever go."[105]

This book operates from a middle ground, envisioning the museum somewhere in between the more romantic imaginings of displays of unbiased information and intentional, oppressive structures of surveilling knowledge. At least where memory of the Confederacy is concerned, this book argues that memory makers have capitalized on the expectations cultivated by the museum field in an attempt to normalize, through appeals to the conventions of museum practice, the myth of Confederate exceptionalism.

When I think about museums, however, I do not think solely of a physical space—a structure that typically houses carefully curated exhibits. Rather, the museum I imagine is capacious enough to include everything from cookbooks to monuments, taxidermied horses to living historians. Far from a static space, the neo-Confederate museum that is Virginia is a dynamic entity that enables continued and continuous engagement with the colliding forces of memory and history.

This book unravels the myth of Confederate exceptionalism in six chapters, each of which considers a different museum practice/artifact that serves to instantiate the myth. These chapters each focus on a specific practice/object and discourse that contributes to the distancing of the Confederate heritage movement from histories of racism and oppression.

Chapter 1, "'Carry Me Back to Old Virginny' and the Neo-Confederate Jeremiad," traces the cultural history of Virginia's state song "emeritus," "Carry Me Back to Old Virginia." From its original composition in the late 1870s, where it gained popularity within the minstrel tradition, to its elevation to a tourism slogan and pageant theme in the early decades of the twentieth century, "Carry Me Back to Old Virginia" and the story of its eventual demise as a statewide emblem of antebellum nostalgia provide critical context for the contemporary neo-Confederate movement in Virginia. The song's dethroning as the state song of Virginia in 1997 served to animate twenty-first-century Jeremiah and Virginia Flaggers founder Susan Hathaway, crystallizing the political contests surrounding memory of the Confederacy as a "cause lost."

Chapter 2, "Stonewall Jackson and Sacred Relics," explores the meanings stuffed into the taxidermied body of Little Sorrel, Stonewall Jackson's warhorse. On display at the Virginia Military Institute (VMI) museum in Lexington, Virginia, the taxidermied horse functions, this chapter argues, as a sacred relic, attempting to forge present-day connections to a past that is no longer, as well as a mounted hide stuffed with allegedly apolitical stories, narratives of a constructed "cast" history intended for future generations.

Chapter 3, "Black Confederates and Performances of Living Reconciliation," follows contemporary Black Confederates—Black men and women who publicly voice commitment to and advocacy for Confederate memory. In exploring the narrative and performative dimensions of these Black Confederates, this chapter suggests that rather than evidence a simple embrace of Lost Cause discourses of Confederate heroism and valor, they celebrate the Confederacy as a "melting pot," attempting to invert historiographic accounts of the Confederacy's commitment to slavery and white supremacy.

Chapter 4, "Cooking Confederate and Nostalgic Reenactment," examines both historic and contemporary "Confederate cookbooks" to explore how the Confederacy is packaged as "heritage" for sale to consumers as a site of both spiritual as well as physical nourishment. Through a close reading of various recipes, narratives, and accompanying visuals, this chapter argues that by offering consumers the opportunity to "cook Confederate" and thereby reenact a sanitized version of the past, the Confederacy is transformed into an object to be both consumed and performed, enabling participants to distance themselves from the histories of enslavement to which they are inextricably linked.

Chapter 5, "Historical Diorama and Protecting the Confederate Habitat," reads Richmond's Monument Avenue, the infamous site of celebration of the "Lost Cause trinity,"[106] as a historical diorama. Analyzing the built environment alongside documents framing Monument Avenue's founding, this chapter argues that contemporary neo-Confederate calls for the preservation of history attempt to frame Monument Avenue as a historic habitat diorama, a beautiful landscape immortalized in a deracialized past, in need of protection.

Chapter 6, "Heroes, Villains, and the Digital Confederacy," explores neo-Confederate social media, with particular focus on the Virginia Flaggers' Facebook posts and tweets in the wake of the August 11 and 12, 2017, violence in Charlottesville. Analyzing neo-Confederates' appropriation of popular films, comic books, and other cultural referents, this chapter argues that neo-Confederates' use of the digital platform facilitates a particular reimagination of Confederate nostalgia—a retreat into a fantastical world suspended in time and divorced from the realities of virulent racism. It is an imagined—and ultimately reimagined—world that has been enacted with continued disastrous effect.

In reading the state of Virginia as a Confederate memory museum, I suggest not that the myth of Confederate exceptionalism is persuasive—that it effectively converts. More likely, these practices tend to "preach to the choir" of the already converted—of the believers. Yet in unraveling the myth of Confederate exceptionalism through the lens of the museum, I seek to unearth the ways in which the particular tactics of these varied memory makers seize on the very expectations the museum as an institution has cultivated over time.

When I look back at the photograph taken of myself and Virginia Flagger Barry Isenhour several years ago, I think about the comments offered to the Facebook page—particularly the one suggesting that I was in need of an "education." My mind needed to be changed, if not my heart. Although the commenter proposed that I was being taught "History 101," what I was being offered by Isenhour was not truly a "history" lesson. Isenhour was narrating a very specific story—a strategic stitching together of the past intended to deflect my skepticism, particularly regarding the Confederacy's historic commitment to the institution of slavery.

The "education" Isenhour offered was the same education my students were encouraged to seek during a class visit to the United Daughters of the Confederacy headquarters several years later. As we sat in the Great Hall listening to archivist Teresa Roane, we were being properly "educated" on the causes and consequences of the American Civil War. At once her commentary seemed wholly rational; she had begged us to be more open-minded about history—to examine historical questions from multiple sides. Yet it quickly became clear to me and my students that there was, in her estimation, only one side to consider—the side that would continue to valorize the Confederate past, claim continued threat in the present, and fight for its future. I sat, and remain, on the other one.

1 | "Carry Me Back to Old Virginny" and the Neo-Confederate Jeremiad

In late April 2014 I attended my first neo-Confederate commemoration in Richmond, a Confederate Memorial Day Service at Riverview Cemetery. I imagined it would be an unabashedly racist event, the Lost Cause incarnate, celebrating "faithful slaves" and "benevolent masters" as participants mourned the loss of their ancestors who fought on behalf of the Confederacy. As I opened the ceremony program, the words to "Carry Me Back to Old Virginny" stared back at me.

> Carry me back to old Virginny
> There's where the cotton and the corn and the taters grow,
> There's where the birds warble sweet in the springtime,
> There's where the old darkey's heart am long'd to go.
> There's where I labored so hard for old Massa,
> Day after day in the fields of yellow corn.
> No place on earth do I love more sincerely
> Than old Virginny, the State where I was born.

Fondly recalling days on the plantation, the song, suffused with racist references to "the old darkey" and "old Massa," crystallized in lyrical form my expectations for the event. Yet I remained horrified. I looked around at the crowd of approximately forty white men, women, and children who convened at the cemetery—the same crowd who would a short while later proudly sing "Carry Me Back to Old Virginny" in unison.

From start to finish, the service lasted approximately an hour, including a presentation of colors, pledge of allegiance to the United States, salutes to the flag of Virginia as well as the Confederate flag, the singing of "Carry Me Back to Old Virginny" and "Dixie," a collective rehearsal of "The Lord's Prayer," a poetry reading, and concluding set of prayers. There was a small group of approximately five women dressed in black period mourning gowns. Most everyone else in attendance wore twenty-first-century clothing, reminding me that the commemorative ritual, despite gestures to the past, was firmly rooted in the present. The pattern would be followed, with little variation, in each of the ceremonies I attended over the next several years across the state of Virginia, from Warrenton to Fredericksburg to Petersburg.

No matter how many such events I attended, I never became comfortable with "Carry Me Back to Old Virginny," refusing to join the chorus. I repeatedly found myself in a state of what theater scholar Anthony Jackson describes as "unsettlement"—of the negative sort—"trapped inside an event they [visitors] find exasperating, irritating, demanding more of them than they wish to give, but from which there is no escape."[1] The repetition of "Carry Me Back" seemed to offer evidence of a most profound disconnect between the Flaggers' and other neo-Confederate heritage groups' disavowal of racism and embrace of it.

After several months of hearing "Carry Me Back to Old Virginny" sung at the various venues in which I found myself an observer, I attended a Sons of Confederate Veterans (SCV) meeting in Virginia Beach, where the elusive Susan Hathaway, founder of the Virginia Flaggers, was scheduled to speak. While I had seen photographs of the brown-haired Hathaway toting her Confederate battle flag, she was never present during my visits with the Flaggers outside the Virginia Museum of Fine Arts (VMFA). When Barry Isenhour emailed to let me know that Hathaway was the guest presenter at the upcoming SCV meeting, I jumped at the opportunity to drive two and a half hours to a roadside restaurant, Gus and George's Spaghetti and Steak House, with my handheld audio recorder.

It was clear this was not her first talk of this kind. Hathaway began by thanking the group of men in attendance and then asking herself the question of how she began her work as an "activist." In response, she said,

> I'd like to think about my time before I became active, as I was sleeping, that I kind of knew what was going on, I would hear about things, like our state song being taken away from us. I remember being upset about that. I remember being angry about it. And I'd like to share that with you all, because now, to me, when I think about now, it's almost like the starting point and maybe some of you all [who] have been around a lot longer can think of other starting points. But to me, the fact that we so easily lost this song, and what it should mean to us and could have meant to us as a state, is kind of the starting point for me.[2]

Although she did not mention the "state song" in question by name, I knew what she was referring to. Hathaway then, in a move that did surprise me, began to sing the first verse of "Carry Me Back to Old Virginny," building to an emotional crescendo, tears welling up in her eyes.[3]

Once she had composed herself, she continued, "That was kind of the starting point where I think of the rich history of that song, and if any of y'all remember when it was taken away . . . the gentleman who wrote this song [James Bland] knew what he was talking about. He lived it, he loved it, this was the song of the people that should be honored as much as anyone else. And that was taken away."[4]

It was then, at Gus and George's, that I began to consider "Carry Me Back to Old Virginny" as more than a mere artifact of racist nostalgia. Written by James Bland, a descendent of freedmen on both sides of his family,[5] the song is both an emblem to neo-Confederates of a bygone era, the "Old South," and a victim of contemporary attempts to be "politically correct," as evidenced by the song's "retirement" as the state song of Virginia in 1997. Unlike "Maryland, My Maryland," the pro-Confederate anthem that was stripped of its designation as Maryland's "official" state song in March 2018, "Carry Me Back to Old Virginny" includes no direct reference to the Confederacy.[6] The song's romanticization of the antebellum (pre-Confederate) southern plantation by an enslaved person instead offers a strategic and harmonic remove from charges of Confederate racism. This remove enables neo-Confederates, the likes of Hathaway and others, to sing proudly, affirming their kinship with the Black man who penned the song's words while paying no heed to his identity.

"Carry Me Back" and the story of its eventual removal as a state-sanctioned public icon in Virginia function in particular relation to history, memory, and emotion, creating what I am terming the "neo-Confederate jeremiad." Further inquiry into "Carry Me Back to Old Virginny" sheds light on not only the source of Hathaway's emotional display but also how that emotion is strategically deployed in the twenty-first century in a plea for the restoration of Confederate "history"—a history that is disassociated from the history of slavery in the United States.

Written in the 1870s, "Carry Me Back to Old Virginny" assumed the status of Virginia's state song in 1940 and state song "emeritus" in 1997. Over its more than 140-year cultural life, the song became a symbol of Confederate heritage and, ultimately, heritage lost. While defined by scholar Laurajane Smith as "a process or a performance, in which certain cultural and social meanings and values are identified, reaffirmed or rejected,"[7] heritage is an abstract concept. There is, as Smith notes, "no such *thing* as heritage"[8] per se. Rather, heritage signals meaning acquired. "Carry Me Back to Old Virginny" has been alternately embraced as a marker of Black achievement penned by a freed Black man, celebrated as a wistful reminder of antebellum plantation life, appropriated as a symbol of racial reconciliation, and denounced as a racist portrayal of Black people that romanticizes the institution of slavery. The song is recognized as both sacred and profane, depending on whose "heritage" is being invoked.

Tracing the political, social, and cultural life of "Carry Me Back to

Old Virginny," culminating in the song's "loss" of status as the state song of Virginia, this chapter argues that "Carry Me Back" offers a parable of a "Cause Lost" for neo-Confederates—a cautionary tale of how "progressive" opportunists leveraged so-called political correctness to dismantle an ostensibly apolitical icon of state pride. The story of the historic song and its eventual dethroning, positioned as the catalyst for Hathaway's activism, her mythical tale of origin, serves as the cultural touchstone providing the impetus for the neo-Confederate jeremiad, anchoring the myth of Confederate exceptionalism. It is the narrative woven throughout Virginia's neo-Confederate museum.

As a rhetorical form, the jeremiad has received close attention from scholars, who have examined it within the context of political rhetoric, as in the cases of Robert F. Kennedy and Barack Obama; religious rhetoric, as in Jerry Falwell; and in environmental rhetoric.[9] The jeremiad, according to rhetorical scholar Katherine Henry, "posits a narrative of national honor and an alternative narrative of national shame."[10] As communication scholar Denise Bostdorff summarizes, "Puritan ministers used the jeremiad to define the community and the situations it faced, thereby leading to greater understanding. The jeremiad was also part of a public ritual that aimed to reinforce community by inducing conformity to community standards. Lastly, the jeremiad allowed Puritan ministers to display their eloquence in ways that entertained and underscored their leadership role."[11]

Jeremiahs, political scientist Andrew Murphy argues, "claim that their societies have gone badly wrong, and offer vivid examples or statistics to back up these claims."[12] Henry describes an "anti-Obama jeremiad . . . invested in making its audience feel that they have been undeservedly shamed and disrespected by an out-of-control executive, even as African Americans had been shamed under slavery and Jim Crow";[13] similarly, the neo-Confederate jeremiad inverts narratives of southern racism by offering a story of Confederate diversity and "progressive" bigotry. As Susan Hathaway proclaimed to her audience at Gus and George's, "Who would have ever thought that the Commonwealth of Virginia, who called thirty-two thousand of her young men to die in her defense would turn her back on them, some one hundred fifty years later, refusing to recognize their service, and dishonoring their memory."[14] Her work, her activism, was situated in opposition to these efforts.

A crisis of Confederate "history" mapping onto a broader crisis of public memory, as articulated by Hathaway, is the source of anxiety underpinning the neo-Confederate jeremiad. As Sacvan Bercovitch argued in his work on the American jeremiad, "From the start the Puritan Jeremiahs had drawn their inspiration from insecurity; by the 1670s, crisis had become their source of strength. They fastened upon it, gloried in it, even invented it if necessary. They took courage from backsliding, converted threat into vindication, made affliction their seal of progress. Crisis became both form and substance of their appeals."[15] "Carry Me Back to Old Virginny" has been made to stand as the casualty of this crisis, this war with "progressives," a symbol of the Lost Cause and the necessity of future defense of Confederate heritage. When Susan Hathaway stood tearful at the makeshift podium set up at the restaurant, she was not only lamenting the loss of a "retired" song; she was also crying for a community she believed under attack, seeking to stave off further loss.

The Making of a Cultural Touchstone

Hathaway's cri de coeur referenced something specific—the protracted public battle that unfolded in the Virginia General Assembly and on the pages of publications between the late 1980s and 1990s, local and national, over the meaning of "Carry Me Back to Old Virginny" and the propriety of its performance. Yet the history of the song is much longer.

First printed in 1878, the same year it was first performed by white minstrel star George Primrose,[16] the song's original lyrics and music were written by James A. Bland, a New Yorker "who apparently never set foot in the Old Dominion."[17] Bland's status as a "Yankee" was a fact that, the *Highland Recorder* noted in 1940, was "difficult for some Virginians to accept."[18] Regardless of whether Bland in fact ever visited Virginia, a historic detail still in dispute,[19] "he knew what he was talking about," Hathaway maintained at that July 2014 SCV meeting. The "Old Virginny" Bland described was the "true" Virginia for the Flaggers and the members of the Sons of Confederate Veterans, a mirror reflecting life on the antebellum plantation, whether Bland actually *lived* that life or not.

Born in Flushing, New York, Bland was, historians note, "the most prolific, famous, and influential black minstrel songwriter"[20] of the nineteenth century, despite his status as a relative unknown. Bland was referred to as "the Negro Stephen Foster," "the World's Greatest Minstrel Man," the "Prince of Colored Songwriters," and "the Greatest Ethiopian Songwriter of All Time."[21] One of his other famous songs, "Oh Dem Golden Slippers" (1879), has been the unofficial theme song of Philadelphia's annual Mummers' Day parade, a white, working-class pageant of costumes, dancing, and blackface, brownface, and redface performance through the center of the city down Broad Street that continues to this day on the first of January.[22] That two of Bland's best-known pieces occupy uneasy positions within the racial landscape stands as testament to the ambiguity surrounding both the author and his works. It is an ambiguity that has been deployed strategically since the works' composition.

The details of James Bland's life and motivations for composing the more than seven hundred songs with which he is credited find little consensus among historians.[23] Robert Toll suggests that Bland's "nostalgic Old Darkies expressed great love for their masters and mistresses; his plantation songs were free from antislavery protests and from praise of freedom. . . . His Northern Negroes strutted, sang, danced, and had flapping ears, huge feet, and gaping mouths."[24] William Hullfish, in contrast, finds in Bland evidence of antislavery sentiment, granting that "Bland may have written about nostalgic and 'happy darkies,' but he never made fun of religion or portrayed blacks as stupid (unable to pronounce words), hoodlums, or thieves." Rather than being a victim of the minstrelsy formula who traded in crass stereotypes of Black people, Hullfish argues, "James A. Bland did not sell out. . . . He paid a heavy price for preserving his dignity."[25]

The "price" to which Hullfish referred was James Bland's eventual death in relative obscurity. Throughout his life, Bland traveled to and lived in England, where his music had been well received, and where he was well known and recognizable for his relative affluence.[26] Toward the end of his life, Bland found himself betwixt and between musical traditions, an icon of minstrelsy as it was being replaced by the emerging vaudeville scene. Largely unknown at the time of his death from tuberculosis in Philadelphia in 1911, Bland was buried in an unmarked grave in Merion Cemetery in Bala Cynwyd, Pennsylvania. His music was revived later in the decade by concert soprano Alma Gluck and W. C. Handy, composer, musician, and "Father of the Blues."[27] Public interest in Bland's life was further stoked by Dr. James Francis Cooke, editor of *Etude*, who uncovered some details of the late composer's life while lecturing at Howard University in the late 1930s.

Whatever James Bland's motivations for writing "Carry Me Back," the song—invoking "Old Virginny" as an idyllic landscape of growing crops, hardworking yet "happy slaves," and chirping birds, where even the Dismal Swamp appears beautiful—played well into the hands of fraternal organizations. In the 1930s the Lions had been "impressed by the patriotic fervor and nostalgic quality of this lyric"[28] and undertook a campaign to have the song adopted as the state song of Virginia. It was an effort to which the Virginia Conservation Commission was sympathetic as it sought to brand Virginia's nascent tourism culture.[29]

"Carry Me Back to Old Virginny" was adopted as the official state song of Virginia by the Virginia General Assembly with House Joint Resolution No. 10 in 1940, more than sixty years after the song was written. On naming the song the official anthem of Virginia in 1940, the Virginia General Assembly changed "Virginny" to the "corrected"[30] "Virginia." The "matter of spelling," according to the *Highland Recorder*, "was one of the centers of debate during consideration of the resolution."[31] Newspapers reported discussion of other textual corrections such as the substitution of "potatoes" for the dialect "taters," which betrayed Bland's roots in the blackface minstrel tradition,[32] but these substitutions never came to pass. The *Richmond Times-Dispatch* would later reflect on the decision to change the title of the song to include the word "Virginia" as an attempt to make the song "more dignified,"[33] code for "more elite and white."

As "Carry Me Back" was being instituted as Virginia's state song, journalist and historian Douglas Southall Freeman, Pulitzer Prize–winning biographer of Robert E. Lee, wrote "The Spirit of Virginia," an introduction for the Virginia Writers' Project's *Guide to the Old Dominion*. In it, Freeman dubbed the Commonwealth "a curious commingling of yesterday and today. . . . There is a deliberate cult of the past. . . . A pleasant society it is, one that does not adventure rashly into new acquaintanceship but welcomes with a certain stateliness of manner those who come with letters from friends."[34] Highlighting Freeman's strategic description of Virginia's "cultured circles" of white people to the exclusion of everyone else, historian Brent Tarter notes, "Freeman's descriptions of what the people of that privileged and self-satisfied population believed about themselves and about Virginia subtly transformed their beliefs into a blanket characterization of the beliefs and attitudes of the whole population. 'The Spirit of Virginia' thereby became a kind of ethnic cleansing of the history and culture of the state."[35]

"Carry Me Back to Old Virginny" captured "the Spirit of Virginia"—what Freeman earlier referred to as "the Virginia Way," a brand of genteel paternalism that, historian J. Douglas Smith summarizes, "wholeheartedly supported segregation and disenfranchisement but rejected the rigid racial oppression and violence trumpeted elsewhere in the South."[36] It was a strategy for managing race relations that enabled white Virginians to enjoy a reputation for relative harmony—promising "to provide a modicum of basic services and even encourag[ing] a certain amount of black educational and economic uplift."[37] Elite whites expected continued deference in return.

This paternalistic system fostered an embrace of the song's "wistful, reverent" tone and helped make "Carry Me Back to Old Virginny" one of

"America's Favorite Songs," according to the *Star-Gazette* of Elmira, New York, in 1923.[38] The song would be sung along with "Dixie" during an August 1919 concert for Eamon de Valera, president of the Irish Republic, who visited Richmond to address the cause of Ireland.[39] One year later "Carry Me Back to Old Virginny" was sung outside the White House for President Woodrow Wilson as a tribute to the commander in chief.[40] The song was announced in advertisements for musical performances printed in newspapers across the United States. The *Star-Gazette* noted that as a symbol the relatively peaceful Virginia was a surrogate for "home—no matter where one's home may be."[41]

This romance for "home" stood in sharp contrast to the reality of racial politics in Virginia. In the early decades of the twentieth century, the passage of Jim Crow laws disenfranchised Black Virginians, the state passed the Racial Integrity Act of 1924, and memberships in local white supremacist Anglo-Saxon clubs, founded in Richmond by musician and composer John Powell, rose. The General Assembly laid the groundwork for the Supreme Court decision in *Buck v. Bell* (1927), which permitted the sexual sterilization of inmates at state institutions.[42] The decision would become legal precedent for the eugenics movement, eventually cited by several Nazi defendants during the Nuremberg trials following sterilizations performed in concentration camps during World War II.[43]

As legislation reinscribed racial hierarchies, labor unions, Tarter writes, "were successfully appealing to the country's working men and women who thought they were underpaid or mistreated."[44] By 1940, while Black people in Virginia had made significant gains, attempting to mobilize in response to repressive laws, "Black residential areas, almost without exception, lacked paved streets, lighting, and sewage,"[45] evidencing neglect by political leadership.

Amid a blinding nostalgia for the past that revealed a certain cultural amnesia among Virginia's leaders and a dire fear of labor unrest, "Carry Me Back to Old Virginia" found its way into Virginians' statewide repertoire. The song had been embedded into the fabric of Virginia state culture as not only a song but also a tourism slogan, titling a 1922 historical pageant. "Carry Me Back to Old Virginia" was also used in promotional booklets shipped throughout the nation for prospective Virginia visitors.[46] By 1938 the Virginia Conservation Commission had used the song in its first motion picture, "Virginia Movietone Travelogue," and in two motion pictures about George Washington being released for distribution.[47]

The extent to which the song had been woven into Virginia's culture was reflected in Gov. William Tuck's stated public support for Bland. At the 1946 dedication of Bland's grave monument, Tuck, an insider of the conservative Democratic political machine run by Harry F. Byrd Sr., proclaimed, "This occasion serves to refute the malicious charge against our fair Commonwealth . . . that there is no mutuality of understanding, no tolerance, no cooperation, no love between members of the white and Negro races below the Mason and Dixon Line."[48] Tuck continued, "We in Virginia have a centuries-old tradition of respectful association between the races, dating back farther than any other locality in the Western Hemisphere."[49] The governor concluded, "We intend to continue this relationship of interracial harmony and will be successful in our objective, unless the seeds of discontent, of mistrust, of misunderstanding and even of hate, sown by perhaps well-intentioned but certainly misguided persons alien to our Virginia and Southern way of life, should take root and spread."[50]

Tuck's points seemed to be further reinforced by Dr. James Francis Cooke, who, when speaking at the ceremony, noted, "there is no color line in music."[51] Tuck's embrace of Bland in an effort to preserve the "southern way of life," a phrase he would later deploy in his efforts to block school desegregation during Virginia's era of massive resistance, revealed a strategic effort to claim Bland as a native son of Virginia. Tuck had "carried Bland back" to memorialize his contributions in offering a "truthful" representation of life south of the Mason-Dixon Line before the Civil War—life that did not include racial animus.

For Governor Tuck, who in 1946 used Bland's lyrics to inoculate against claims of Virginia's racism, "Carry Me Back to Old Virginny" should be read as eyewitness testimony of racial harmony. While Virginia at the time "did not usually share in the rabid forms of racism which plagued the lower South," according to historian William Crawley, Virginia was "affected by the general deterioration of racial feelings which occurred in the postwar era."[52] The song, Tuck suggested, should be read at face value, absolving Virginia of its history of racism and oppression, instead proffering a narrative of "faithful slaves" and "benevolent masters." Tuck's praise of the song echoed in Hathaway's meditation on its meaning more than fifty years later.

Carried Back To . . .

By 1987, when Sen. Charles L. Waddell (D-Loudoun) claimed that his "constituents don't want to be carried back anywhere,"[53] the state had done its fair share to inscribe the slogan onto the national consciousness for more than half a century. Tourists were lured to Virginia to literally revisit the past and a particular past at that—the past Hathaway romanticized with her tearful rendition of "Carry Me Back" at that restaurant in Virginia Beach.

Even before its inauguration as Virginia's state song in 1940, the lyrics to "Carry Me Back to Old Virginia" were considered "magic words, drawing thousands of visitors to the historic city [of Richmond] on the James during the week of May 22 [1922]" for the 1922 Virginia Historical Pageant.[54] The words, the pageant's slogan, sought to "appeal to Virginians, descendants of Virginians, and lovers of American History, wherever they may reside."[55] The pageant was advertised in publications throughout the South, from the *Twin City Daily Sentinel* in Winston-Salem, North Carolina, to the *Tampa Tribune* to the *Washington Times* in the US capital.[56] The pageant program, depicting men in period dress spanning more than two centuries, appealed to tourists' sense of history, offering to "carry them back" to an earlier time—one they themselves might never have experienced but to which they were intimately tied.

Produced by Dr. Thomas Wood Stevens, the pageant was intended to "commemorat[e] in Tableaux, Song and Story the wonderful progress of Virginia from the early days of Jamestown, through the stirring and eventful periods of Colonial, Civil and Foreign Wars to the present time, and prophesying the even greater Virginia of the future."[57] First suggested by a member of the Virginia Historical Society in February 1916, with a program draft published in the journal of the Richmond chamber of commerce the following April, the pageant was imagined to be a model, receiving not only national but international attention.[58] Billed as "the first historical pageant to combine on a huge scale the parade of the day time with its floats depicting historical events and industrial progress in the state,"[59] the only reason it had not taken shape sooner had been the advent of World War I.

The six-day affair was designed to have each day corresponding to a historical period, from the colonial era through the Confederacy, complete with processions through the streets of the city. On Thursday, May 25, Confederate history was to take center stage. In reporting the event, the *Times-Dispatch* announced "Veterans of Old South to be Picturesque Figures in Pageant Process." In addition to the "usual formation of the mounted police, followed by a band, and the queen's float," the paper announced "Major Dallas Coghill, who, on his charger, will impersonate General Robert E. Lee."[60] Gen. W. B. Freeman, commander of the Virginia Division of the United Confederate Veterans, was scheduled to marshal. The Confederate Memorial Society was said to have a float "showing the 'White House of the Confederacy'" with Davis and family on the porch.[61] The United Daughters of the Confederacy had a float inspired by the words of James Barron Hope: "In the future some historian shall come forth both great and wise, With the love of the republic and the truth before his eyes. He will hold the scales of justice; he will neither praise nor blame. And the South will stand the verdict and will stand it without shame."[62]

In addition to reporting a re-creation of the Battle of Chancellorsville, the fateful battle during which Confederate general Stonewall Jackson was accidentally shot by his own men, the *Richmond Times-Dispatch* took particular note of a Henrico County float, dubbed "perhaps the most unique float which has thus far appeared in any of the period parades."[63]

> It represented an old Southern plantation with the picturesque mansion home. On the veranda sat a white-haired old colonel and his wife. In the rear appeared old-time Southern "negroes" singing, "Carry Me Back to Ole Virginny," as they bend to their labors. It brought a spontaneous roar of applause all during the parade march. Led by Donohue's Municipal Band, several musical units played the stirring notes of "Dixie" at intervals along the line.[64]

It was a literal reenactment of James Bland's "Old Virginny" as visualized on versions of reprinted sheet music (see fig. 1.1).

While the pageant was advertised as a spectacle to behold, "a series of great moments in ye history of ye state,"[65] according to a *Richmond Times-Dispatch* advertisement, local department and drugstores seized the pageant as an opportunity to sell wares, from the mundane to the pageant-specific. From Tragle's Luncheonette, which advertised a "Special Pageant Menu," "Pageant Week Candy Specials," and Kodak cameras to "give you a picture story of the great Historical Pageant events,"[66] to Richmond's famous department store Miller & Rhoads, advertised as "headquarters for costume materials suitable for the balls and other events tipifying [sic] the several periods represented during Pageant Week,"[67] local businesses capitalized on the pageant's connection to the past as a commercial opportunity aimed at Richmond participants, spectators, and out-of-towners.[68] E. J. Conway wrote in the city's Black press, the *Richmond Planet*, of pageant preparations serving to "stimulat[e] business in many lives."[69]

If being "carried back" offered economic opportunities for local businesses, Black and white, the pageant, too, offered unparalleled educational opportunities. Leading into the final day of the pageant, the *Richmond Times-Dispatch* asked, "What about the school children? Are the school authorities awake to the educational values to the pupils of one night at this great drama?"[70] The educational value was echoed by the *Richmond Planet*, which stated, "The historical displays were of a kind that

Figure 1.1, "Carry Me Back to Old Virginny": Song and Chorus/Words and Music by James A. Bland [sheet music] (Library of Virginia)

the student could read at a glance and the ordinary individual could think about for some time to come."[71] The *Planet* deemed the event a "superb achievement of the progressive white citizens of this locality."[72] Reflecting on the pageant's accomplishments one week later, however, the *Planet* noted that "the colored people were apparently forgotten."[73]

The resignation with which the *Richmond Planet* covered the Virginia Historical Pageant might lie with the fact that months earlier, in February 1922, a group of forty-two members of the Ku Klux Klan, dressed "in their robes and hoods of white" and seated in the Academy of Music's boxes, arose during the last night of the rerelease of D. W. Griffith's *Birth of a Nation* with their left arms extended—an action repeated twice during the film. "Mysterious and silent," the Klansmen sat quietly throughout much of the film, "in which the most thrilling scenes depict the Ku Klux Klan in reconstruction days in the South coming to the rescue of the oppressed white people."[74] On the conclusion of the film, the group, which had roused the watchful eyes of the audience, dispersed with little sound.

While the Klan's very public appearance in February 1922 was followed by the relatively uneventful Virginia Historical Pageant—at least in terms of its potential for violence and intimidation—it became clear that engaging with the past had become very much a part of Richmond's, and by extension the state of Virginia's, present. It is thus unsurprising that "Carry Me Back to Old Virginia" became the title of the state's tourism pamphlets between the 1930s and 1970s, appealing to potential visitors by narrating the story of the state, its sites, and its people, whose "native sons," including George Washington, Thomas Jefferson, and James Madison, were responsible for "many of the fundamental principles of democracy."[75] Woodrow Wilson even received brief mention as another Virginian who "burned with a passionate desire to extend the fruits of our successful democracy to larger fields."[76] These tourist pamphlets textualized the 1922 pageant, including an absence of nonwhite peoples (see figs. 1.2–1.4).

Seemingly immune to the passage of time, each pamphlet, whether from 1941, 1950, or 1964, trades in an appeal to the past. While none of the covers explicitly invokes the Confederacy, Confederate history was by no means hidden from readers. The covers instead provided a point of origin for Virginia. In the period between the three covers, the United States underwent a series of political, social, and cultural changes. White mobs rioted in cities such as Detroit and Harlem (1943) following the movement of Black people into urban centers as part of the Great Migration. Latino youth were attacked in the Zoot Suit riots (1943). A twenty-seven-year-old Black woman by the name of Irene Morgan was arrested

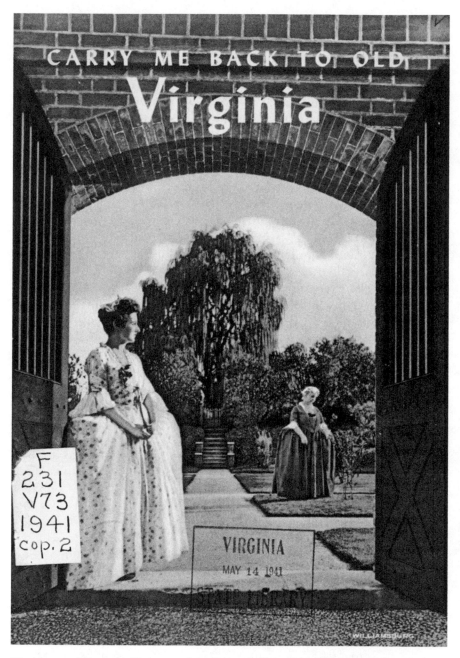

Figure 1.2, Virginia Conservation Commission, "Carry Me Back to Old Virginia" [pamphlet], 1941 (Library of Virginia)

Figure 1.3, Virginia Dept. of Conservation and Development, "Carry Me Back to Old Virginia" [pamphlet], 1950 (Library of Virginia)

for refusing to give up her seat to a white passenger as she traveled from Gloucester, Virginia, to Baltimore, Maryland (1944). As the Supreme Court overturned the 1896 decision in *Plessy v. Ferguson* that inscribed the "separate but equal" doctrine with its decision in *Brown v. Board of Education* in 1954, southern governors convened in Richmond to develop a plan to resist *Brown*.[77] Amid a changing nation and a changing Virginia, the interior text of the brochures changed little, if at all, over time.

The history of Virginia, the 1941 booklet claimed, "is a moving story of an uphill yet successful march in helping to declare, establish, defend and strengthen a government dedicated to assure freedom for all its people."[78] The state's history could be distilled into a linear narrative of progress—successful in its pursuit of freedom—despite the fact that there is only one person of color depicted in the book's close to a hundred pages—"A little Virginian" seen "pluck[ing] ripe cotton."[79] Inviting visitors "one and all to come and share her glorious heritage with her people,"[80] the 1941 booklet presents, with particular aplomb, Richmond. The capital of the Confederacy "until the tragic Cause was lost" where "in the end, valor gave way to despair," Richmond is celebrated as the home of Monument Avenue, "a roster of the South's greatest leaders in the 'sixties."[81]

Figure 1.4, Virginia Dept. of Conservation and Economic Development, "Carry Me Back to Old Virginia" [pamphlet], 1964 (Library of Virginia)

Monument Avenue is but one of the hallmarks of "old Virginia," which a 1952 brochure titled "Enchanting Virginia" claimed is "a charming land that will open new vistas for you—like the absorbing pages of a dramatic novel come to life."[82] Not only was Virginia a mythical land where the past is undeniably present, it is also a place where fiction comes to life.

This appeal to the past was among the draws of Virginia, a state that, a 1966 brochure titled "Moving to Virginia" boasted, had seen an influx of new residents, including in 1950 "a quarter-million white people from New England, the Middle Atlantic States, and the northern Midwest."[83] While the state also attracted retirees and military personnel, likely due to its proximity to Washington, DC, and the presence of military bases in Norfolk and Hampton Roads, the pamphlet noted a decline in the state's nonwhite population. Between 1870 and 1950, Virginia's nonwhite population diminished from 42 to 22 percent. The brochure explained, "*The point of this is that Virginia is highly favored as a place of residence by a large and increasing number of people from many States and countries.*"[84] The state's influx of white residents, coupled with the departure of nonwhite people, was cause, at least as far as the state was concerned, for celebration.

In 1970, then Virginia senator Douglas L. Wilder, also the first Black elected governor of any state in America (1990–1994), first attempted to dethrone the song he claimed to be a racist relic. The next year, the booklet "Carry Me Back to Old Virginia" sought to captivate potential visitors by harking back to "the magic of Virginia," a place "where the charm of an older era blends with the wonders of the new in a setting of natural beauty unmarred by time."[85] The booklet was an even more romantic meditation on the state's history than earlier versions, literally dubbing Virginia a "Land of Romance." It vividly describes romance as it "wove a golden pattern through the lives of the Cavalier colonists and their share in the struggle for independence, which had its source and center in Virginia. Romance, mingled with tragedy, lingers in the bugle echoes of the Civil War—with Virginia the principal battleground."[86] Richmond was lauded as "no finer spot" for history buffs, "a city with a long, colorful past, a charming present, and an exciting future."[87] Richmond's charms remained, like the state's more generally, mired in its whiteness.

A pamphlet announcing, "You haven't seen America until you see Historic VIRGINIA," published in the late 1970s, encourages visiting the "birthplace of the nation," where "our modern union was forged in the fire of war." Offering visitors a remarkably optimistic interpretation of the American Civil War, the brochure reminds tourists that Virginia is home to "the plantation birthplace of Robert E. Lee, who rose above defeat to become a hero of both North and South." Reconciliationist narratives appealed to North and South, drawing visitors to "make a pilgrimage to the homes of Washington, Jefferson, Monroe, Wilson and other Virginia-born Presidents."[88]

By February 1987, when the Senate Rules Committee passed a resolution, sponsored by Delegate Thomas M. Moncure (R-Fredericksburg), to appoint a joint subcommittee to study the adoption of new lyrics or another state song to the cost of an estimated $8,000,[89] the stakes had increased dramatically. While tourism pamphlets throughout most of the twentieth century attempted to lure visitors to Virginia, highlighting the state's historic connections to freedom and liberty, by the mid-1980s attempts to reconsider the song reached a climax. Wilder, along with other Black leaders in the city, criticized the song and called for its repeal, while former governor Mills E. Godwin Jr. publicly attacked Wilder's proposal and Wilder himself for foregrounding race in the discussion.

The conservative *Richmond Times-Dispatch* rushed to Godwin's defense, claiming, "Exactly why it was an act of racism for Mr. Godwin to defend the song and not an act of racism for Sen. Wilder, who freely admitted he was motivated by racial considerations, to denounce it was not made clear." Godwin, the *Times-Dispatch* argued, "appointed blacks to many important state posts, breaking, in the process, the color barrier in Virginia's judiciary by naming the first black circuit court judge. He is entitled to most of the credit for establishing the community college system, which has contributed dramatically to black educational and economic progress."[90] The paper paid no attention to Godwin's own political history, which included a formative role in Virginia's resistance to public school desegregation in the wake of the *Brown* decision.[91] By the mid-1980s, "Carry Me Back to Old Virginia" was a political football.

As with twenty-first-century discussions of the future of Confederate monuments, there was hardly consensus in the 1980s regarding what to do with the song. Delegate Moncure spoke of the reluctance to change the song in 1987, summarizing a few of the varied perspectives: "One is that blacks should be proud that they were able to endure slavery. If you follow that reasoning, the starving time at Jamestown would be a wonderful thing to celebrate in a state song. . . . The other line of reasoning is that it's history and it should be left alone."[92] Supporters of the song articulated a version of the "it's history" argument that lingers in the air close to thirty years later.

Despite efforts to position the song as a form of depoliticized "history," calls for the General Assembly to dethrone the song came from the Richmond chapter of the Southern Christian Leadership Conference (SCLC), which claimed the song was "a reminder to a great number of the citizens of a painful era—the era when blacks were referred to as 'darkies,'" according to Rev. Robert Jones, SCLC chapter president. Jones continued,

"It (a state song) should be a song that can be sung in any public gathering among any group of persons with no shame, feelings of resentment or bad memories."[93]

The *Richmond Times-Dispatch* disputed the charge that the song could inspire shame among those singing it. In a 1988 editorial, the newspaper named the song's lyrics "merely relics from Virginia's past" and, when "viewed in that context, [they] ought not to offend anyone. It's the song's message that matters. Written by a black man, James Bland, it speaks movingly of love of and loyalty to homeland, of Virginia's beauty and its pull on the heart. It is a hymn of sincere praise."[94] This sentiment was echoed by the Lancaster chapter of the United Daughters of the Confederacy, who encouraged chapter members and Virginians to "write their senators and delegates, immediately, to let them know how you feel about 'desecrating our well-known and well-loved state song.'"[95] The *Smithfield Times*, which shared that then governor Linwood Holton suggested keeping the tune but changing the lyrics, commented, "That might be prudent policy for the commission to consider. Keep the baby but throw out the bath water." The editorial comment was accompanied by a political cartoon depicting a doctor looking to make an incision into the "racist lyrics."[96]

In January 1989 a state senate subcommittee rejected attempts to add Charlottesville resident Adele Abrahamse's "Old Dominion" as the second state song of Virginia. Recommended by the study committee, "Old Dominion" was selected from a group of thirty to forty proposed songs.[97] Described as "a catchy song that heralds Virginia's landscape, heritage and spirit," "Old Dominion," the song's supporters assured, would be appropriate for public functions.[98] The rationale for the proposal for a second state song was, according to Abrahamse, "If we have two songs, each can serve a purpose. Nobody loses."[99] Abrahamse's argument did not win with the state senate.

For the next several years, the House of Delegates debated ways to wordsmith "Carry Me Back," replacing terms considered offensive. The exercise, the *Richmond Times-Dispatch* suggested in January 1991, resulted in a song that "resembled a bad travel-agency jingle."[100] Several other alternative songs were proposed. Each proposal was killed.

This Old Dreamers' Heart

In 1994 the debate surrounding the song was revived again with House Joint Resolution No. 179, offered on January 25, 1994. That the future of the song was debated within the Virginia General Assembly points to the stakes involved in the song's fate. The resolution acknowledged that "certain portions of the official song are offensive to many citizens of the Commonwealth" and noted that "the Secretary of Health and Human Services appointed a committee of five citizens to review the official state song and make recommendations for changes to the lyrics which would eliminate such disturbing features."[101] Senate Bill No. 231 proposed that the lyrics of "Carry Me Back to Old Virginia" be amended by Robert Bluford Jr., replacing the "darkey's heart" with "dreamer's heart" and "old Massa" with "my loved ones."[102] The bill's sponsor, Sen. Madison E. Marye (D-Montgomery), stated, "If we start with schoolchildren and they sing together a song about their state, I think we will make great strides in harmony."[103] Marye noted, "I think it's time we can sing this song together without one trace of racism. I believe that millions of people long to hear this song sung again."[104] Although the measure passed the senate with a vote of 35–2, the house voted 87–9 to repeal. As Michael Hardy summarized for the *Richmond Times-Dispatch*, "The House debate was sometimes emotional, with opponents, both black and white, decrying the offending lyrics."[105]

While the debates surrounding the song in the mid-1990s tended to fall broadly into one of two camps, the rationale for revising the song or not assumed a variety of forms. Wayne Byrd, president of the Danville, Virginia, chapter of the Historical Preservation Society and supporter of the original lyrics, said they "dispel the myth that all Southerners were terrible people who 'beat and abused the slaves.'"[106] Following suit, the Coalition for American Heritage blamed "politically correct liberal activists" for wanting to ban the song, along with Lee-Jackson Day.

The *Smithfield Times*'s Mary Wakefield Buxton agreed, claiming,

> Poor James Bland. He had the unmitigated nerve as an artist to write in his times a song that reflected the real world, and his real feelings living in such a world. It included mentioning words like "massa" and "missus," words that reflect that blacks were once enslaved in this great country. One must never breathe a mention of such terrifying truth. . . . After all, how politically correct is it to suggest that some Virginians then and even now might have spoken or speak in uneducated dialect?[107]

She continued,

> Yes, slavery happened. No matter how many songs, poems, and stories are rewritten in order to try to make us feel better about the past . . . slavery happened. Right here in Virginia. And the damage it did to blacks was devastating. And the damage it did to whites was devastating. We are still suffering from it. Isn't it time to confront our feelings rather than just rewrite another song?[108]

Buxton's central claim—that slavery had been historically devastating to Black *as well as white* people—evokes Hathaway's tearful rendition of "Carry Me Back." Hathaway's emotion, her quivering voice, revealed the sense of loss among white Virginians. The song, after all, was their attempt to demonstrate that they were not racists. They had embraced the words—the dialect—written by a Black man celebrating the antebellum southern plantation. James Bland could be no better spokesperson for the past for Hathaway and the Virginia Flaggers, and any detractors who took issue with Bland's "truth" did so only in the name of "political correctness." Those detractors who cited the song for its racism, Hathaway and the Flaggers maintained, were the real racists.

Buxton followed up the next week by elaborating on her understanding of slavery. She wrote, "If only slavery was about whips and shackles and one race subjugating another. If only it were that easy to recognize. . . . The concept that government knows best what you need and is best set up to provide it to you in the form of government welfare programs has enslaved whole multitudes of people. Many Americans no longer take responsibility for their own lives and behavior and have become dependent on the new 'massa.'"[109] Echoing segregationist Governor Tuck's 1946 commentary at the dedication of Bland's grave site close to fifty years earlier, Buxton invoked the song as evidence that slavery was about more than "whips and shackles." What Buxton offered was an implicit critique of the welfare state, part of the broader conservative jeremiad warning against the consequences of big government.

While Buxton and others remained committed to the song's provenance as a historical testament to the past, criticism of such a stance was just as easy to find. *Richmond Times-Dispatch* progressive Black columnist Michael Paul Williams noted in March 1994, "A state's song should evoke a sense of pride in all of its residents. 'Carry Me Back' produces little more than pain and loathing for many. The song is an embarrassment that has been kept in the closet rather than sung publicly at events."[110] Delegate William P. Robinson (D-Norfolk) agreed with Williams and as the chairman of the thirteen-member Black caucus noted that no revision could make the song acceptable to Black people: "You can change the spots, you can change the stripes, but the song is still offensive."[111]

While the bill to change the song's lyrics in 1994 failed to gain state approval, in 1997 Sen. Stephen D. Newman of Lynchburg sponsored Senate Bill No. 801, proposing that "Carry Me Back to Old Virginia" be retired as the state song "emeritus." In an attempt to combat the critiques of "racists, traditionalists and preservationists," Robert Mason Jr. summarized, "Our song should reflect our proud progress, not our peculiar past."[112] The bill was passed in February 1997, signed by Gov. George Allen on March 20, 1997. "Carry Me Back to Old Virginia" became the state song "emeritus."

Since the song's 1997 "retirement," a soft pedal on an open denunciation of the offensiveness of the song's lyrics, Virginia has pursued a replacement song. While this selection process was by no means easy, in 2015, by a vote of 39–0, "Our Great Virginia," typically sung to the tune of "Shenandoah," was approved as the official state song of Virginia, with "Sweet Virginia Breeze" designated the official "popular song" of Virginia. "Our Great Virginia" celebrates the state as "the birthplace of the nation / Where history was changed forever," with "rolling hills, majestic mountains . . . rivers wide and forests tall." Beyond its history and beauty, Virginia, the song boasts, is where "all of us, we stand together."[113] "Sweet Virginia Breeze" similarly invokes the state's natural landscape, with mention of the Blue Ridge Mountains and dogwoods (Virginia's state tree). It also states, "When I get back to the city of the monuments, / It doesn't matter where I hang my hat, it's home to me."[114] Mention of "the monuments" is about as political as the song gets.

The "loss" of "Carry Me Back to Old Virginia" marked an ideological shift, from the segregationist politics of William Tuck and later Mills Godwin that viewed Black people as suited for plantation life, to the more progressive politics of leaders such as Doug Wilder, who became mayor of Richmond in 2005 and, along with many Black leaders in the city, saw the song as an offensive homage to a past that was idyllic for a particular, white subset of the population. For Susan Hathaway, however, the loss of the song, like contemporary contests surrounding the propriety of flying the Confederate battle flag, signaled a greater loss—the loss of Confederate memory. At Gus and George's in 2014, Hathaway recounted, along with her story of "Carry Me Back," the recent trials and travails of the Confederate battle flag, a historical ground that has been well trod.[115] She remarked, "By buying into the guilt-by-association hogwash, our own folks have shunned the battle flag, leaving the impression that we are all ashamed of it, and prefer it to stay in a museum. I don't know how many times I've heard that, either. Belongs in the museum, hidden from public view."[116]

With these words, Hathaway foreshadowed the many words that would be uttered in debates surrounding the future of Confederate monuments. For Hathaway, as she spoke, "It is my belief, once this battle flag is gone from view, and folks, we're getting close . . . Once this is gone, they're gonna start coming after the next ones. It's not about this flag, it's about us. It's about our ancestors. It's about pretending like it never happened to make people feel a little more comfortable."[117] Hathaway's vague references to "it" signaled an assumption on her part of a common, collective understanding of the cause for which they were organized. Her speech reflected her efforts to rally the collective, seated in that room and across the country, to thwart attacks on Confederate heritage. "Carry Me Back to Old Virginia" had been one of the casualties of the battle.

Following the tradition of the jeremiad, "Redemption is achieved through the efforts of the American people, not through a change in the system itself."[118] Redemption, for Hathaway, is continuing to sing proudly the words of James Bland, to continue to fly the Confederate battle flag, and to vilify those who question the Flaggers' racism. She elaborated,

> With every flag that is raised, return it to its rightful place of honor, or add it to the landscape, we gain a victory for the Confederate veterans who fought and died under them. And when they are not the focus of our efforts, the veterans, such efforts are truly in vain. Our heritage is under attack in ways that we could never imagine, and I have no doubt that victory will be ours, even in the midst of these assaults. I may not know what lies ahead, but I'm certain that there will be many more such attempts to stop us, but I know one thing is for sure; I'm determined to stand, fight, and never back down, but I'm gonna fight like [Nathan Bedford] Forrest, not Sherman. I think that's where we need to make sure we're a little bit different.[119]

In framing this fight, Hathaway lays claim to a moral high ground in an attempt to restore the heritage lost when "Carry Me Back to Old Virginia" was retired. For Hathaway fighting like Forrest is to suggest, as one commenter noted, a "fair and heroic fight," not a fight like a "COWARD and TERRORIST."[120] There was no attention to the fact that Forrest, first grand wizard of the Ku Klux Klan, was known to lead an organization whose very aims were to inspire terror among Black people.

That the song was "retired," allowed to retain its status as an honorable, sacred part of state history, and not *repealed* suggests a broader, more complicated relationship to Confederate memory that is not as "lost" as Hathaway asserts. Rather, memory of "Carry Me Back to Old Virginny" and its celebration of the antebellum plantation continue to linger, a subtle hum reminding of the neo-Confederate memory museum's capacity to mediate different registers of experience. Yet on one account Hathaway is correct: the story of "Carry Me Back to Old Virginny," the story of the neo-Confederate jeremiad, is one of contest, of the struggle to define racism in twenty-first-century America. As my later journey to Lexington, Virginia, would reveal, not all artifacts engaging with memory of the Confederacy are discussed as acrimoniously.

2 | Stonewall Jackson and Sacred Relics

Writing about Gen. Thomas "Stonewall" Jackson's taxidermied war horse for the newspaper of the Virginia Military Institute (VMI), the *VMI Cadet*, in 1949, T. L. Marr noted, "It may be a 'stuffed horse' to those of this atomic age, but to those who are historically minded, and it is to be hoped, to those descendants of those V.M.I. cadets who saw him—who may themselves see the animal now in Lexington—'Little Sorrel' was a part of 'Stonewall' Jackson."[1] When Marr wrote these words, Jackson's faithful steed had been dead more than fifty years. Little Sorrel died in 1886 on the grounds of the current Virginia Museum of Fine Arts (VMFA) in Richmond, the former Lee Camp No. 1 for Confederate Veterans. Curiosity led me on a drive to Lexington, Virginia, some two hours west of Richmond, to visit the museum at VMI where Little Sorrel stands, then as now, on display.

The home of Little Sorrel's taxidermied body, Lexington is also the site of the Stonewall Jackson House, the general's residence from 1858 to 1861. Walking distance from Jackson's house is the general's tomb, a popular stop for tourists visiting the Stonewall Jackson Memorial Cemetery. Visitors often deposit lemons around the tomb's base, paying homage to the legend that the eccentric Jackson had an affinity for the fruit—a detail that has been shown to be more fiction than truth.[2] Tourism brochures and the Lexington website identify the locales of the final resting place of Gen. Robert E. Lee, interred in the lower level of the chapel beneath Edward Valentine's imposing recumbent statue at Washington and Lee University, as well as the grave of Lee's horse, Traveller—outside the Lee Chapel. Little Sorrel, these promotional materials note, "stands nearby on exhibit,"[3] at the VMI Museum.

While I was drawn to Lexington to visit Little Sorrel, "part" of the famous general, I soon learned that there were, in fact, pieces of Jackson throughout the state of Virginia. In the family plot on Ellwood Manor near Spotsylvania, a small granite stone marks the site where Jackson's left arm, amputated after the general was mortally wounded during the Battle of Chancellorsville, lay buried. The Stonewall Jackson Shrine in Guinea Station, marking the site where the general succumbed to pneumonia a week after being shot at Chancellorsville, boasts a blanket that lay with

Jackson in his final hours. In Lynchburg, the deteriorating hull of the packet boat *Marshall*, which carried Jackson's body (minus his left arm) to Lexington for burial, stands on display under a roof constructed to protect the historic artifact.[4] A small portion of the boat is in the same display case as Little Sorrel at the VMI Museum. Read in isolation, these sites of memory reinforce the significance of Jackson as a historical actor whose life was cut tragically short. Taken together, they curate a set of experiences across the Commonwealth that instantiate the myth of Confederate exceptionalism through museal practice.

For visitors walking into the VMI Museum in Jackson Memorial Hall, a site that "stands today as tribute to a man [Stonewall Jackson] who served the Virginia Military Institute with distinction,"[5] the taxidermied Little Sorrel is displayed in profile. "The oldest mounted horse in America and one of only about six historically significant mounted horses in the world," according to Col. Keith Gibson, museum director,[6] Little Sorrel has been on display for more than half a century—far longer than women have been permitted to enroll at VMI, a grim reality easily missed if one is unacquainted with the history of the school.[7]

As I stood in front of the taxidermy encased in protective glass at the VMI Museum, I was dumbfounded. Surrounded by several families with small children, an elderly couple, and a young man and woman about college age who appeared to be on a date quietly and reverently inspecting the animal's remains, I stared—at them and then back at the hide (fig. 2.1). What I had not realized when I arrived in Lexington was that although I had made the journey to bear witness to a taxidermied horse, I had indeed traveled to visit a sacred relic, much like the monument to Jackson's amputated arm, the shrine containing the blanket that lay with him at his death, and the boat that carried his body to its eventual resting place.[8]

As a conceptual category, "relic," historian Teresa Barnett notes, has never been an especially "rigorous classification."[9] While within religious studies, the term refers to an object that possesses a special quality or power by virtue of its connection "with the body of a saint, martyr, or other holy person,"[10] the relic, as imagined in the nineteenth century, was capacious enough a category to include all objects tied, however loosely, to a historical figure or event, a fragment of the past, or even a natural object.[11] A relic could be anything from a handkerchief touched by Robert E. Lee to a button from George Washington's uniform to a piece of Plymouth Rock. The relic was envisioned as "the metonymic equivalence by which a material piece of the past stands in for a larger event to which it is closely allied." In standing in for a larger event, the sacred relic, Barnett

Figure 2.1, Little Sorrel (VMI Museum, Lexington, Virginia)

notes, is "a thing that could be interacted with on an intimate level and used to achieve certain emotional states. It created a relationship *with* the past rather than a stance *versus* the past."[12]

Despite their affective power, sacred relics were largely dismissed by museum professionals in the early twentieth century as lacking evidentiary authority, forsaken for the less sentimental and more "scientific" object.[13] While the term "relic" has since been consigned to "a synonym for antiquated and irrelevant,"[14] equated with quaint curiosities, sacred relics such as Little Sorrel remain foregrounded in places such as Lexington, where Confederate memory is largely divorced from history.

Within the VMI Museum, Little Sorrel stands frozen, halting time's inexorable march while simultaneously communicating a certain "liveliness," reinforced by the museum text panel quoting Jackson's wife, Mary Anna, about the horse's expressive eyes, "as soft as a gazelle's." If the very act of taxidermy seemed macabre, Mrs. Jackson's comment about the horse's eyes—the one part of the horse's exterior that was fake—was particularly jarring.

Little Sorrel is unquestionably the main attraction at the VMI Museum, featured prominently in promotional materials found across Lexington and on the Internet. On one of my visits to the museum, I heard a woman exclaim, "This is the place with the horse!" Visitors to the museum can purchase magnets, T-shirts, and an array of other objects commemorating the horse, which a tag for a stuffed "Little Sorrel" from the museum gift shop describes as "tough, tireless, and loyal." Such souvenirs offer visitors opportunities to buy mementos of their experience at the VMI Museum, capturing "the adventure, mystery, escape, or pleasure experienced at the [vacation] destination."[15] In this chapter I consider the taxidermied Little Sorrel as both cultural artifact and metaphor, a sacred relic attempting to forge present-day connections to a past that is no longer, as well as a mounted hide stuffed with stories, narratives of a constructed, "cast" history intended for future generations.

Little Sorrel is more than a mundane exemplar of historic pet taxidermy, an object of remembrance to his owner that reflected common practice in the nineteenth century. As a sacred relic, Little Sorrel reinforces the broader mythology of martyrdom surrounding Jackson and, by extension, the Confederacy—a mythology, historian Wallace Hettle has argued, intimately tied to the writings of Presbyterian theologian, Lost Cause proponent, and Jackson biographer Robert Lewis Dabney. A Confederate perhaps only surpassed in the popular imagination by Robert E. Lee, Stonewall Jackson is a historical figure who has long preoccupied the American imagination, likely, Hettle hypothesizes, "because of his peculiar combination of religious piety and martial ferocity."[16] The taxidermied Little Sorrel anchors memory of Jackson and the Confederacy in the twenty-first century in its attempt to reanimate the deceased—to give life to an entity, the Confederacy, which is now more than 150 years defunct.

"The horse's innocence," historian Drew Gilpin Faust notes, "has remained an important part of twentieth-century memory. . . . Glorified as soldiers and campaigners, themselves honored as veterans of war," horses occupy a critical part of the American imaginary as "relics," serving as surrogates for the men they carried.[17] Yet Little Sorrel's body comes to stand in not simply for Stonewall Jackson, as T. L. Marr wrote for the *VMI Cadet*, but for the Confederacy as whole: dead but ever present. In this way, it becomes difficult to see Little Sorrel (and the Confederacy, by extension) as truly gone, an artifact of the past. If anything, the taxidermied body assures us of the Confederacy's presence, which tourists can visit on a daily basis. Functioning in much the same way as taxidermied animals romanticizing the West, such as Roy Rogers's Trigger, the taxidermied Little Sorrel fosters in visitors an emotional nostalgia for the Confederacy by proffering a myth of the Confederacy as an apolitical "animal" and endangered species. Little Sorrel serves as an icon, a noble and virtuous companion whose cause is to be praised.

Moving between the twenty-first-century museum where Little Sorrel stands on display, documents surrounding Jackson's horse at the time of its death, and other relics conjuring the deceased general, this chapter explores how these sacred relics serve to cast the Confederacy as an entity divorced from histories of racism and oppression. If "Carry Me Back to Old Virginny" offered fodder for public, political debate about the definition of racism, played out within the state's General Assembly, the sacred relics harking back to Stonewall Jackson inspire no such controversy. Rather, they exist as benign vestiges of history, antiquarian phenomena to be revered.

"VMI Tells a Story"

The Lexington Historic District communicates its history through a variety of architectural styles, from Greek revival and Queen Anne to picturesque cottages.[18] Lexington is a town, its website boasts, where "the legacy of great leaders . . . [isn't] limited to dusty textbooks." Rather, the leaders' "commitment to civility, honor and education remains an important part of the culture at W&L and VMI as well as the surrounding city."[19] This "legacy" is vague, with the website only offering passing reference to the Confederacy.

In 1995 Rick Killmeyer, an alumnus of VMI, encouraged readers of the *VMI Cadet* to visit the Institute's museum with the reminder, "The Virginia Military Institute is a place where some of the greatest men in the history of the United States of America have walked. I am sure, that George C. Marshall, Robert E. Lee, and Thomas J. Jackson have had their fair share, and walked in our footsteps at one time or another. We are not alone. Let us continue this proud and noble lineage that has been put before us."[20] This "proud and noble lineage" defining the so-called West Point of the South remains the story told today. A marble statue of Gen. Stonewall Jackson, which first-year students are required to salute each time they pass, stands guard at the Barracks' main entrance.[21] As the museum's webpage notes, "Since 1839, VMI alumni have helped mold the history of America. The museum traces the amazing civilian military careers of many alumni. Among the ranks of the alumni are Nobel Prize winners, explorers, film stars, national, state and local political and civic leaders."[22]

VMI's commitment to extending the narrative of a "proud and noble lineage" should not be a surprise. A military school that, as scholar Philippa Strum argues, was a bastion of "Southern white manhood," VMI became the focal point of the landmark equal rights case in 1996, *United States v. Virginia*, which struck down the school's males-only admission policy. VMI, according to Strum, "embodied the values of patriotism and machismo, tradition and fraternity, and it knew in its collective heart that white men were superior to everyone else."[23] This history and tradition is largely unspoken at the VMI Museum, though it is communicated powerfully.

Although there is no explicit reference to the Confederacy on entering Gothic revival–style Jackson Memorial Hall, a sign in the entry of the building explains that the structure was funded with a $100,000 federal government grant "to pay for damages done to the Institute by union [*sic*] soldiers during the Civil War." The phrasing of the sign, which notes "damages done *to* the Institute," suggests that VMI, like the unnamed Confederacy, had been victimized during the Civil War—targeted by the vandal enemy.

The Confederacy's centrality to the identity of VMI despite its lack of specific mention is amplified by the massive painting of the Battle of New Market that takes up much of the central wall of Jackson Memorial Hall's large, nondenominational chapel. The painting is flanked by portraits of Stonewall Jackson and Robert E. Lee, two men whose legacies loom large, particularly in Lexington where seemingly everywhere one turns, buildings bear the name of one or the other revered Confederate.

During the Battle of New Market on May 15, 1864, ten VMI cadets died or were fatally wounded, and forty-five were injured.[24] The contributions of VMI cadets to the success of Confederate forces under the leadership of Gen. John C. Breckinridge, who drove back Gen. Franz Sigel's Union army, are commemorated annually on the battle's anniversary at the New Market Monument, known officially as *Virginia Mourning Her Dead* by sculptor and VMI alumnus Moses Ezekiel. While at the time of its 1903 campus dedication the monument was intended to memorialize the bravery of cadets who served in the 1864 battle, since then the commemoration has evolved to include "the sacrifice of all Institute alumni who have served our nation."[25] VMI's alignment of the cadets' service in the Battle of New Market on behalf of the Confederacy and more recent military service implicitly suggests that sacrifice for the Confederacy was, indeed, a service to the United States. This connection is a trope woven throughout the VMI Museum, located on the two floors beneath the chapel.

On descending by elevator one floor, visitors entering the museum are immediately confronted by the gift shop. With no orienting label text, visitors' only sense of the museum's purpose is shared by a brochure available on entry into the building. Including photographs of Jackson Hall's exterior, Little Sorrel, a soldier's uniform and hat, and a sword, the brochure states, "Explore the history and inspired architecture of America's first state-sponsored military college through the lives of those who changed world events." Boasting about more than 450 rare firearms, the bullet-scarred raincoat worn by Gen. Stonewall Jackson the night he was mortally wounded, and the helmet worn by Gen. George S. Patton, the brochure exclaims, "Explore the Lives of Great Americans!" What I did not immediately realize was that the brochure's emphasis on artifacts—firearms, a raincoat, and a helmet—foreshadowed the veneration of relics that I would soon confront.

While the museum is called the VMI Museum, the exhibit begins with Stonewall Jackson's death and the mounted Little Sorrel, foregrounding the Confederate general and his faithful steed. The once Major Jackson, the introductory panel notes, served as professor of natural philosophy and artillery tactics at VMI, a position he was ill equipped to handle, as he "struggled to stay one lesson ahead of his students." The panel highlights Jackson's first command of the Civil War: "when he marched the VMI cadets to Richmond to serve as drill instructors." Introducing Jackson as an "eccentric" if not inept professor, known around grounds as "Tom Fool" and "Old Hickory," the panel presents a skilled "Civil War" commander. Precisely who the major was commanding, however, the panel leaves unclear. The word "Confederacy" is not mentioned. Rather, reference is made to General Jackson's "12-mile march around the Union Army" and his later attempts to "determine the Union position," leaving visitors, if they are unfamiliar with the contextual history, to infer Jackson's status as a Confederate general.

Save for mention of Commodore Matthew Fontaine Maury, the "Pathfinder of the Seas," whose nephew Dabney Maury "became a Confederate general and later served as Ambassador to Columbia [*sic*] for President Grover Cleveland," a reference that appears in a case one floor below Little Sorrel, the Confederacy receives brief mention in the museum, used periodically as a modifier: Confederate. A text panel describes John Mercer Brooke as a lieutenant who "resigned his U.S. navy commission and joined the Confederate Navy." The same case describing Dabney Maury displays a US Navy sword carried by Commodore Maury, who wore the weapon, the text notes, "when he met with President Lincoln on the eve of the Civil War, attempting to avert the impending conflict." Maury, a man the city of Richmond commemorates on Monument Avenue, its homage to icons of the Confederacy, bears no immediate association with the Confederacy, per the display case.[26] Even as the museum notes Czar Alexander II's appeal to Maury to become the chief scientist of Russia, the naval commander's decision to decline the position to "commit himself to his native Virginia during the Civil War" reads as an artful dodge.

These passing mentions of the Confederacy and the involvement of VMI cadets underscore the museum's attempts to universalize the experiences of those who fought. This point is emphasized by a quote attributed to President Franklin Roosevelt (November 1939) in large letters: "The whole history of VMI is a triumphant chronicle of the part which the Citizen Soldier can play in a Democracy." VMI's "whole history" is framed as standing in for the service of citizens on behalf of democracy. Given the popular positioning of FDR within neo-Confederate circles as a treasonous socialist, the use of FDR's appeal to VMI as representative of the nation is a surprising and significant move, aligning the Confederacy with broader American patriotism. Without historical specificity, it is easy to draw parallels between Confederate soldiers in the American Civil War and those who fought in Afghanistan and Iraq in the early 2000s, who are commemorated in the museum as well. The museum panels implicitly reaffirm the Confederacy's commitment to freedom, even as the Confederacy waged war on the United States.

Little Sorrel, Jackson's "favorite mount during the Civil War," is by far the most striking "object" in the museum's first case. The label text summarizes Little Sorrel's significance in terms of his association with Jackson, the horse's temperament, and his death.[27] Visitors learn that Jackson purchased the horse from a Baltimore & Ohio train in 1861 (nothing is made of the horse's "Yankee" roots);[28] the horse was initially intended to be a gift to Mrs. Jackson, but the horse's calm temperament led Jackson to keep him; Jackson rode Little Sorrel the night he was mortally wounded, and the horse lived at VMI until being moved to the Old Soldiers' Home in Richmond, where he died in 1886.

While Little Sorrel's authenticity and historical significance are indisputable, he is accompanied in the museum's first case by several artifacts of varying degrees of provenance. The British Pattern 1850 saddle, owned by Jackson, *may* have been the one he was riding when he was wounded accidentally, the text panel notes. "The blood stained handkerchief *may* have been with Jackson the night he was mortally wounded" (italics added). Jackson's camp stool, a pamphlet available to museum visitors notes, "became a fixture around the Jackson camp. . . . The stool was a weathered reminder of home." The India rubber raincoat, in contrast, was worn by Jackson when he was accidentally wounded on May 2, 1863. To affirm its authenticity, the raincoat is positioned sideways in the case so as to expose the bullet hole in the upper left sleeve. Taken together, however, these relics amplify the sacredness of Little Sorrel, who stands towering over them, the contemporary of Gen. Stonewall Jackson.

Within the world of taxidermy, the "trophy," the taxidermied body, "represented a powerful signifier of the hunting moment, a theatrical artifact around which the hunt could be extrapolated and experienced—in other words, performed once more."[29] Yet Little Sorrel is not a trophy. Unlike most taxidermied animals, Little Sorrel stands not as testament to superior marksmanship but rather to endurance. Little Sorrel stands in spite of the fact that Stonewall Jackson fell. More than 150 years after Jackson was killed atop his faithful steed, Little Sorrel remains, behind museum glass, ready to be observed by visitors.

The decision to taxidermy Little Sorrel reiterates a desire to ensure the horse's "liveliness" for visitors. The positioning of more contemporary VMI cadets involved in the war efforts in Afghanistan and Iraq throughout the museum only serves to strengthen the connections between past and present, threat and sacrifice. The sense of threat endured by Little Sorrel as a surrogate for the Confederacy is further advanced by a display featuring the work of artist Eugene "Gene" Leoncavallo in lower level of the museum. A wood carver whose work evidences a folk art sculptural aesthetic, Leoncavallo produced *Solitude* in 1986 (see fig. 2.2).

Although the sculpture gives off the appearance of a carousel horse, the label text notes, "Closer examination reveals the riderless horse's real identity." Though the horse seems to stand as if ready to embark on the endless circuit of carousel ridership, the carved debris at the horse's feet points to a relief of a wheel, a sword, rocks, and a soldier's hat. The horse is not one of play or childhood amusement. It is a horse who stands alone without his rider amid a battlefield littered with the remnants of men. The sculpture's eyes communicate a sense of panic, of concern—likely due to the loss of his rider. The eyes are not unlike the eyes used to communicate the "liveliness" of Little Sorrel. The label text notes, "Leoncavallo captures loss and survivorship of the battle. The horse is left alone—in solitude." Leoncavallo's solitary horse stands as a wooden analog to Little Sorrel, who stands upstairs alone in his case, surrounded by the noncorporeal remains of his master. *Solitude* reminds us that the horse

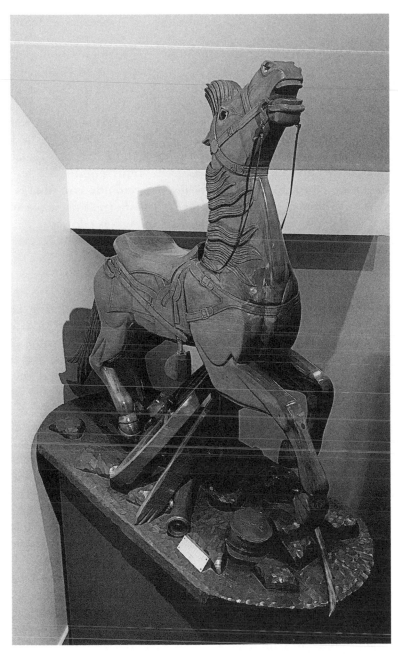

Figure 2.2, *Solitude*, Artist: Eugene "Gene" Leoncavallo (VMI Museum, Lexington, Virginia)

endures as a symbol of strength in the face of unspeakable death and devastation.

It is a message echoed in Leoncavallo's other sculpture on display, *The Soldier's Cross*, produced in 2008. *The Soldier's Cross* is an explicit tribute to the sacrifice of VMI alumni during the War on Terror. The label text states, "The artist captured the universal symbol of a fallen comrade—upturned rifle with bayonet topped by the soldier's helmet." However, *The Soldier's Cross* emphasizes a critical distinction from *Solitude*. In the latter case, the thing being used to commemorate loss, the horse, is visualized, like the body of Little Sorrel. *The Soldier's Cross* represents the soldier without manifesting the soldier's body. Its absence reminds us of what is missing, a sense of human presence, whereas Little Sorrel's presence recalls Jackson's noncorporeal presence, with his belongings encased.

Little Sorrel: "Jackson's Favorite Mount"

While the VMI Museum offers a narrative of Little Sorrel befitting a hero, inquiry into reports surrounding Little Sorrel's life and death underscores precisely why Jackson's "favorite mount" was taxidermied as opposed to simply buried. Little Sorrel is not the only Civil War horse to be preserved, either in part or in whole, following his death. As Faust has noted, the skeleton of Gen. Robert E. Lee's beloved "Confederate gray" Traveller was on display at Washington and Lee until 1971, when the horse's remains were buried next to the Lee Chapel at W&L. The head of Union major general George G. Meade's Old Baldy, wounded fourteen times throughout the course of his life, was mounted and placed on display in the Grand Army of the Republic Civil War Museum and Library in Philadelphia. Union general Philip Sheridan's black horse, Rienzi, also known as Winchester, was taxidermied and ultimately placed on display in the Hall of Armed Forces History at the Smithsonian Museum of American History in Washington, DC.[30] Little Sorrel, however, was a horse with a story molded to become the stuff of legend.

Unlike Lee's Traveller, who died in 1871 at the age of fourteen after stepping on a nail and developing tetanus, Little Sorrel lived an impressive thirty-six years—three years shy of Jackson's thirty-nine-year life. Unlike General Meade's Old Baldy, Little Sorrel had an active life after the Civil War's end. Unlike Sheridan's Rienzi, Little Sorrel was a horse known not only for the vaunted rider he carried but as an exemplary animal in his own right.[31]

Little Sorrel was not only the "tough little horse," a Morgan, who, when forced to stop and allow Jackson to dismount, was said to lie down like a dog.[32] The wily animal who "acquired the knack of lifting the rails with its mouth until the fence could be jumped"[33] was analogized to both his master and the man whom he enslaved—simultaneously personifying the admirable traits of a war hero as well as of a steadfast servant. The horse has been cast to transcend the history of oppression to which he is inextricably linked.

Little Sorrel rode with Jackson, "his master," until Jackson's death in 1863. T. L. Marr noted in 1949 that on the night Jackson was mortally wounded, Little Sorrel, responding to gunfire, became "mad with terror and began frantically to gallop through the woods toward the dangerously close Federal lines."[34] Fortunately, reports noted, the horse was intercepted before veering into Union territory, enabling the wounded general to be brought to a field hospital near Guinea Station, Virginia. Jackson died there eight days later at a site that today is known and advertised along Interstate 95 as the Stonewall Jackson Shrine. Reflecting on Jackson's death, the *Richmond Dispatch* noted that the general's passing marked "the clos[ing] of a wonderful career and gave to the Confederacy a shock from which it never recovered."[35] The reverberations of said shock could be felt close to a century after Jackson's death. Writing for the *VMI Cadet*, Marr argued, "The little horse is important more than in his own right; he is a reminder of one of the greatest leaders our world has known."[36] In the wake of Jackson's death, Little Sorrel bore the burden of Confederate mythology.

Little Sorrel offered Confederate veterans an opportunity to ruminate on what could have been had Jackson not been killed so early in the Civil War. First taken to Mrs. Jackson's home in Charlotte, North Carolina, Little Sorrel was eventually donated to VMI, where he was cared for by the cadets. In the words of Mrs. Jackson, "He was such a pet that he was allowed to do anything and was taken to county fairs, where he was an object of as much interest as one of the old heroes of the war."[37] The horse toured the New Orleans Exposition and Civil War veterans' reunions to benefit the Soldiers' Home in Richmond and the Jackson Monument Fund,[38] becoming something of a celebrity—so much so that, as journalist Tony Horwitz would later comment, "souvenir seekers tugged so many hairs from his [Little Sorrel's] mane and tail that the horse required guards."[39]

While the horse's association with Jackson undoubtedly led to this celebrity, Little Sorrel's allure was about more than affiliation. As the *Peninsula Enterprise* reported in 1882, Little Sorrel bore something of a resemblance to his master: "He is . . . as good on a flank movement on a corn field as the General was on a Yankee line of battle. 'Little Sorrel' is also of noble heart. When contemplating a foraging tour, he has been seen to go around and let the other horses out of the stable, and then take the lead for the corn field."[40] The similarities between master and horse were communicated more pointedly by the horse's epitaph:

> Old Sorrel
> Of obscure birth.
> He achieved fame.
> The faithful servant
> Of a noble master.
> He died March 17, 1886,
> Aged 36 years.[41]

The *Richmond Dispatch* noted in the horse's obituary that the horse "fittingly closed his life at the Soldiers' Home [at the Lee Camp in Richmond], where he was petted and nursed as tenderly as a child; where war-worn veterans wept at his death, and where his form, when passed from the taxidermist's hands, is to remain and long be an interesting link in the history of one of the greatest of the world's soldiers."[42] While he had gained fame as Stonewall Jackson's faithful steed, Little Sorrel came to be seen in the eyes of Confederate veterans as a hero. Like his human counterparts, Little Sorrel received a hero's funeral, complete with mounted cavalry and infantry, a fife and drum corps, a bagpiper, and ladies in period dress. Reverend William Klein, pastor of Lexington Presbyterian Church, gave a blessing and benediction.[43]

The same respect accorded Little Sorrel, however, was not extended to Jackson's enslaved cook during the Civil War, a Black man named Jim Lewis. Little is known of Lewis.[44] Most historical accounts conjure the oft-quoted passage by Congressman Alexander Boteler,[45] a member of the Confederate States House of Representatives from Virginia (1862–1864), who described the commonalities between Lewis and Jackson's horse:

> The servant and "Old Sorrel" being about the same color—each having the hue of gingerbread without any of the spiciness—their respective characters were in a concatenation accordingly. For they were equally obedient, patient, easy-going and reliable; not given to devious courses nor designing tricks; more serviceable than showy and, altogether, as sober-sided a pair of subordinates as any Presbyterian elder with plain tastes and a practical turn, need desire to have about him. Both man and horse seemed to understand their master thoroughly and rarely failed to come up fully to all his requirements.[46]

Congressman Boteler's dehumanizing analogy between Lewis and Jackson's horse is more than evidence of the plantation-owning politician's racism. Used as evidence by many neo-Confederate authors of Jackson's inscrutable belief that all, regardless of race, had a right to pursue the kingdom of heaven,[47] Jackson's relationship with Lewis speaks, more pointedly, to the general's paternalistic attitudes toward Black people, whom he believed to be godless heathens in need of saving. While Jackson's financial support for a "Colored Sabbath-School"[48] in Lexington is often cited by neo-Confederates to diffuse charges of the general's racism, even Jackson biographer James Robertson Jr. acknowledges, "Yet in his [Jackson's] mind the Creator had sanctioned slavery, and man had no moral right to challenge its existence. The good Christian slaveholder was one who treated his servants fairly and humanely at all times."[49] Despite this implicit acknowledgment of Jackson's paternalism, Robertson, whose extensive tome betrays a deep reverence for his subject, suggests, "Jackson neither apologized for nor spoke in favor of the practice of slavery. He probably opposed the institution,"[50] a claim that echoes in neo-Confederate literature. Jackson was, as the subtitle of Richard G. Williams Jr.'s 2006 book suggests and neo-Confederates reaffirm, "The Black Man's Friend."[51]

The same argument was made by John R. Blackmon of the Sons of Confederate Veterans in a letter published in the *Columbian-Progress* (Columbia, Mississippi) in February 1998. Blackmon cited Lewis's service to Jackson as evidence of the elusive Black Confederate, "some of the least recognized role players in American history."[52] Invocations of Lewis's service to Jackson hark back to traditional Lost Cause narratives of the "faithful slave," the happy servant who was nothing if not part of the family.[53] Regardless of the care that Lewis provided Jackson on his deathbed, a point the Stonewall Jackson Shrine in Guinea Station makes for visitors, the fact remains that the relationship between Lewis and Jackson was an unequal one. Lewis had been enslaved; Jackson was his enslaver.

Unlike Little Sorrel, who remains a central part of the story of the Civil War and whose bodily remains were eventually interred on VMI grounds, Jim Lewis's life and death reveal no such respect and honor accorded. Initially buried in a segregated cemetery along with Jackson's enslaved Amy, Lewis's remains were allegedly reinterred at Evergreen Cemetery in Lexington, a historic Black cemetery created in 1880. However, the move was never confirmed; the whereabouts of Lewis's body are today unknown. The original cemetery where he was buried was sold in 1946. Today houses stand there—likely atop the remains of many within Lexington's nineteenth-century Black community.[54]

Little Sorrel's life and death, in sharp contrast, are well documented, as is the fate of Stonewall Jackson's arm. On one Saturday morning, I

Figure 2.3, Arm of Stonewall Jackson burial site (Nicole Maurantonio)

traveled with two of my students north from Richmond on Interstate 95 to Ellwood Manor, where Stonewall Jackson's left arm is allegedly buried (see fig. 2.3). The lone marker in the Lacy family cemetery near the site where Jackson was shot, the small granite gravestone identifying the general's amputated arm was dedicated in 1903, roughly thirty years after the limb was removed from Jackson's body. Coinciding temporally with the dedication of Confederate monuments throughout the United States but particularly across the South, the dedication of the monument to Jackson's arm imparts a certain reverence for not only the general himself but for the Confederacy. The humble stone states, "Arm of Stonewall Jackson May 3, 1863." Providing only the date of amputation, the stone suggests the date of the arm's "death."

The dedication of a marker commemorating Jackson's arm might seem a bizarre and even irreverent decision, particularly given the lack of attention accorded the enslaved Lewis's deceased body. However, the monument to Jackson's arm conjures medieval practices memorializing the body of a deceased holy person, often a saint. Examples such as the tongue and jaw of Saint Anthony of Padua and Saint Claire's fingernails and hair clippings remind us that the veneration of a dismembered body is part of its sacralization.[55]

While the site is not declared officially the Jackson "shrine," a term used on signage to advertise the aforementioned death site in Guinea Station off I-95, there is nonetheless a sense of devotion the site inspires. The National Park Service panel quotes Robert E. Lee: "He has lost his left arm; but I have lost my right arm." For the cynic, Lee's line might read as an absurd cliché, yet like Little Sorrel, the part gestures back to the larger whole.

The Afterlife of Little Sorrel

Little Sorrel, journalist Tony Horwitz later commented, would encounter a fate much like his master's, buried in pieces.[56] On his death, Little Sorrel's body was placed in the hands of Professor Frederick S. Webster of Rochester, New York, recommended by the directors of the Smithsonian Institute. Webster, protégé of Jules Bailly,[57] was one of the most renowned taxidermists in the country and had been entrusted with mounting the remains of General Sheridan's horse, Rienzi.[58] The decision to taxidermy Little Sorrel had been made in advance of the horse's death. Webster had taken measurements of Little Sorrel prior to the horse's demise.[59] As Webster himself stated, Little Sorrel was taxidermied "because of the record of having carried the famous and beloved General through the heat and blast of a desperate war."[60] Undoubtedly an attempt to preclude the possibility that the body would be treated as callously as the skeleton of Lee's Traveller, on which students inscribed their initials as a talisman of good luck, the taxidermied Little Sorrel would be afforded no similar disrespect.[61] His bones were presented to Webster as partial payment for the taxidermy. Webster stretched Little Sorrel's hide over a plaster of paris frame in a technique that was, for the time, revolutionary.

The taxidermy process for Little Sorrel was to take three to four days and cost approximately $250, with an additional $250 required should an enclosure for the body be desired, with the goal of giving Little Sorrel "the most life-like appearance possible."[62] Richmond newspapers accepted donations. If taxidermy, as Dave Madden summarizes, "is the arrangement of an animal's skin over a premade form in an attempt to make that arrangement look alive," the practice "traffic[s] in acts of resurrection"[63] as well as illusion.

While, according to historian Karen Jones, "taxidermy emerged as an elite artistic vocation in the seventeenth century," bolstered by interest in natural history and its concomitant museums, the nineteenth century could be labeled "the age of the taxidermist." Although taxidermy had been viewed as a largely private endeavor, museum culture, beginning in the 1870s, "embraced taxidermy as a way of communicating colonial encounters, educating the public on natural history, engaging in civic display, and offering triumphalist and scientific commentary on conquered spaces and their species complement."[64] In March 1880 William Temple Hornaday and six coworkers formed the Society of American Taxidermists (SAT), an organization founded with the purpose of sharing new methods with a broader audience.[65] Webster was selected the first president of SAT. Taxidermy became a vehicle for educating the public on a variety of animal species, endangered and mundane, while underscoring the dominance of man over nature.[66]

In considering the practice of pet taxidermy, scholar Rachel Poliquin summarizes, "We remember departed companions because of their spirit, their charisma and personality. Once dead, this liveliness departs, and all that remains is a husk. Preserving that husk and claiming that it is still the creature is a disturbing confusion of corporeality for presence, or worse: it suggests that what has departed is not particularly missed."[67] The public display of the taxidermied Little Sorrel at the VMI Museum works strategically to materially and narratively conflate corporeality with presence.

Although perhaps not the "model" horse in the physiognomic sense, described as "compactly built, round and fat," Little Sorrel offered a symbolic model primed for public display. As Poliquin argues, "Pets are not preserved in order to ease their journey into the afterlife or to capture some spiritual essence. They are stuffed so that their owners might find solace."[68] While by the time of Little Sorrel's death Jackson was more than twenty years deceased, Little Sorrel's meaning rested with the solace his hide offered the former Confederacy. It is thus little surprise that the decision to taxidermy Little Sorrel was made as monuments to Confederate generals were being erected and dedicated throughout the South. Just four years after Little Sorrel's death, in 1890, Richmond would dedicate the first of the monuments to eventually line what would become Monument Avenue—the statue to Robert E. Lee.

On the completion of the taxidermy process, Little Sorrel arrived back in Richmond the morning of November 22, 1887, to be placed in the carriage house of Mrs. George A. Ainslie and Son on Tenth Street. The *Dispatch* reported that "Mr. Webster did his work finely, and the horse looks as well as he ever did in life." The article took particular note of the horse's stance, described as follows: "The front legs are together. The left hind leg, however, lags behind the right in an unnatural manner. With the exception of this the pose is correct and graceful. The erect position of the head and the pricked up ears give a startled, listening position, as if while grazing he had heard some unusual, unexpected sound."[69] Despite the minor quibble with the horse's stance, Webster's work was the object of much praise. The taxidermied horse eventually served as the model for Richmond's 1919 Stonewall Jackson statue, sculpted by William F. Sievers, now located on the city's Monument Avenue.

Despite the temporal coincidence of Little Sorrel's taxidermy with the emergence of monuments to the Confederacy's most revered generals, there is a crucial difference between the two forms of commemoration: unlike the monuments, Little Sorrel *was* alive. This was a fact readers were eager to remind others in letters. Writing to the *Lexington Gazette* in August 1902, T. C. Morton sought to correct the "reminiscences of Rev. R. M. Tuttle," who claimed that Little Sorrel was buried in North Carolina. Morton wrote,

> I don't like for Mr. Tuttle, or any other admirer, to think that Little Sorrel has returned to dust and can no more be seen in this world. If not "in the flesh," he is in his skin and can be seen any day at the Soldiers' Home in Richmond, saddled and bridled and holstered, with the same accoutrements that his famous rider used upon him. He holds his head a little higher indeed than when "Old Jack" used to sit him but here is Little Sorrel, "as large as life and just as natural," under strict guard and the object of much attention on the part of visitors and almost veneration by the old soldiers of the Home and other pilgrims to the shrine. . . . I hope this little correction of horse history will relieve the minds of many veterans and lead to an opportunity for them to look once more upon the familiar form of the steed they once delighted to follow.[70]

Morton's letter represented a factual corrective—Little Sorrel was not buried in North Carolina. More significantly, Morton conveyed a sense that Reverend Tuttle had lost a critical part of history with the inaccuracy. What had been lost was the opportunity to *see*—to bear witness to the horse as a site of pilgrimage, a spiritual experience honoring a noble hero. Visiting Little Sorrel was not simply about observing a formerly live horse; visiting his body was likened to visiting a shrine to the Confederacy, wholly distinct from the experience of going to a cemetery. To visit Little Sorrel in person, *in the flesh*, was to pay homage to the Confederacy and display "appropriate" reverence to an entity that was, while defunct, still present.[71]

While the taxidermied body of Little Sorrel stands in the VMI Museum, his cremated remains are mere feet from Jackson Hall at the VMI parade grounds. The horse's burial site, however, is not advertised in the VMI Museum, as if to shield visitors from the fact that the horse is indeed dead.[72] The horse's remains were buried in 1997 in front of Jackson's statue beneath a stone that lays flush to the ground, easily missed or even stepped on by the casual observer.

Given Little Sorrel's grave is not mentioned in the museum, visitors are left to happen on the grave site or learn about it via other means. According to reports, Little Sorrel was laid to rest to the tune of "Dixie," played by a fife and drum corps, and a gathering of approximately four hundred people.[73] The horse was said to have had a particular energy in his step on hearing the unofficial Confederate anthem, which made it especially apropos.[74] Attendees at the 1997 burial who came to pay their respects placed apples at the graveside of the horse—an homage to the horse's owner, who was said to have spoiled Little Sorrel with apples when no one was looking.[75] The grave site, news reports noted, would be landscaped by the Virginia Division of the United Daughters of the Confederacy.

The burial of Little Sorrel attracted much attention. A eulogy was delivered by Jackson biographer and Virginia Tech professor James Robertson Jr. At the ceremony, Robertson noted solemnly, "Old Jack and Little Sorrel were more than a man and his mount. They were for a time, the inspiring symbol of a nation's hopes. Man and horse imparted to each other great care, service, and dependability. The little horse also gave something else: love."[76] Little Sorrel was the ideal companion—a universal symbol of compassion and service.

Little Sorrel's remains had been kept in storage since 1989, when the skeleton was put away on the construction of a new biology building at VMI. The skeleton had previously been on display in a biology class for almost forty years.[77] The skeleton came to VMI in August 1949, first on indefinite loan and then ultimately as a gift.[78] The burial of the horse's cremated remains in 1997 elicited strong responses from mourners, who were invited to toss onto the horse's casket soil collected at major Civil War battlegrounds, marking sites where Little Sorrel and Stonewall Jackson had been.

As bystander Gale Lawson stated after attending the ceremony, "To be here made you feel like you were living a part of history and commemorating it." Libby Fosso of Lexington remarked, "It's unusual that we get a chance to see how much an animal is appreciated like that. The horse was as loved in his memory as he was by Jackson in his life." Professor Robertson noted, "I think it's really nice that an animal got this much love and attention."[79] For Mrs. Mark R. Allen, president of the Virginia Division of the United Daughters of the Confederacy, the burial was the appropriate end to Little Sorrel's "saga." She noted, "I know it must seem a bit strange to some people to make such a fuss over a horse, but Southerners are a very devoted people in honoring heroes of all types. It's quite thrilling—and an honor—to be able to do this, particularly so many years after the fact. It connects us in a very real way to our past."[80] Mourners felt not only that they had participated in an act of historical commemoration, of remembrance—they felt a certain connection that transcended emotion regarding the deceased animal. Journalist Tony Horwitz would later comment on the ceremony, in a play on the Gettysburg Address, "The world will little note nor long remember what was said here, but many will never forget the weirdness of what they did here."[81]

Despite the absurdity inflected in Horwitz's account, the fact remained: supporting Little Sorrel in death was a way of reconnecting to "history" in the present. It begged the question, as historian Drew Gilpin Faust posed at the time of the bones' burial, "if Southerners wanted to stuff Stonewall Jackson but stuffed his horse instead."[82]

While it is widely acknowledged that Little Sorrel is, in fact, deceased, the horse's trials and travails since it entered the VMI Museum are well documented, emphasizing the ways in which he continues to live metaphorically as a symbol of pride and a reminder of those committed to the cause for which he was put into service. Yet Little Sorrel's "liveliness" has been more than a metaphor. References, particularly to the horse's restoration, have gestured to a sense that he is to be treated as a living, albeit endangered, animal—like the Confederacy itself.

Refurbished in 1969 at the Smithsonian, Little Sorrel was said to have "never looked better in his memory," by VMI Museum director Lyon G. Tyler.[83] Almost two decades later, in 1985, the horse was further restored due to funding from Ms. Lise Putnam Liddell, who also funded the restoration of the flag carried by Jackson at the Battle of First Manassas.[84] Over the next decade, VMI Museum director Keith Gibson sought to preserve Little Sorrel with calls to the Smithsonian every few years, in recognition that "He's done with the Yankees—humidity's his worst enemy now."[85]

The twenty-first century has seen even greater attention to Little Sorrel and a commitment to ensuring both his "liveliness" and living memory. Acknowledging that years of wear had taken their toll on the hide, journalist Mark Hinson's wife, Amy, noted, in April 2007, "He [Little Sorrel] looks like one of those mummified cats they dig up in Egypt. Maybe he should have used moisturizer."[86] As a result, in October 2007 VMI's *Institute Report* ran a story announcing the "Civil War Steed['s] . . . Spa Treatment," referring somewhat flippantly to the conservation efforts being undertaken by Smithsonian taxidermist Paul Rhymer. While the horse's third restoration, it was, Gibson stated, "the first time the horse will be receiving a major conservation effort," necessitated by more than 140 years of dust and beeswax buildup. The report noted, "The horse then received a shampoo that filled the room with an aroma that Jackson himself might have smelled when he bathed his horse."[87] It was, in the words of the *VMI Cadet*, "the ultimate makeover," costing approximately $16,000.[88]

Such attention was similarly bestowed on the Jackson monument in Richmond, where local conservator Andrew Baxter was said to have enlisted his company, Bronze et al., in an attempt to ensure the statue of Jackson and Little Sorrel did not fall victim to the corrosive elements. After burnishing the statue with a "lemonade-looking mixture," Baxter said of Jackson, "He took it [the mixture] well. He seemed pleased someone took an interest after all these years,"[89] as if the general were a living, albeit neglected, older person.

While a taxidermied horse's "makeover" might seem to signal a certain humor, with the *Richmond Times-Dispatch* taking note of the horse being shampooed using "Pert Plus, the original 2-in-1 shampoo plus conditioner—and dyed . . . to restore the old steed back to his medium-brown color,"[90] such descriptions were more than tongue in cheek. Commenting on Little Sorrel's "bath," Colonel Gibson remarked, "Scent is one of those things that is missing from history."[91] Colonel Gibson's comment on scent as "missing" from history points to an affective level on which the horse operates as well as an attempt to avoid conjuring the stench that is often associated with death and, more specifically, death during the Civil War.[92] By attending to the horse's body—to restore it to its natural appearance and with a pleasant odor—conservators seek to remind of a bygone era recalled fondly. The conservation project was made possible with the support of the Virginia Division of the Daughters of the Confederacy, who raised funds for the conservation by selling stuffed replicas of Little Sorrel. The stuffed replicas provided purchasers with opportunities to not only contribute to the continued "liveliness" of Little Sorrel. They offered visitors another opportunity to claim a relic, leading to the further sacralization of not only Little Sorrel but of his rider.

Despite these conservation efforts, not all have been equally supportive of VMI's attempts to preserve Little Sorrel. In a bold expression of resistance to the taxidermied horse, Mike Robertson, a *Cadet* opinion writer, described Jackson's steed in 2009 as a "rotting piece of furniture, . . . look[ing] like something that one of the Four Horsemen of the Apocalypse would ride. Mangy and smelly and whinnying his horrible whinny. I can picture the dread rider, surrounded by locusts and gnats, wielding a terrible scythe and ready to exact vengeance upon mankind . . . the ground turning to ash and bone in his wake. Little Sorrel looks, for lack of a better term, gross."[93] Drawing attention to the more potentially disturbing dimensions of taxidermy—particularly taxidermy that has existed for more than 140 years—Robertson offered the one critique of Little Sorrel's preservation, conjuring the death that surrounded the animal. What is significant about Robertson's critique is that it stems not from objection to preservation as such but rather from the sense of decay. Looking "gross," the horse reflected not the honor of VMI but rather its decrepitude.

"Putting Civil War Horses on a Pedestal"

Little Sorrel is one Civil War horse whose story is woven into a complex tapestry of mythology surrounding the American Civil War. The significance of horses to the story of the Civil War has not been lost in Virginia, where in Richmond, in front of the Virginia Museum of History and Culture (formerly the Virginia Historical Society [VHS]) near the former home of Little Sorrel, stands a bronze statue honoring Civil War horses. The statue was unveiled in September 1997, the same year Little Sorrel's remains were buried. Designed by Tessa Pullan, a British sculptor, and commissioned by philanthropist Paul Mellon, the statue's inscription reads: "In memory of the over one and a half million horses and mules of the Confederate and Union armies who were killed, were wounded or died from disease in the Civil War."[94] The statue is gaunt, head bowed, speaking to deprivation throughout the history of the Civil War. As Faust notes, Pullan's design was revised multiple times in an attempt to ensure that the displayed horse was sufficiently haggard-looking,[95] expressing the physical as well as emotional toll of war.

On the statue's unveiling, Dr. William M. S. Rasmussen of the VHS stated,

> This is one of the best pieces of outdoor sculpture to be introduced to the Richmond landscape since Jean-Antonin Mercié's Lee was unveiled a hundred years earlier. It's only a horse, but the sculpture can be viewed as more, as a symbol of the suffering inflicted on so many living creatures in Virginia during the Civil War. People from all ways of life were affected. This is a message that is very easy for us to forget today, partly because it isn't offered at all by the Monument Avenue sculptures.[96]

The horse stands as icon of pain and suffering, a stark contrast to the built environment that celebrates Confederate generals and the animals on which they sat, mere blocks away. The horse sculpture draws together Union and Confederate sacrifice in one bronze piece—a reminder of a reconciliationist past revived in the present. The emaciated beast remains noble, courageous, and true, like Little Sorrel, a symbol of wartime sacrifice suffered by all, animals and humans.

Tessa Pullan's sculpture continues to stand peacefully outside the Virginia Museum of History and Culture mere blocks from Monument Avenue, the site of much debate, reminding us of the horse's ability to unify through its capacity to reduce history to its most instrumentalist and apolitical players. The sacred relics of Stonewall Jackson recall the capacity for the object—the remnant or residue—to be venerated uncritically through abstract invocations of history, divorced from racial trauma. Horses, unlike the men they carried, had no capacity to resist—to challenge or question the cause for which they were employed. The same cannot be said for those who reenact Confederate memory.

3 | Black Confederates and Performances of Living Reconciliation

On my first tour though the United Daughters of the Confederacy (UDC) headquarters in Richmond in May 2014, Virginia Flaggers spokesman Barry Isenhour and I were guided by Teresa Roane, UDC archivist. As we walked through the building, Roane shared stories of her experiences speaking on Confederate history. She noted,

> People that look like me all the time [say]: "We want to know our history." They want to know certain history. They don't want to know about the Confederate connection. Last year, I went and talked to a black Baptist church. I told them straight up. I said, "If you take away Confederate history, you're taking away your own people's history," and it never occurred to them. One of the women said, "That's when I stood up in my chair and realized I should pay attention to you."[1]

Although, as Roane suggested, Black people were indeed integral to Confederate history, I quickly realized that our reasons for making that argument did not neatly line up. As I thought about the Confederacy as an entity founded on the commitment to preserving the institution of slavery, placing millions of Africans in bondage, Roane considered the system of labor as not so clear cut. This perspective made our first interaction that much more perplexing to me, a white northerner. Roane is a Black southerner.

Regularly delivering lectures that can be distilled into variations on two themes—the importance of Confederate history broadly and the necessity of remembering so-called Confederates of Color specifically, Roane seeks to debunk the taboo "C word," *confederate*, as she referred to it, that leads many to assume that "you are racist or you're about racism."[2] She bristles at the mention of slavery as typified by "whips and chains," instead preferring to consider enslaved people as having particular agency within their story, as having choice.[3] Championing Black self-determination, Roane simultaneously resists narratives describing the brutality of slavery as an institution. Her stance—a seemingly progressive articulation of the agency of enslaved people yet also a deeply conservative view rooted in paternalism—echoed of a historiographical tradition that has been challenged by more contemporary scholars of slavery.[4]

Roane is not the only person of color who espouses such an intense loyalty to the Confederacy. Isenhour would later introduce me to Sgt. Maj. James Haymes,[5] who refers to himself as Roane's "cousin." A retired member of the US Army, Haymes was museum operations assistant at the Museum of the Confederacy and guide at the adjacent White House of the Confederacy, positions he held until 2016, when he was let go due to restructuring.[6] Karen Cooper gained notoriety as the regular Black Flagger protesting with the Confederate battle flag outside the Virginia Museum of Fine Arts. Cooper was profiled as part of an article for the *Washington Post* in 2015 and in a documentary, *Battle Flag*.[7] An iconic model to Roane, Haymes, and Cooper, H. K. Edgerton, former local NAACP head in Asheville, North Carolina, is a Black southern heritage activist who can regularly be seen donning a Confederate uniform and carrying the battle flag.[8] Edgerton is known for his outspoken support for the "Confederate Heritage" license plate,[9] appearing as a guest columnist in several publications[10] and publicly denouncing Michael Brown, murdered by Ferguson, Missouri, police officer Darren Wilson in August 2014. Edgerton referred to the slain Black teen as a "thug."[11] Edgerton is the subject of the book *The Historical March across Dixie*. While for the Tea Party and its subset of neo-Confederates, Edgerton is an "American hero"[12] whose face is plastered on T-shirts available for purchase for $29.95 on the CSA II website and through other online retailers such as Dixie Outfitters (see fig. 3.1),[13] Edgerton is, according to a group of artists who report on right-wing racism, "hated by most black people for his love and support of glamorized phony Confederate myths."[14] Edgerton has also been protested by the Ku Klux Klan (KKK) in Jacksonville, Florida, a detail that makes his pro-Confederate stance all the more confusing.[15] In late August 2018 Edgerton showed up with his Confederate battle flag on the campus of the University of North Carolina at Chapel Hill where the Silent Sam statue had been recently toppled by protesters. Edgerton sought to show his continued support for the statue and pride in the Confederacy.[16]

Each of these individuals, they will readily admit, elicits, as one writer noted of Edgerton specifically, "curiosity and emotion."[17] However, such a detached description would underestimate the emotion Edgerton and his fellow Black Confederates provoke.[18] Rather, as one blogger wrote in response to a description of Edgerton, "are you fuckin' serious?"[19] One does not expect to see a Black person espousing deep admiration for

Figure 3.1, H. K. Edgerton T-shirt (CSA II's Confederate Corner Store)

the Confederacy—at least I didn't. Karen Cooper, who presents herself as something of a public provocateur, said in an interview with Salon.com, "I know what people think about when they see the battle flag—the KKK, racism, bringing slavery back—so I knew it would be something for people to see a black woman with the battle flag."[20]

My predominantly white students at the University of Richmond sat flummoxed by Roane in February 2017 when she asked the group, sitting in the Great Hall at the headquarters of the United Daughters of the Confederacy, how someone like her could be comfortable in the space. By "someone like her," she meant quite pointedly that if a Black woman could walk the halls of the UDC with comfort, then, by extension, it would be difficult to level the critique of the organization's racism. As my students walked throughout the UDC with Roane and the other docent, an older, white UDC member, they looked visibly disturbed. When we returned to campus I asked students to join me to debrief, if they wanted. I was surprised how many students stayed after class ended in an attempt to process—to understand what they had seen and what it meant. Following our guided tour of UDC headquarters, Roane emailed me to share what she perceived to be my students' discomfort (she was not wrong) and misconceptions surrounding the Confederacy. Among those misconceptions were "that we [the Confederacy] advocated for slavery." She additionally noted that my students "did not realize that there were still States within the Union at the time of the war that had slavery" or that "we pledge to the United States Flag."[21]

My students, who hailed predominantly, but not exclusively, from the Northeast, where the Civil War is often taught as a battle between North and South, freedom and enslavement, were stunned not merely by the narrative but by the messenger. What they had experienced, however, was more than cognitive dissonance. They witnessed a woman who performed the historical actors she described. She had shared with my students, reified by her repeated use of "we," a form of ethnic autobiography, functioning in ways not dissimilar to the autobiographies shared by the ethnic impersonators of American studies scholar Laura Browder's *Slippery Characters*: "offer[ing] the authentic voice of a minority group to a reading audience composed of primarily white, middle-class Americans."[22] Yet, I learned, this—the discomfort elicited—was part of the performance: the performance of the mythical Black Confederate. It is part of what makes the Black Confederate the most powerful weapon of neo-Confederates in the twenty-first century.

The story of Black Confederates is part of a larger narrative circulated by contemporary neo-Confederates: that of a multiracial and multiethnic Confederacy.[23] More recently described as the so-called Rainbow Confederacy, the story can be summarized as follows: tens of thousands of Black combatants, ranging from ten to fifty thousand in number, served on behalf of the Confederacy. Neo-Confederates maintain that historians of the Civil War have heretofore concealed the existence of these numerous brave men in an effort to vilify the Confederacy and exalt the North. Beyond providing evidence of academics' conspiracy against "the South," the story of Black Confederates enables Confederate heritage sympathizers, in the words of historian Bruce Levine, to reframe the "southern war effort . . . as the cause not merely of slave owners, nor even of southern whites more generally, but of *all* southerners, white as well as black, free as well as slave."[24] Within this narrative arc, the Confederacy stands as an exemplar of a diverse, yet cohesive, collective, united by a common cause that, by virtue of the diversity of its protectors, could not be inherently racist. This rhetorical move, while "naming and voicing the typically silent experiences of people of color,"[25] denies racism. It is racial neoliberalism performed.

Historians have dismissed the Black Confederate as a mythical figure whose presence is overstated at best. In the words of historian Kevin Levin, contemporary Black Confederates such as H. K. Edgerton should be best understood "as a form of entertainment, not entirely unlike the presence of former camp slaves, who attended parades and veterans reunions at the turn of the twentieth century."[26] In this chapter, I explore how the Black Confederate is performed in the present: how individuals leverage their identities as Black people to narrate a version of the Confederacy that not only embraces traditional Lost Cause discourses of Confederate heroism and valor, complete with the image of the "faithful slave/servant," but also crafts a more complex story celebrating the Confederacy as a "melting pot," a metaphor that appears antithetical to the Confederacy's white supremacist reality. While the "melting pot" metaphor most often conjures images of European immigrants flooding New York harbor in the early twentieth century, their huddled masses pouring through Ellis Island to become assimilated, "Americanized," the "melting pot" in question in this chapter—the melting pot being proselytized—I argue, is the Confederacy. The "melting" taking place among Black Confederates, however, is not only ethnic but racial. Simply put, the Confederate melting pot achieves what immigrant assimilation could not.

The concept of the "melting pot" emerged in response to the influx of predominantly European immigrants into the United States and progressives' concerns with societal capacity to adapt to social, political, and economic change, even if it did not find universal support.[27] Standing in stark contrast to nativist arguments opposing immigration,[28] the melting pot offered an alternative vision of so-called immigrant adjustment, albeit a confusing one.[29] As sociologist Rubén Rumbaut notes, the "mischievous metaphor" of the melting pot offers a "vivid and seductive image"—"an inclusionary image of the mechanism by which an *unum* is forged from the *pluribus*," thereby legitimizing the nation as a "beacon to the world."[30] Significantly, particularly within an early twentieth-century context, the phrase was used to describe the process by which white ethnicities became white, as Israel Zangwill's popular 1908 play of the same name recalled.[31] It was not used to describe a process experienced by Black people. As Rumbaut notes, "race" cannot be melted.[32] The trope thus offers a paradoxical referent that would, at first glance, seem to preclude the sort of agency contemporary Black Confederates espouse.

Despite having been forsaken more recently in favor of other culinary heuristics such as the salad bowl, the melting pot metaphor signals more than a process of cultural homogenization and repression in the service of "Americanization." During my first one-on-one interview with Virginia Flagger spokesman Barry Isenhour in April 2014, he referred to the South explicitly as a "melting pot," celebrating fondly the region's capacity for melding cultures. He noted then, "We don't look at the black people and say, 'You're here now, forget your African roots.' We don't do that. In fact, we say, 'Wow! Okra's pretty damn cool. Can we fry it?' That's part of the culture. It's southern culture; it's all of us. Not just the music, the food, the people, the history, the heritage."[33] While Isenhour used the phrase to mark the "South," what he meant was a specific vision of the South: the Confederacy. Although I explore the connections this discursive slippage materializes via food and foodways in chapter 4, here I examine the work of the Black men and women who enact this melting pot, performing as living historians. In this capacity, they engage in a form of historical reenactment, embracing their identities as people of color while emphasizing their status as historical actors making choices. As with the stories they tell of enslaved peoples, they have a choice: they choose to celebrate the Confederacy in the present as a reconciliationist model for the United States.

Reenactment and Living History

While the genre of historical reenactment is vast,[34] I use reenactment to describe a mode of cultural heritage performance whose purpose "is to present an aspect of a (located) culture's past to an audience." Reenactments, following scholars Elizabeth Carnegie and Scott McCabe, "include elements of both affirmation of community/culture *and* celebration for its own sake, to provide a means of escape from the modern through dramaturgical performance which *requires* the participation of many to achieve these ends."[35] In other words, reenactment offers groups an opportunity to retreat from the contemporary moment to relish a past that is no longer.

As a global phenomenon, reenactment benefits from its populist appeal, attracting those with "an interest in colorful, familiar history," as well as its capacity to provide voice to marginalized populations as a form of "history from below." As a result, reenactments foster a sense of the past's elasticity, operating as an "emancipatory gesture . . . [that] allow[s] participants to select their own past in reaction to a conflicted present."[36]

Over the past two decades, interest in reenactment as a performative genre has grown, with tens of thousands participating in battle reenactments such as the Battle of Gettysburg, despite the genre's considerable expense.[37] Public fascination with Civil War reenactment in particular crystallized with the publication of journalist Tony Horwitz's 1998 best seller *Confederates in the Attic*.[38] Often emphasizing the minutiae of everyday life—"dress, diet, bodily maintenance, domestic space, material objects, the management of human relationships, and the organization of time"—reenactment is "a body-based discourse in which the past is reanimated through physical and psychological experience."[39] In *Confederates in the Attic*, Horwitz enabled a broad, public audience to experience the Confederacy vicariously as he attempted to make sense of it.

Beyond battle reenactments, however, organizations such as the Sons of Confederate Veterans continue to sponsor social events that provide opportunities for twentieth- and twenty-first-century participants to play historical "dress up." Richmond, Virginia, made national news in February 1996 when the White House of the Confederacy announced it would hold a Confederate ball, the Bonnie Blue Centennial Ball, which an estimated four hundred people were expected to attend. The ball "feature[d] hoop skirts, Rebel uniforms, and a color guard's presentation of the Stars and Bars."[40] Although not "true reenactment," the costume ball nonetheless sought to glorify, in the words of the first Black governor in the United States, Virginia's L. Douglas Wilder, "an inglorious past." However, for many participants the costumed event was embraced benignly as "a part of the history of the United States of America." The "dressing up," for those participants, was all in good fun, as many sought to model their gowns on Scarlett O'Hara's from *Gone with the Wind*.[41] The only Black people at the event, *New York Times* reporter Mike Allen would later write, "were at the catering stations, pouring bourbon and dishing up black-eyed-pea salsa and sweet-potato biscuits."[42]

In December 2010 the Sons of Confederate Veterans sponsored a "Secession Ball" in Charleston, South Carolina.[43] Such events follow a much longer history of nostalgic commemorations such as the "Old South Ball," "Rose Ball," and "Plantation Ball," which often featured the Confederate battle flag prominently, and young people, most often university students, in period garb.[44] Flipping through the pages of 1950s and 1960s yearbooks at the University of Richmond, I was confronted with photographs of white students, similarly donning the dress of their Confederate ancestors as they partook of events celebrating the antebellum South.[45]

Taken together, these various forms of reenactment advance a central narrative, cultural critic Vanessa Agnew suggests, "one of conversion from ignorance to knowledge, individualism to sociability, resistance to compliance, and present to past."[46] In the case of Civil War reenactment specifically, historian Melvin Ely noted,

> There was a widespread understanding in this country that the Civil War was just an unfortunate spat between both sides, that both sides meant well, and,

in the end, the two belonged together and should and could respect one another. And that understanding downplayed the centrality of slavery to the Civil War, it downplayed anything having to do with Reconstruction, and it downplayed the rolling back of black civil rights in the 20th century. Basically, it was a white fantasy entertained by Northerners and Southerners alike who were over all of that.[47]

The presence of Black Confederates, I suggest, enables white fantasies to come to life. Within this chapter, however, I focus on a particular subset of historical reenactment: "living history." Defined as "an attempt by people to simulate life in another time,"[48] "living history," as sociologist Stephen Hunt notes, "in the majority of cases is bound up with the presentation of heritage. . . . In this definition, heritage is also reduced to a commodity which is 'consumed' by an audience that pays to observe and experience its contemporary representation and interpretation."[49] For American studies scholar Jay Anderson, "it is the intrusion of the *past into our present*, and it can be both a fascinating and threatening experience."[50] Most commonly associated with sites such as Colonial Williamsburg and Old Sturbridge Village, living history tends to entail interpreters dressed in period clothing who demonstrate period craft. Design historian Judith Attfield has argued that living history "is intended to transform the everyday object in a way that evokes a *sense* of history, and therefore empathy."[51] I see the Black Confederates at the center of this chapter attempting to evoke precisely this sentiment.

While living history "can range from costumed tour guides to actors performing prepared materials, from craft demonstrations to hobbyists doing historical playacting or historical researchers studying the complex interactions of people, things, and environments of the past,"[52] I use living history in this chapter to signal the latter. With the exception of Edgerton, the individuals I discuss in this chapter do not dress in period garb to reenact battles or enact historic crafts.[53] They are not impersonators. Rather, in performing historic roles in the present, they embrace the tradition of the ethnic autobiography and its particular emphasis on self-fashioning so as to speak for Black people more broadly, making a case for their agency in the story of the Civil War and, more controversially, their support for the Confederacy.[54]

The individuals I consider in this chapter position themselves as "ordinary" people seeking to teach the "truth," correcting what they deem to be historical inaccuracies regarding Confederate history propagated by the Left. Edgerton stated that people, white and Black, have been "shamed and beaten down" and consequently led to deny their (Confederate) heritage.[55] Edgerton, as well as Roane, Haymes, and, to a lesser extent, Cooper, seek to fulfill what they imagine as a larger educational responsibility, like the museum as an institution more broadly. They do so in a way that makes "history come alive" in spaces that might otherwise be "considered stuffy and dull."[56]

While the traditional interpretive exhibit trades in movement through a circumscribed space, anchored by objects, living history functions, as scholars Richard Handler and William Saxton argue, "as part of a larger constellation of modern values that urge individuals to fulfill themselves by having experiences they can define as authentic."[57] According to archeologist James Deetz, living museums, of which Colonial Williamsburg is perhaps the most iconic example, should "re-create, within the limits of their boundaries and resources, facsimiles of entire cultures—not just the houses, fences, fields, and other appendages of the cultural, man-made landscape, but the social context as well: people going about their everyday lives, working, playing, praying, celebrating, and so on."[58] Such efforts at re-creation, however, are not without controversy. In 1994 Christy Coleman, then director of African American interpretations and presentations at Colonial Williamsburg, orchestrated a reenactment of the auction of enslaved people, drawing local as well as national criticism. Vocal critics, including the Virginia chapter of the NAACP and the Virginia branch of the Southern Christian Leadership Conference, attempted to block the program, with leaders expressing concern that history would "be trivialized in a carnival atmosphere." The event, however, went forward with Coleman, a Black woman, playing one of the enslaved people being sold. After the reenactment, Jack Gravely, political action chairman of the Virginia chapter of the NAACP, expressed a change of perspective regarding the program, dubbing it "passionate, moving, and educational."[59] Coleman would later go on to become chief executive officer of the American Civil War Museum and ultimately cochair Richmond mayor Levar Stoney's appointed Monument Avenue Commission.[60]

Yet, as with all forms of reenactment, there are limits to what will be relived. The performances I discuss in this chapter function in a specific manner. They "confirm nostalgia rather than challenge it" by often resorting to a simplified rendering of the past that "distorts the lives of the majority of past people." In this way, I suggest, "they do not teach *history.*"[61] Instead, they seek to inscribe a particular version of Confederate memory that stands divorced from a historical record of white supremacy culture and racism.

Living Historians and Living History

None of the individuals at the center of this chapter explicitly refer to the Confederacy as a "melting pot." The metaphor that imagines a beautifully eclectic, if at times chaotic, fusion of races undergirds their narrative of a Confederacy that is a paragon of inclusion. Rather than deny difference, this narrative celebrates it so as to refute critiques of neo-Confederate racism. For scholars such as Rumbaut, "the 'melting pot' does not, cannot, square with the seamy side of the country's history and the detritus left in the collective memory of those who must locate themselves in a narrative of wounds."[62] The metaphor casts the United States as an "immigrant haven,"[63] a refuge for the persecuted, yet as Rumbaut reminds us, it neglects to acknowledge its own limits.

A member of the United Daughters of the Confederacy since 2013, Roane traces her Confederate lineage to a free man of color from Gloucester Point named George Washington. Washington performed "fortification work," which Roane notes today translates to a "combat engineer."[64] Born in 1963 to parents who grew up in the Jim Crow South, Roane wields particular social and cultural capital as a tour guide and historian with Confederate ancestors. She has been recognized by groups throughout the South for her commitment to preserving Confederate heritage. Called to speak before the City-County Committee on Confederate Monuments and Memorials in Durham, North Carolina, in August 2018, Roane includes the Heritage Preservation Award from the National Sons of Confederate Veterans (2012) and the Commander-in-Chief Lady's Appreciation medal (2014) among her many awards and accolades.[65] She is light-skinned, a feature she tends to draw attention to when introducing herself to her audiences, describing her physicality as a motivator for her research. When speaking to an audience at a Memorial Day weekend ceremony in Fredericksburg, Virginia, in 2016, she stated,

> One of the reasons why I ended up doing this is because of my skin tone. I started doing genealogy because I wanted to know why I'm this light. My grandmother and my great-grandmother on the census were enumerated as mulatto, but I don't know what that means. I don't know if I'm mixed with European; I don't know if I'm mixed with Indian; I could be tri-racial, who knows.[66]

A living embodiment of the "melting pot" phenomenon, a fusion of racial groups, Roane's desire to learn more about her ancestors is as personal as it is historical. The popularity of Henry Louis Gates's television program inquiring into heritage, *Finding Your Roots*, following celebrities as they uncover stories of their pasts, coupled with the emergence of websites such as Ancestry.com and 23andMe.com seeking to help individuals uncover their genetic makeup, points to a collective preoccupation with genetics and ancestry. Roane's quest to understand her heritage not only provides a glimpse into her connections to the Confederacy; the quest makes her deeply relatable. By inserting herself into her work, Roane follows J. Christopher Holloway's conclusion that guides "adopt a variety of practices designed to break down the physical and psychological barriers."[67] While a historical authority at the UDC as archivist, Roane is also, her stories remind audiences with whom she speaks *not* as a representative of the organization, a "regular person."

As she positions herself in relation to her research, whether on a tour or in front of a lecture audience, Roane jokingly shares her age, reminding audiences of the era during which her parents grew up. She notes that life during Jim Crow was not easy, yet she reflects fondly on a photograph from her parents' wedding reception, which includes the faces of many white people who knew her mother, whom she describes as "a domestic." The photograph is a source of pride and evidence of a form of racial reconciliation, a congenial melting pot Roane does not see at present. She recalls the advice she received from her now-deceased mother that "there are good people and bad people" regardless of skin color.[68] The statement, while certainly not untrue, and fairly commonplace, offers important insight into Roane's positioning of race and racism within narratives of the past.

Beyond her strategies for connecting with her audiences, Roane legitimates herself as a tour guide through her positioning as a public history "insider," a status she has honed for more than twenty years in Richmond. Roane was trained in history at Virginia Commonwealth University (VCU). Formerly employed at the Valentine Museum and the Museum of the Confederacy,[69] visible and respected historical establishments in Richmond, she has worked with many of Richmond's key players in the public history world. Sharing a personal connection with almost all members of the mayor's appointed Monument Avenue Commission, she is no newcomer to the Richmond public history scene.

Confident and friendly, Roane has graciously made arrangements with me over the years to allow groups of University of Richmond students and faculty to visit. She is also, when confronted on issues of history, particularly regarding the Confederacy's relationship to slavery, an impassioned defender of Confederate memory and critic of "soundbites" that "do not reflect the true and actual [historical] complexities."[70] I have seen her deliver an emotional diatribe against liberals who claim the Confederacy's history is tethered to white supremacist ideologies. I have also seen her nervously speak before the Monument Avenue Commission as she called for monuments honoring "Confederates of Color." She is, for the most part, measured in her responses to critics, yet one senses that she delights in opportunities to engage in historical confrontation—to verbally spar with "naysayers."

Like Roane, Haymes reiterates that, despite differences during the years of the American Civil War, "there were no good guys. There were no bad guys. There were Americans."[71] Yet Haymes is not a naive adherent to what sociologist Eduardo Bonilla-Silva and others have called "colorblind racism."[72] A man who described himself as "married to the military," he avows that he will not "apologize for my slow talk" or "my heritage."[73] He recounts an extended military career that began with his draft notice from the Department of Defense on September 15, 1968, and took him to Vietnam, Baghdad, and Somalia over the course of thirty years, and then right back to Richmond. A site he had first visited in 1961 at the age of eleven, the Museum of the Confederacy captured his interest and imagination thirty years later, when a visit with his children and grandchildren prompted him to pursue a position as a docent, then ultimately a job as a guide.

The position of museum operations assistant at the Museum of the Confederacy was created for him in October 2004, at which point, he notes, "some of the staff there, they were not pleased to see me. . . . Look at me. I was a man of color. . . . No matter what I did in the early stages of my tenure, some of them were not pleased to see me. . . . I had a hard time." While Haymes's story of his coworkers' discomfort with a Black man working at the Museum of the Confederacy might seem to suggest a narrative of his coworkers' racism, in his telling Haymes persevered, "because I do my job, and I do it well . . . I don't let anyone trample on my honor. I have seen them come. I've seen them go, but, by God's grace, I have persevered."[74] He attributes his longevity at the Museum of the Confederacy to his personal fortitude and desire to remain free of politics.

Within the context of his work, Haymes does not engage with the issue of slavery nor does he acknowledge it as the cause of the American Civil War, or "The War Between the States," as he refers to it. Haymes identifies as "the student of the granddaughter of General Robert E. Lee, Mrs. Mary Custis Lee deButts of Winchester, Virginia."[75] He approaches his tours of the White House of the Confederacy as opportunities to "disseminate the history of this beautiful home,"[76] and in so doing ensure that visitors gain an appreciation for the space.

Focusing on the home's aesthetic qualities and the stories of the family who lived inside, evidenced in my first visit to the White House of the Confederacy, when Haymes proudly announced his role in maintaining the house, polishing the banisters, Haymes renders the history of slavery invisible. Emphasizing the beauty of the period wallpaper and toys of the Davis children, much like the many pins and pewter spoons on display within the headquarters of the United Daughters of the Confederacy, Haymes, like Roane, shares "history" as an amalgam of "authentic" objects, characterized by texture, material, and architecture. Little attention is paid to the stories these objects tell. Instead, Haymes and Roane make themselves the story, sharing an embodied history devoid of racial trauma. While Haymes might point to the difficulty of "melting," he narrates his story as one of self-determination and individual resilience. Haymes's narrative is a narrative of racial reconciliation.

Less preoccupied with preserving the past, Karen Cooper is an activist whose work is firmly rooted in the present. Also from the South, Cooper was born in Georgia and raised in New York. This experience gives her particular perspective when asked to consider the relationship between the South and racism. She noted in an interview with me in May 2014, "There's more racism up in the cities, in New York and Boston, than down here in the South. There were more black people killed in white neighborhoods up where I came from than I ever heard of down here." For Cooper, the contested Confederate battle flag is about "standing up for freedom." She stated, "And the notion that somehow I'm free when I don't feel free. I can't smoke what I want, I can't drink what I want, I can't go out certain places at certain times. They have these curfew restrictions. You can't be here, you can't be there."[77] Anchoring her protest in her beliefs as a twenty-first-century member of the Tea Party, Cooper is antigovernment, vying for the preservation of individual freedoms at the expense of the whole.

When asked about her support for the Confederate battle flag, she noted, "I look up to Confederate soldiers because I believe they were brave men. They fought the United States government. They knew they was outnumbered, outgunned, but they'd rather die than be ruled by another man."[78] Seeing H. K. Edgerton only reassured her in her efforts:

And then what he [Edgerton] said made sense. It did help that . . . at least there was another black person that realized that it wasn't about slavery. A lot of black people, slaves, actually fought with their masters. There were free black people who fought on the southern side because there were black slaveholders, especially in Louisiana. There were the black men that had a large plantation in Louisiana. People don't want to hear that.[79]

The presence of another Black person on the front lines advocating on behalf of the Confederate battle flag steeled Cooper. Like Roane and Haymes, Cooper recognizes difference. However, she is unfazed by the overwhelming participation of white men in the neo-Confederate movement. She noted, "it's more white men because mostly white men are conservative, and they feel that they are being attacked nowadays. It's true. I see it. They're being attacked. They're being vilified, like every day in the media and on TV. If black people can be black, why can't white people be proud to be white?"[80] Such a claim works well in the hands of the Virginia Flaggers and other Confederate heritage groups, for whom race is a weaponized term.

Cooper's recognition and validation of their stance grants it legitimacy, along with their denial of racism. As Panama Jackson, senior editor of Very Smart Brothas, wrote in the weeks following the 2015 Charleston massacre, "Folks like Karen are the kind of people you want to bring in as keynote speakers at your 'southern heritage' events. Except, she's Black. Dave Chappelle was joking about Clayton Bigsby . . . or was he?" Invoking one of Chappelle's most famous characters, the blind, "black white supremacist," Jackson more seriously concludes, "she [Cooper] is LITERALLY the Black friend they can always resort to when somebody calls them racist."[81] Cooper thus serves a strategic purpose for the Virginia Flaggers and Confederate heritage sympathizers.

Cooper's comments, particularly regarding slavery as a choice years before Kanye West made a similar claim, have drawn the attention and criticism of many. She has been cited for seeking her fifteen minutes of fame and called an "idiot."[82]

Yet in a less publicly recognized story, Cooper wound up at the center of debate. In July 2015 Raymond Agnor placed an ad in the (Lexington, Virginia) News-Gazette that announced, "No black people or democrats are allowed on my property until further notice."[83] Agnor cited "all the trouble the democrats and black people are causing." Not only did Agnor's action prompt an online petition calling for an apology from the News-Gazette for printing the ad, it prompted historian and Confederate memory critic Brooks Simpson to ask, "Are we to assume that Karen Cooper's no longer welcome to go to Billboard Hill north of Lexington to look at her beloved Confederate flag while reminding us that 'slavery's a choice'?"[84] The Flaggers were silent in response to Agnor's explicit racism, begging the question, posed by Simpson, as to the extent to which Cooper has been exploited by the very organization to which she claimed allegiance.[85] If one attempts to visit the Flaggers' commentary today, one finds a broken link, suggesting that there might have been something the Flaggers recognize might not reflect well on their organization.

A public disagreement with outspoken Flagger Tripp Lewis in summer 2016 launched Cooper into the spotlight yet again. This time, the disagreement led to Cooper's decision to distance herself from the Flaggers. Conflict erupted after Cooper shared that she would not vote for Donald Trump.[86] Lewis responded with anti-Muslim attacks; Cooper is a former member of the Nation of Islam, which has its own complicated history with the Confederacy. Nation of Islam leader Louis Farrakhan defended the Confederate flag, claiming it is just as upsetting as the American flag.[87]

Cooper's tenuous place within the Virginia Flaggers ultimately led Daryle Lamont Jenkins, founder of One People's Project, to argue, "I don't think Karen Cooper is a bad person. I definitely don't think she's a stupid person. I think she has bad politics, or at the very least a bad approach to them. But I truly hope that this particular episode [her clash with Lewis] causes her to realize that the people around her might not be her friends."[88] The One People's Project seeks to raise consciousness about the work of right-wing groups and individuals in an effort to provide deeper understanding of "the hate politics" of the contemporary moment.[89] In an episode of the podcast *Love + Radio* that aired in November 2018, Cooper described the words leading to her departure as "really nasty." When prompted, however, as to whether the comments were "racial," she replied, "No, I don't think he meant it that way."[90] While Cooper suggested that racism could be read from the comments, she maintains that there are only a "small amount of them [southerners] who are truly racist."[91]

Despite Cooper's parting of ways with the Virginia Flaggers, H. K. Edgerton continues his campaign, as president of Southern Heritage 411, to reify the gallantry of the Confederacy, attracting audiences including the South Carolina Secessionist Party.[92] Edgerton's connections to southern heritage groups, however, can be traced back to his days as president of the Asheville branch of the NAACP. While Edgerton was suspended from the NAACP for noncompliance due to the branch's debt, his meeting with Kirk Lyons and Neil Payne of the Southern Legal Resource Center, whose slogan reads "Justice for Dixie,"[93] made many suspicious of Edgerton's allegiances. A photograph of the three holding white dinner napkins in a way so as to resemble KKK hoods only reinforced such suspicions. Edgerton said the photo captured "a lighter moment" during a meeting to "discuss how to avert potential violence during a Ku Klux Klan rally being planned at the same time."[94] Edgerton's eventual removal from his post suggested that not all were as convinced of the moment's innocuousness.

Beyond mere celebration of the Confederacy and its protectors, Edgerton has been outspoken in his opposition to contemporary civil rights activists, calling "these so-called leaders in the black community" "poverty pimps."[95] Edgerton's targets have also included North Carolina council-man Cecil Bothwell, an atheist or "post-theist," who was sworn into office without reference to God.[96] Edgerton's activism demonstrates the difficulty of divorcing politics from the larger cause to which he is committed.

The Stories They Tell

Beyond their embodied performances, Roane, Haymes, Cooper, and Edgerton offer narratives of the spaces they inhabit, serving to bolster myths of the Confederacy's heroism and diversity. In the cases of Roane and Haymes, these narratives are woven into their tours of the United Daughters of the Confederacy headquarters and the White House of the Confederacy, respectively.

When it was dedicated, more than fifty years after the United Daughters of the Confederacy was founded, UDC headquarters served, as a *Richmond Times-Dispatch* editorial noted, "to remind us of a heritage from our forefathers which must never be forgotten."[97] As Susan Quinn wrote for the newspaper on the day of the UDC headquarters' dedication in 1957, "Their [the UDC's] monuments and historical markers are everywhere. . . . They have worked to have fair and unbiased histories used in schools, marked the graves of countless Confederate veterans, and collected the records of at least 40,000 of those veterans, which are now housed in the new building."[98] The UDC was an organization, Richmond's newspaper of record reminded its readers, whose contributions to history were to be revered. More than sixty years later, the imposing structure's continued presence in one of the most trafficked tourist sites in the city—also the site where the Flaggers were once most visible on the Boulevard next to the Virginia Museum of Fine Arts (VMFA)—makes the Confederacy present in Richmond and difficult to ignore.

The sense of the site's historicity was part of the earliest conversations for UDC headquarters. A January 1954 article in the *Fort Lauderdale News* reported of a row between members of the UDC and the city of Richmond following a proposal to create a parking lot next to the VMFA—the site where the UDC headquarters would later stand. In a statement to the state legislature, the UDC wrote, "Do . . . visitors come to Virginia to see an art collection? Oh, no! They come to see Jamestown, the very beginning; Yorktown, where Cornwallis surrendered; and Williamsburg! . . . They come to see Monticello, and Stratford Hall, and the city which sits on seven hills—Richmond, Virginia, the capitol of the Confederacy!" While the land in question, the UDC noted, "is sacred and hallowed ground,"

Virginia's rich history transcended, in the UDC's members' minds, the provenance of the art housed in the museum.[99] The city *was* a historical museum.

While the land on which the eventual UDC headquarters was built was envisioned as a site worthy of public reverence, the building is not open to the public. Guided tours are offered by appointment only. The fortress-like building, designed by Louis Ballou, with a Georgia marble façade, two large (11' × 16') bronze doors gifted by the Children of the Confederacy (CoC), brick walkways, marble wainscoting and columns, marble floors, and a twenty-four-foot ceiling,[100] communicates a sense of distance—remove—at least to those who are not members. The interior, by contrast, feels more like a home, displaying greater warmth. The corridors are dimly lit, the dining room is grand, and portraits romanticizing the first daughter of the Confederacy, Winnie Davis, and her successors decorate the walls. At the UDC, visitors are regaled with the story of Winnie Davis's love for a Yankee, transforming her into a modern-day Juliet, whose love for her Romeo from the opposing clan led to her tragic end. While Winnie Davis did not commit suicide, she died young and unmarried at the age of thirty-four.

It is thus unsurprising that Roane would assure visitors to the headquarters of the UDC that the organization is "very patriotic."[101] Her strategy of attempting to authenticate the UDC by testifying to the organization's "aesthetic, historical, monetary, recreational, and social values"[102] is neither new nor unique. She noted, "Our Chapter every month donates canned goods for the food bank, and another woman at Chapter was involved in Feed More. She just passed around a hat and like that, she got seventy-five dollars. We do a lot of stuff with the VA and not only with the VA hospital, but you know, all the soldiers that are over in Afghanistan, Iraq . . . People don't realize, we're benevolent, we're educators."[103]

Roane's emphasis on the UDC's education and philanthropy is wholly consistent with the historic ways the organization has been described by members. In a 1957 article, President General Miss Edna H. Fowler of Los Angeles reported that the UDC's "per capita patriotic contributions . . . have been greater than those of any other group." This same article noted, "Ever interested in education," the UDC has "given scholarships and essay prizes, as well as yearly awards to outstanding students at the United States Military and Naval academies."[104]

Years after my first tour with Roane, she sought to reassure my students that UDC members are not "traitors" but rather patriots—women who see themselves as part of the United States as well as the historic Confederacy. This is a point on which she elaborated publicly in August 2018: "I know that slavery existed. But we have to realize that it was a United States issue. . . . All the blame cannot be put on the South."[105] That same month, an online debate ensued after Brendan Wolfe, editor of *Encyclopedia Virginia*, publicly responded to a series of letters received from members of the UDC. Ginger R. Stephens, president of the Virginia Division of the UDC, had encouraged the "ladies" to request that the UDC *Encyclopedia* entry be corrected, given its "very biased" portrayal of the organization. The "bias" was evident, letter writers suggested, in the entry's emphasis on race. According to one letter writer, the entry was evidence of a "Good old smear campaign!" Wolfe identified the "crux of this philosophical argument": "white supremacy."[106]

To diffuse critiques of the UDC's work to instantiate white supremacy culture, Roane seeks to debunk data released by the Southern Poverty Law Center (SPLC) citing the proliferation of Confederate monuments during the eras of Jim Crow and the civil rights movement. Referring to the invocation of Jim Crow as "convenient," Roane notes, "The South was devastated by the war. Regardless of the videos and other nonsense that has been produced lately, it took southerners years to find the funds to erect these memorials."[107] Distancing Confederate monuments from issues of race and racism, Roane valorizes the Confederate cause.

Haymes, like Roane, emphasizes the benevolence of the Confederacy and the honor associated with the cause at the White House of the Confederacy. Preserved to be the bearer of "very intimate treasures of the heroes of the Confederacy," the White House of the Confederacy housed sacred relics including "a lock of General Lee's hair, the blood upon a handkerchief of the immortal Jackson, the baby shoe found clasped in death to the heart of an unknown soldier," reported Maude Waddell of the *Asheville Citizen-Times* in March 1929.[108] It was described as home to the "relics of the war between the states."[109] For Waddell, "Any lover of the dear dead cause, of the Southland with its noble ideals, history and tradition could but behold in ecstasy the memorials presented here."[110]

Touted as "among the places history-conscious Americans will visit during the centennial," the White House of the Confederacy clarified its position in the city in 1960 when then museum director India Thomas stated, "This is a memorial museum, dedicated to the memory of Southern soldiers and responsible for displaying and caring for the things they used."[111] In 1976 a new building adjacent to the White House of the Confederacy was opened to house the Museum of the Confederacy, enabling the former Confederate White House to be restored to its 1860s appearance. More recently, tours of the White House of the Confederacy have exhibited a less celebratory bend—as evidenced in the removal of guides such as Haymes. Promotional materials now describe the site as encouraging the stories of "enslaved and free African Americans, European immigrants, and personal staff who worked in the home, as well as house visitors like Robert E. Lee and Abraham Lincoln."[112]

When I spoke with Haymes in 2014, two years before he was let go and some four years before the Museum of the Confederacy's September 2018 closure to facilitate the new American Civil War Museum's opening in May 2019, he described his lexical decisions in framing the past to his tour groups at the Confederate White House with no prompting:

> When I talk about the Southern Confederacy, I talk about the *glorious* army, one of the *greatest* infantries to ever walk the face of the earth, the Army of Northern Virginia, commanded by the legendary General himself, Robert E. Lee. I talk about the *honorable* Jefferson Davis. I talk about his *major contributions* to the fabric of this great nation. The *gallant* Jeb Stuart, the last cavalier that America has ever produced. . . . I talk about the *great* men who served the Confederacy and their connection to the American Revolution.[113]

Haymes is unapologetic about his use of language. While the use of such terms might seem heavy-handed, Haymes's and Roane's claims to authenticity stem not merely from their reliance on terms that underscore the bravery and benevolence of the Confederacy. Haymes, in his words, tells the story of great Americans. They are the men who can be linked historically to the American Revolution, the founding fathers who fought against the tyranny of the British—as the Confederacy fought against the "tyranny" of the Union.

While the language of valor and gallantry harks back to traditional Lost Cause themes, Roane introduces her groups to details that serve to further complicate this narrative. Along our tour of the UDC, we stop, for instance, at an image depicting Judah Benjamin, who had been part of Jefferson Davis's cabinet as secretary of state (1862–1865) during the Civil War. She noted that Benjamin was Jewish, a point that Virginia Flagger Barry Isenhour, who accompanied me on my first visit to the UDC in May 2014, followed up with, "so you always have the fact that the Klan hates Jews and Catholics; so the South not only venerated the Jewish members but that's why we designed the flag the St. Andrew's cross."[114] It was as if Benjamin's presence as a member of the Confederate cabinet negated any racism or anti-Semitism that had historically characterized the entity—or that the St. Andrew's cross neutralized the movement's racial intolerance. To Roane and to Isenhour, Benjamin was a part of the melting pot—a metaphor that was often used in discussions of Jewish assimilation and the process of becoming white.[115]

Isenhour presented the KKK as fundamentally misunderstood—a point that Roane would reiterate after my visit with my students years later. Rather than acknowledging the Ku Klux Klan as a terrorist organization with deep roots in Virginia—parading down Richmond's Broad Street in the mid-1920s and running recruitment ads in Virginia newspapers as recently as 2018[116]—Roane reiterated a desire to "correct" what she framed as a misidentified KKK. The image of Benjamin was used to feed the larger narrative of the Confederacy's inclusivity, counteracting claims of the Klan's racism. Certainly, Benjamin was not the only person of Jewish heritage to be implicated in the Lost Cause. As historian Matthew Gottlieb argues, there are questions to be asked of other Richmonders as well.[117]

When I visited the UDC with my class in February 2017, Roane asked students to flip through registers to see if they could find their last names, in an attempt to discern their Confederate ancestry. In this way, she sought to remind students that they, too, could be part of the community—regardless of who they were or who they believed themselves to be. They might just not be aware of it yet.

The language of the Confederacy's inclusivity was further advanced by Haymes at the White House of the Confederacy, where an attempt to reframe the labor in the house is made explicit. In our conversation, Haymes explained his logic for casting the Black laborers in the White House of the Confederacy in particular ways.

> I talk about the servants, the people of color who are servants in the house. Many of my guests who come want to see whips and chains and people getting beat and escaping. A lot of my coworkers have yet to learn the finer details about these people who had employment there. They were free people of color. They would come in, do their job, and then they would go home. I've got a couple of employees who think every black person was a slave and that's not true.[118]

While Haymes is not incorrect to caution against casting all experiences as the same, his concern, like Roane's, that the "whips and chains" narrative does a disservice to the past begs the question as to how.

Anticipating queries as to what she means when she resists the "whips and chains" narrative, Roane shows her experience to audiences. When I listened as she delivered a lecture in a cemetery in Fredericksburg, Virginia, on Memorial Day weekend in 2016, Roane presented a narrative of a labor system to her audience offering enslaved people greater agency. Roane explained to her audience, seated as the sun set,

They're going to pay the slaves. Now isn't this interesting because we're taught that slaves had no agency. They had nothing. However, there was the hired-out system. I'm going to use me as an example. I'm a slave out there in the country, my owner decides he's going to hire me out. I'm going to go to Richmond, Virginia. First of all, as a slave, I get to pick where I want to live. Did you hear what I was just saying? I get to pick where I want to live.[119]

Presenting her audience with this hiring out and living apart scenario—one that, as historian Midori Tagaki notes, did distinguish urban slavery in Richmond from its rural counterparts[120]—Roane speaks from the perspective of an enslaved person. She portrays the system as ultimately an empowering one in which enslaved people had choice. *She* has choice. In performing this character, Roane emphasizes her contentment with such a prospect. Slavery, by extension, appears less cruel, a critique Roane often encounters. She states, "They [skeptics] say, 'Oh, that's just so cruel. I can't believe that the slaves had to find his or her . . .' I said, 'That's freedom.'"[121]

For Roane, the story of slavery in the South is not one of human bondage and brutality; it is of agency and possibility. That enslaved people had a modicum of choice is offered as evidence of self-determination. Although, as Tagaki argues, "Richmond's slave system did . . . create certain opportunities for slave men and women not only to survive—which in itself is extraordinary—but also to build a rich, complex community supported by strong family ties, the African Baptist Church, and mutual aid societies, among other institutions . . . it was no less brutal, oppressive, or legally constraining than any other form of bondage."[122] This latter point receives no acknowledgment from Roane. Rather, in her estimation, living within the so-called melting pot, enslaved people wield the potential to make decisions—to retain elements of their culture in the process of becoming Americanized. It is the ultimate freedom. This is a point echoed famously by Cooper, with more extreme consequence: "I say because of what Patrick Henry said: 'Give me liberty or give me death.' To me, if we had went back to that kind of slavery, no I couldn't do it. Give me death."[123] This statement was reprinted in publications across the world, likely due to the incredulity with which it was often met. However, for Cooper, the answer was simple: if given the choice between enslavement and death, she would choose the latter, and she would do so in full recognition of the situation. It would be, in her view, a definitive act of freedom. She would have *chosen* death.

While Roane's desire to ensure that the historical narrative does not relegate enslaved people to the status of passive victims of circumstance is admirable, both Haymes and Roane narrativize the lives of those enslaved as well as free as an either/or proposition: either they were passive victims of a brutal system of human bondage *or* they were agents in determining their futures. There exists no possibility for resistance within institutional oppression, a historiographical tradition that has been in existence for several decades.[124] This move might seem to undercut the melting pot metaphor's more pluralistic qualities. Haymes's and Roane's stories emphasize the individual to the exclusion of the collective. They maintain the primacy of the individual's choice, leading to the greater good. This emphasis on "agency," which historian Walter Johnson argues became "the antidote to the indignities of exploitation,"[125] comes at a cost: a tradition that "unwittingly reproduce[s] the incised terms and analytical limits of a field of context (black humanity: for or against) framed by the white supremacist assumptions which made it possible to ask such a question in the first place."[126] Haymes's and Roane's stories reinforce this critique.

Part of Roane's desire for a narrative that speaks more directly to the experiences of enslaved people stems from what she describes as a sense of shame among Black people. Roane stated, "Sometimes I can't get people that look like us to understand there is nothing to be ashamed of. If your ancestors were slaves, so be it. . . . I said how can you be ashamed of people who had the skills that were needed to run the South?" She continued, "I think about the men and women who were freed from bondage. They had to get on with their lives and figure out what they had to do. I don't think they sat around going, 'woe is me. I was a slave. I've been put down.' That really bothers me."[127] Roane sees contemporary discussions of reparations therefore as an attempt to be compensated for a history one did not experience—refusing to consider the residual effects of slavery.[128]

Offering "evidence" to those who claim racism to be at the center of the American Civil War, Roane states,

> The United Confederate Veterans would have an annual reunion. Who went to those reunions? It wasn't all white. Look at that, men of color. They went, they wanted to be there, they were welcomed. If they couldn't afford to go, white people helped them to go to the convention. We always hear about all the tension between the races, but yet they were welcome. You know why? If you serve in the military and I know some of you have, there is a bond that you cannot break.[129]

While there were Black men in the photographs at the dedication of the Robert E. Lee Monument in 1890, for example, their presence by no means translated into their unequivocal support for the valorization of Lee, as the editorials of John Mitchell in the *Richmond Planet* make clear. More so, her appeal to the military bond as one that transcends race again points not to a naive colorblindness but to reconciliation.

Beyond these evocations of the past, Roane narrates a reconciliationist present whereby a Black woman such as Ms. Mattie Clyburn Rice could attend a marker dedication for Confederate soldiers in December 2012 in Monroe, North Carolina, where people, white and Black, stood together. "The only thing we didn't do was sing Kumbaya. Okay? It was a wonderful service."[130] Ms. Mattie's father, Weary Clyburn, "was honored for being a proud soldier in the South Carolina Troops of the Confederate States of America." In the words of Ms. Mattie, "My father was born a slave but he died as a hero for his honorable service as a Confederate soldier."[131]

The story of Ms. Mattie, neo-Confederates write, is one of persever- ance. The conservative *Times Examiner* described "Ms. Mattie" as spending "decades searching for documents that supported her father's war stories, despite those who tried to tell her there was no way her father, being a man of color, would have been a soldier for the South." However, the *Times Examiner* noted, "This courageous lady did not ever give up, because she knew what her father had told her was true. This determination was rewarded when she discovered her father's application for pension and records verifying his service as a Confederate Soldier."[132] She was the ul- timate Black Confederate. Her story is reposted often to social media—a reminder of the possibilities not only for peace in a reconciliationist pres- ent but also for citizenship. Ms. Mattie's father, neo-Confederates remind us, was a Confederate "citizen," welcomed into the melting pot.

When Ms. Mattie died in October 2014, Roane announced,

> There was a twenty-one-gun salute, cannon fire and it was a three-hour service and none of us cared . . . What's even more important this is her stone right here. Why is it so important? Because four organizations are on there. The United Daughters of the Confederacy, Sons of Confederate Veterans, Order of Confederate Rose, and the Military Orders of Stars and Bars . . . This woman brought together four organizations, that's how much she was loved.[133]

Ms. Mattie, a Black woman who people like me might assume would see the Confederacy as a symbol of racism and hatred, instead is champi- oned as a testament to the Confederacy's love for people of color. The Confederacy was not only a "melting pot," it is a place where the "metals" harmoniously fused.

Far from being resigned to playing a supporting role as an arbiter of memory, Roane is a leader, seeking to complicate narratives of Black passivity by reassuring audiences of Black agency and self-determination. Enslaved and free people alike were not passive victims of a brutal, oppressive system. They persevered, she reminds us, making choices whereby they positioned themselves as historical actors. She is simultaneously an actor, continuing their legacy.

Although this claim of Black agency and self-determination, at face value, appears one worthy of praise and in concert with existing historiography, Roane's and Haymes's commitment to ensuring that not only did enslaved people have power but they were actively welcomed, embraced by the white people of the Confederacy, alongside whom they fought, suggests that the most pernicious part of the melting pot metaphor has found a place within neo-Confederate discourse. That which ultimately led to the concept's comparative fall from critical favor—its uncritical celebration of the melding of cultures and people—is most central to their story. Yet, as neo-Confederates' opposition to Black Lives Matter and other social justice movements suggests, the characters they perform— the characters accepted by neo-Confederates—conform to a mold that strategically bolsters their cause. Roane, Haymes, and Cooper, to a lesser extent, alongside Edgerton, thus became model minority Confederates— exemplary exceptions regaled with praise by neo-Confederates who reassure themselves of their non-racism.

In the end, Roane, Haymes, Cooper, and Edgerton maintain that they, like all people of color in the South, had a choice, opting to become part of the melting pot—the hybridized cuisine that is custom in the South while retaining the authenticity of their individual "flavor." They embody this stance as they actively narrate it, enabling a larger collective to be fortified by claims of an apolitical Confederacy clinging nostalgically to "heritage." They have written themselves into the story, demonstrating the ways they have gained power through historic invisibility. As was written in the One People's Project,

> When you are a Black Republican, it is rather questionable. If you are a full on Black Conservative, you are sad. If you are a Black Conservative that makes a lot of apologies for white racism while attacking what is seen as black racism, you are pathetic. If you are a Black Conservative that not only makes apologizes for racism but actually endorses it, you are downright despicable and need to be especially routed. . . . Here we have a black man [H. K. Edgerton] who disregards that legacy [of white supremacy] and will count among his friends those that want to further it. Calling him scum is disrespectful to scum.[134]

As "living historians," contemporary Black Confederates reify the lived experience of the melting pot, eschewing charges of the Confederacy's racism by amplifying their agency as the museum's storytellers. And yet they do so at a price. As I learned, there would be other ways for white Americans to partake of this story, this melting pot, in very literal terms.

4 | Cooking Confederate and Nostalgic Reenactment

In August 1987 *Richmond Times-Dispatch* columnist Bill Lohmann introduced readers to the "scene at Mary Mac's, a downtown Atlanta restaurant that attracts taxicab drivers and bank presidents."

> Southern cooking was born in the melting pot of its people. . . . Perhaps because of the Civil War or perhaps because of the nature of the people themselves, the South has always been a bit protective—some would say defensive—of its customs and determined to pass them along to the next generation. Because of that, no regional cuisine is more steeped in tradition or better reflects the ingredients at hand.[1]

With these words, Lohmann painted a nostalgic picture that transcended its particular Atlanta locale: of diners talking "jovially with each other as they shovel in forkfuls of country fried steak, stewed corn and pickled beets, sop gravy with homemade bread and wash it all down with iced tea."[2] He described what Barbara Sullivan of the *Chicago Tribune* would later call "honest-to-goodness, down-home Southern cooking,"[3] a form of cooking immortalized in South Carolinian Nathalie Dupree's *New Southern Cooking*, a companion cookbook to her fifty-two-part public television series bearing the same name.

Since Dupree's emergence on the culinary scene, her popularity rivaling that of Julia Child,[4] public figures such as Ree Drummond, the Pioneer Woman,[5] and butter-loving Paula Deen have been similarly able to capitalize on their southern roots, parlaying their popularity into television cooking shows, restaurants, books, and even magazines, inscribing "southernness" as a particular brand of "whiteness." One need go no further for evidence than the pages of *Southern Living* magazine, featuring "exquisite" decor for homes in downtown Savannah bearing "historic charm" alongside recipes for Lowcountry Shrimp and Grits and recommendations for "The South's Best Soul Food" with not a person of color in sight.

Paula Deen is a mainstay in *Southern Living*, which tracks the "Georgia food doyenne" and her restaurant openings and real estate holdings while sharing her recipes.[6] Yet Deen's cachet extends beyond the pages of the popular magazine. Portrayed by journalists across the country, from the *Detroit Free Press* to the *Atlanta Constitution*, as "sincere," praised for "her easy Southern charm and inviting personality," Deen has been dubbed "the uptight Martha [Stewart']s salty Southern antithesis."[7] Deen's warmth and accessibility, hallmarks of that aforementioned southern charm, stand in sharp contrast to New England's Martha Stewart, described by *New York Daily News* writer Judith Schoolman as "the high priestess of hausfraus" who "answer[ed] the call of gracious living"[8] by transforming her image into one of the most successful brands in the United States.

Known as the consummate businesswoman, Stewart was selected in 2000 as one of *Vanity Fair*'s top fifty leaders of the Information Age and ranked among the *Forbes 400* list—that is, until she was found guilty of insider trading in 2004. Deen, in contrast, built an empire with its "devoted legion of fans"[9] on an entirely different model. While as a young mother Deen had been "living the American dream," experiences of personal tragedy led her to spiral, she notes, into "[near] poverty, self-doubt, and health challenges." Deen rebounded in a remarkable journey that, her website assures, enables the southern chef to remain "every bit as genuine, real, and full of love as she was the day the first meals left her kitchen."[10] Deen *was* the "American Dream." If ever Deen needed a sign that she had "made" it, it was being publicly lampooned in 2012 by comedian Kristen Wiig on one of the nation's best-known comic variety shows, *Saturday Night Live*.[11]

Wiig's Deen, seen buttering her hair and referring to her diabetes diagnosis as "the sugars," was a comic caricature, yet the impetus for the southern celebrity chef's public roasting came with allegations that she had used a racial epithet, sharing with a former employee a vision to orchestrate her brother's wedding with a "southern plantation" theme, complete with Black waitstaff dressed in white shirts and bow ties as "in the Shirley Temple days, [when] they used to tap dance around."[12] The almost instantaneous fault lines dividing Deen's fans made clear that while fans might continue to consume her peach cobbler or Not Yo' Mama's Banana Pudding, the deployment of the past in the name of spectacle was not without bounds. Precisely where those lines lie, however, has been the subject of much debate.

Some, like Rod Dreher, editor of the *American Conservative*, "reluctant[ly]" defended Deen, noting that "every younger white Southerner who holds enlightened opinions on race knows that you have to allow for the cultural deformation of older white Southerners."[13] Others saw the revelation of Deen's racism as a reminder, as Amy Maclin wrote for Oprah.com, that "homemade sin is part of our [southern] legacy, just like lard—which might be delicious but is poison, too."[14]

Although Deen's contracts with the Food Network, Walmart, Target, QVC, JCPenney, and Kmart, among other retailers, were cancelled in the wake of the controversy, Deen's cookbooks "surge[d] to top spots on Amazon best seller lists," noted the *Washington Times*, a week following the chef's public apology in June 2013. Years later I would pass by Deen's restaurant while walking through Savannah, only to find it bustling. As restaurant sales boom, so, too, do plantation weddings, which remain popular for nuptials throughout the South.[15] The tensions between these phenomena emphasize a disconnect among consumers regarding whether and how to engage with the very public figure's blatant disregard for the plantation's history and the enslaved people who built and maintained it.

Paula Deen's fall from grace coupled with her continued popularity captures a reality of food history, making it a particularly apt site for study. As American studies scholar Marcie Cohen Ferris notes, "Contradiction is a central theme in the history of southern food, where the grim reality of slavery, Jim Crow segregation, extreme hunger, and disenfranchisement contrast with the pleasure and inventiveness of the region's cuisine."[16] Within this chapter, I consider the ways in which southern and "Confederate cookbooks" attempt to resolve this contradiction by capitalizing on the slippage between the two terms, often deployed as synonyms. I thus use "Confederate cookbooks" in quotation marks in recognition that not all the books I analyze are period cookbooks dating to the Confederacy or even explicitly associated with the Confederacy. Yet they are united, I suggest, by a common frame instantiated powerfully by women.

Reading various cookbooks' narratives, recipes, and accompanying visuals, this chapter explores the strategies deployed by women to sell the Confederacy as a site of both physical and spiritual nourishment. As historian Janet Theophano has argued, the themes woven throughout cookbooks are "timeless: life and death, youth and age, faithfulness and betrayal, memory and forgetfulness." The medium "tells us how to make beauty and meaning in the midst of the mundane—a concept especially important for women, whose lives often are punctuated by the demands of feeding others."[17]

Beyond offering insight into the everyday lives of women much like a diary, journal, or scrapbook, the cookbooks examined in this chapter underscore women's central role as stewards of Confederate memory. White women, particularly members of the United Daughters of the Confederacy (UDC), have been understood by historians as "authorities of collective memory"[18] whose legacies can be readily observed through the persistence of the Confederate monuments and memorials for which they raised funds at the turn of the twentieth century. This chapter suggests that "Confederate cooking" offers a place for women in a contemporary Confederate landscape, reinforcing historic images of the "demure southern belle," marked by stereotypical whiteness[19] and popularized by *Gone with the Wind*'s Scarlett O'Hara. "Confederate cooking" also offers a platform for ritualized performances that enable women to continue to resist the history of slavery and its legacies, with which "southern" cooking is intimately connected.

By fetishizing food, the "Confederate cookbooks" at the center of this chapter reduce the Confederacy to a delicious consumable, often a delectable and allegedly apolitical confection, available within a capitalist system accessible beyond the confines of the South. Forging a connection between consumer and the past, such books and their concomitant commentary cast off the yoke of "tourism" with its attendant connotations of distance. Rather, they embrace the pasts with which they engage as part of "heritage," yet unlike Deen, they neglect to engage with that heritage's history in any material way.

If the Virginia Flaggers publicly claim "heritage not hate," these cookbooks suggest that heritage can be reduced to what their ancestors *ate*. Taken together, these books propagate the myth of Confederate exceptionalism by enabling the Confederacy to creep into the American home under the guise of an appeal to reenact history through heritage—to commune with the past in a "neutral" way.

The cookbooks I examine in this chapter not only champion the agrarian, antebellum South, a cornerstone of Lost Cause ideology; by encouraging a form of historical reenactment through the cooking of food, these books firmly locate the Confederacy in the present as a paragon of both individualism and communitarianism.[20] Performance studies scholar Scott Magelssen has argued, "because living history's museum staffs, public relations, and literature emphasize their historical accuracy and commitment to detail, the three-dimensional, historical environments provided for the visitors are not just an appearance of the real—a mirror image representation—but *real* history . . . by convention of the museum and by audience agreement[,] not by ontological essence."[21] In this way, cookbooks provide a way for memory of the Confederacy to live on through continual reenactment and literal consumption.

In chapter 3, I considered reenactment through an exploration of persons who I argue function as "living historians." Within this chapter, I suggest that cookbooks engage with readers by appealing to a desire to make history "'come alive' for secular audiences."[22] Like scholar Alexander Cook, I do not mean to suggest that there is no value to reenactment as a mode of engaging with history. Rather, in this case, I argue that

"Confederate cookbooks" crystallize one of the primary critiques leveled against reenactment as public history: namely, its "privileg[ing] [of] a visceral, emotional engagement with the past at the expense of a more analytical treatment."[23]

Food, Foodways, and Reenacting Historic Food Culture

The connections between food, foodways, and politics are woven throughout history. Foodways, defined by culinary scholar Megan Elias as "the combination of what people ate, how meals happened, and what diners thought about food—which dishes were considered normal, what materials were deemed edible, [and] which preparations are appropriate to which groups," in general, and cookbooks specifically have recently experienced a surge in interest.[24] For scholars, this interest stems from the sense that "ideas about food are not mere fads but instead part of an extended discourse that involves ideas about national identity—who is American—as well as what is good and bad taste."[25] Food and foodways offer insight into cultural norms and practices often under the guise of a cozy escape.[26] Yet the realities of food history have shown that the past was hardly so peaceful or apolitical.

During World War I, sauerkraut was renamed "liberty cabbage." More recently, in 2003, amid anti-French sentiment, french fries were rebranded "freedom fries."[27] Sometimes, historical names of food seem overtly racist today. Thomas Germain notes that "in the first half of the 20th century, MSG was still nothing more sinister than what the 1953 edition of *The Joy of Cooking* would later call 'the mysterious 'white powder' of the Orient."[28] Irma and Marion Rombauer's 1960s reprint of *The Joy of Cooking* offered readers instructions on how to make "Mohrenkoepfe or Moors' Heads,"[29] a variation of which appeared in a New York bakery in 2009 in an attempt to "honor" President Obama. The cookies were called "Drunken Negro Face."[30]

If such examples exemplify the politics of food and foodways, food nonetheless continues to be romanticized. Popular television programs such as *Diners, Drive-Ins, and Dives* have devoted entire episodes to the quest for the best southern barbecue, around which its own deeply rooted mythology orbits. Wilbur Caldwell's book, *Searching for the Dixie Barbecue*, whose subtitle references the "Southern psyche," typifies the genre, likening barbecue to a "religion involving hallowed rites and ancient rituals reaching all the way back in time and place to the twisted myth of true Southernness."[31] In Richmond, locals debate the best barbecue in town, much as Philadelphians have an almost religious affinity for the cheesesteak. Beyond preoccupation with "southern" cuisine, fascination has also grown with the culture of Appalachian alcohol production, evidenced in the popularity of *Moonshine Nation*, penned by award-winning author Mark Spivak.[32]

Such examples underscore the extent to which "southern" food and foodways in particular have inspired not only wide interest but also an incredibly lucrative industry that capitalizes on a romanticized version of "the South"—a region whose cuisine is distinctly "international,"[33] as Helen Worth wrote in her 1979 book, *Damnyankee in a Southern Kitchen*. Such a sentiment was echoed in my first interview with Barry Isenhour of the Virginia Flaggers, who described southern fare as a multicultural "melting pot" where the flavors of diverse cultures meld into a singular cuisine, much like Lohmann had in the late 1980s. Food therefore becomes the consummate way of presenting the South, and the Confederacy in particular, as an amalgam of rich flavors to be consumed.

Cookbooks remind us of these flavors often with nostalgic aplomb.[34] Diane Pfeifer's 1992 collection, *Gone with the Grits*, capitalizes on southern nostalgia, featuring a *Gone with the Wind*–like scene sketch with the Rhett Butler character holding, in addition to his Scarlett O'Hara, a bowl of grits. While Scarlett O'Hara famously declared, "I will never be hungry again," a powerful meditation, the *Washington Post*'s Alyssa Rosenberg has argued, on the limits of Confederate nostalgia,[35] Pfeifer's book takes the character's word at face value, presenting recipes that evoke the past in name only, including such dishes as George Washing-Grit Cherry Crisp and Grits-Topher Columbus Herb Grits.

Beyond such crass appropriations of popular southern nostalgia, there is today an unmistakable market for historical-themed recipes and cookbooks such as Anne Carter Zimmer's *The Robert E. Lee Family Cooking and Housekeeping Book*, written by the maternal granddaughter of Robert E. Lee Jr., and volumes such as *Dining with the Washingtons: Historic Recipes, Entertaining, and Hospitality from Mount Vernon* and *Dining at Monticello: In Good Taste and Abundance*.[36] Consumers are, for lack of a better term, hungry for history—or at least a particular, prepackaged version of history made for their consumption, literal and figurative.

Readers of *The Tennessean* in Nashville were tempted in December 1997 with Zimmer's recipe for Roman Punch—a "holiday punch packed with history."[37] *Dining with the Washingtons*, wrote Bill Daily of the *Chicago Tribune*, is a book whose "liberal use of glorious color photos of the house (Mount Vernon) and grounds, sprinkled with contemporary sketches and the laudatory memories of Washington family and friends, evokes a familiar, almost patriotic, scene of privilege, of cozy family teas and festive feasts for the nation's founding fathers and mothers."[38] Such books, however, do not simply appeal to the consumer's penchant for beautiful visuals and historical recipes but also gesture to the likes and dislikes, preferences and pet peeves of historical actors, presenting personality and peculiarity. The Washingtons, "renowned for welcoming anyone who showed up at their door," were also *people*.[39] George Washington's favorite dessert was ice cream.[40] Martha Washington had an affinity for artichokes.[41]

Demystifying the lives of historical icons along with nostalgia for food cultures past was not new in the late twentieth and early twenty-first centuries. Mrs. George Lyman's 1942 *Recipes: From the Time of Washington until the Second World War* attempted to capture the range of dishes referencing different periods within American history. The profits from the World War II–era compilation, published in Massachusetts, were to benefit the American Army and Navy Relief Funds and the United Nations Relief Fund. The volume's recipes, which included the decidedly ahistorical and nonregional beef stew and Society Rice, also explicitly invoked the past, with Daniel Webster's Chowder and Jim Crow, a children's dessert composed of "slices of slightly buttered toast" that was then covered with "molasses which has boiled three minutes."[42] The origins of Jim Crow are unknown, let alone why it references both a stereotypical character that posited the inferiority of Black people and a caste system that enforced racial segregation.[43] Yet the fact that Lyman's book presents the recipe so casually suggests a normalizing of this past, or perhaps its outright denial.

This distancing from history, and in some cases complete erasure of it, is, according to food scholar Megan Elias, typical of southern cookbooks.[44] While *Dining with the Washingtons* is praised for not only its "90 well-chosen historical recipes adapted for today's cook" but also its distinctive ability to contrast the "oft-told lives of the president, his family and his famous guests with those of the unsung slaves who toiled long to produce the hospitality for which Washington was famous,"[45] the book, despite its gestures to the lives of enslaved people, remains fundamentally a nostalgic ode to the Washingtons' hospitality. It is little wonder that the book was featured during programming sponsored by the Atlanta chapter of the Daughters of the American Revolution as recently as 2012.[46]

Each of these books engages with readers through historic narratives of famous figures, yet the cookbooks do not only provide a glimpse of past persons and cooking practices. They enable readers to reenact those pasts. This became clear to me as I leafed through the pages of Zimmer's *Robert E. Lee Family Cooking and Housekeeping Book* in the gift shop of Pamplin Historical Park and the National Museum of the Civil War Soldier in Petersburg, Virginia, the site where, on April 2, 1865, Union soldiers, under the leadership of Gen. Ulysses S. Grant, broke through General Lee's defensive line, a move that spelled the beginning of the end for Confederate forces.

Although the appeal of Zimmer's book undoubtedly stems from its author's blood ties to one of the most iconic families of the Confederacy, the allure, too, is deeply linked to her commentary in working through a notebook filled with the historic "receipts," as they were called, that belonged to Zimmer's great-grandmother, Mary Lee, more than a century after the Civil War's end.

The style is not dissimilar to the one further popularized by Julie Powell, the New York City–based writer who famously worked her way through Julia Child's magnum opus of 524 recipes, *Mastering the Art of French Cooking*, in a year.[47] Like Powell's 2005 book, in which she catalogued the trials and tribulations of living up to one of the culinary "greats," Zimmer is a player in her story, who presents herself as a somewhat unwilling participant in the period cooking endeavor due to her own history of adult dieting, coupled with the recipes' propensity to use high-fat ingredients such as cream and butter.[48]

Zimmer introduces her book as an experiment of sorts, on which she embarked with the Ohio State University Gourmet Group to cook through her ancestor's notebook and ultimately learn more about herself. To cook, then, is to not merely witness the past; it facilitates the opportunity to live and taste it. It is a complete sensory experience that has historically enabled many women, as Theophano has argued, to "acknowledg[e] their blood ties and hoped-for continuity of relationships that transcended time and space."[49] "Confederate cookbooks" enable precisely this engagement with "heritage."

"Embattled Nationhood and Womanhood at Its Best"

The American Civil War might seem an odd historical juncture to have produced a cookbook and subsequently an even odder set of recipes to reenact. In many ways it was and is. As US Army general Silas Casey said in 1862, "The cooking is everything. . . . If not well done it is positively injurious; if well done, it is wholesome."[50] The implications of cooking during the Civil War meant life and death for not only soldiers on the battlefield but also families on the home front. This was a reality recognized by northern military strategists who undertook the tactic, as food historian Andrew Smith has argued, of "starving the South."[51]

A time when access to fresh foods was limited, the Civil War necessitated thrift and rationing, leaving women of the household, to whom the responsibility of cooking fell, with the challenge of developing recipes from the available store of goods. So was born the 1863 *Confederate Receipt Book*, published in Richmond, where the Bread Riot occurred that same year on April 2.

Spawned by the lack of food and fuel into the capital of the Confederacy, the so-called Bread Riot took place after hundreds of women marched to Capitol Square to demand a meeting with Virginia governor John L. Letcher.[52] Receiving no relief, the women headed to the city's central business district, seizing food and clothing. According to a *New York Times* report, "they broke open the Government stores and took bread, clothing and whatever else they wanted."[53] An act that seemed to disrupt the dominant image of the "Southern lady," a white woman who was a "genteel, obedient, guardian of the home,"[54] the Bread Riot reinforced women's simultaneous desperation and dedication to protecting their families.

The only recipe book printed during the Confederacy, *The Confederate Receipt Book*, advertised in August 1863 as the "little book" "no housekeeper should be without," was deemed a manual, of sorts.[55] Recognized by historians as one of the earliest community cookbooks published for charity, a genre associated with the efforts of northern women attempting to raise funds for Union efforts during the Civil War,[56] *The Confederate Receipt Book* offered homemakers substitutions for household items. For instance, "coffee" was made "from roasted acorns, flavored with 'cream' from beaten egg whites and butter."[57] The substitutions were cited in the 1940s by a letter published in the *Saturday Evening Post* to remind contemporary readers that the shortages experienced during World War II paled in comparison to those "in the Confederate states during the War Between the States." The letter writer reminded readers, "Before it was over people of the South were reduced to such makeshift as tea made from raspberry leaves and home spun clothing dyed with nut juices. . . . So what are you kicking about in this year of 1942. Signed, A Daughter of the Confederacy."[58] The clipping was so powerful the *Marshall News Messenger* reprinted the letter ten years later, in December 1952.[59]

The Confederate Receipt Book offered a stark contrast to Mary Randolph's 1824 *The Virginia Housewife, or the Methodical Cook*, the first regional cookbook credited with placing "southern" cooking on the map. Inspiring Lettice Bryan's *Kentucky Housewife* (1839) and Sarah Rutledge's *The Carolina Housewife* (1847), *The Virginia Housewife* betrayed its antebellum origins in a home of a privileged, white enslaver through its attention to her relationship to her "servants."

While Randolph's elite pedigree likely had much to do with the *Virginia Housewife*'s initial success, Thomas Jefferson's cousin was well known for her skills as a cook and hostess. An invite to the Randolphs' home was sought out—so much so that legend has it that Gabriel,[60] who orchestrated an insurrection of enslaved people in Richmond in 1800, "announced that he would spare her [Randolph's] life so that she could become his cook."[61] The mythology surrounding Randolph has even led reenactors such as Donetta Bantle to portray the Chesterfield native.[62]

If Randolph's work celebrated pre–Civil War Virginia as a place of relative abundance, an image that would be invoked in the 1950s in columns such as the *Tampa Tribune*'s "Ante Bellum Advice"[63] and 1960s stories about bread pudding's "rich American heritage,"[64] the appeal of *The Confederate Receipt Book* was of a different sort.

A historic artifact testifying to lack of access to adequate food during the years of the Confederacy, *The Confederate Receipt Book* was reprinted in the 1960s, on the eve of the Civil War centennial. Southern historian and Confederate apologist E. Merton Coulter[65] wrote in the book's 1960 introduction, "The war which broke out in 1861 in defense of the independence of the Confederate States of America plunged the Southern people into great privation before the struggle was two years old."[66] While, according to Jefferson Davis Freeman, who penned the reprint's preface, the 1960 version was adapted in an attempt to allow readers to "get a taste of Confederate times," the "taste," for Freeman, was quite literal. Containing recipes for tallow and "confederate candles" as well as home remedies for everything from dysentery to croup, the book offers recommendations for caring for clothing and home. Readers were encouraged to consume the Confederacy at a moment when memory of the Confederacy surged in American culture, with the dedication of monuments and the renaming of schools across the nation, but particularly in the South. This pride arose in tandem with resistance to such efforts at commemoration, conveyed by the burgeoning civil rights movement. If *The Confederate Receipt Book* celebrated the Confederacy's ability to persevere in the face of privation, the lunch counter sit-ins across the country, from Greensboro, North Carolina, to Richmond, Virginia, would amplify the power of consumption within the public sphere and active efforts to curb it.[67]

Rather than celebrate the Virginia of plenty, *The Confederate Receipt Book*'s 1960s readers fetishized the Virginia of scarcity. Offering a powerful historical referent within a Cold War context, *The Confederate Receipt Book* was a cultural touchstone. As Americans dug fallout shelters fearing the outbreak of nuclear war, readers of the *Montgomery Advertiser* were assured, in 1961, "in an incomparably smaller way, citizens of the embargoed South of 100 years ago had something of the same problems. Their response to lean times is suggested in old cookbooks that show a stout resourcefulness."[68] Readers could take solace that their problems in the 1960s were certainly not unique. Americans had before faced scarcity.

The "resourcefulness" of the southern people, repeatedly identified in mainstream publications across the United States,[69] was exemplified in the most commonly cited recipe in *The Confederate Receipt Book*, reportedly shared during a UDC meeting in Arkansas more than a decade after the pamphlet's reprinting, in 1971.[70] The recipe explained how to make an apple pie without the use of apples. The pie was made with crackers, tartaric acid, butter, and nutmeg. A variation of this recipe existed on the back of the Ritz crackers box,[71] encouraging consumers of the buttery cracker to try the recipe themselves. It was a recipe that became popular during the Depression and into World War II, given the scarcity of apples and the ease with which crackers were available. The recipe last appeared on the cracker boxes in 1993.

The accessibility of the recipe made it one many felt compelled to imitate. In 2009 Lisa Abraham wrote about her experience with the recipe, "mak[ing] a mockery of an apple pie." While the process of making the pie was "easy" in her estimation, it was met with mixed reviews. Whatever the perspective, Abraham concluded, "What this pie lacks in apples, it makes up for in American history."[72] The recipe may not have been a unanimous hit, but it nevertheless enabled Abraham to faithfully reenact a historic American ritual.

Abraham's experience with the mock apple pie revealed that more than forty years later, *The Confederate Receipt Book* continued to have, as Coulter wrote in the 1960s, "as much quaint and amusing appeal to present-day readers as it had practical value to a beleaguered people fighting for their national independence which they finally lost after four years of struggle."[73] Coulter's nostalgic sense of the book's "quaint" and "amusing" appeal was borne out, and when the recipes were difficult to follow, contemporary cooks could comment, as one writer did in 1961 in an attempt at levity, "In the name of Jefferson Davis"![74]

The Confederate Receipt Book enables its readers to engage with the past by reenacting the creative recipes. Eating history, within this frame, was just as valuable as learning about it narratively. One could literally consume the past, in a selective and ostensibly apolitical way given one does not have to be descended from Confederates in order to cook the mock apple pie. Like the women of the UDC at the turn of the twentieth century who then presented themselves, as rhetorical critic Amy Heyse has argued, as "merely doing what republican mothers, true women, and Southern ladies normally do at home"[75]—not engaging in a political act—the act of "cooking Confederate" in the 1960s and beyond reminded that the past could be consumed from a safe distance. The contemporary cook, existing in a world of plenty, could return to making a *real* apple pie if she so desired. The past was ephemeral, to be engaged on the contemporary cook's terms, much like the present from which she could opt to escape.

Subsequent reprintings throughout the latter part of the twentieth century displayed continued warmth toward the thin pamphlet. It was declared by the *Jackson Sun* in the early 1980s a "delightful reissue" as well as "embattled nationhood and womanhood at its best."[76] The Georgia Room of the Cobb County Library near Marietta Square boasted in the mid-1980s of owning copies of *The Confederate Receipt Book* and Annie R. Gregory's *The New Dixie Receipt Book* (1902).

While the cookbook enabled contemporary cooks to reenact the process of "cooking Confederate" with its attendant old-fashioned appeal, it stood for many as an exemplar of not only southern resourcefulness, as women "discovered and developed many new ways of providing old remedies and articles of food and dress or substitutes for them," but also community. As one 1971 news story in the *Danville Bee* notes, "When anyone hit upon something that seemed valuable, the secret was not kept, but was published in the newspapers or written down in recipe books, or told by word of mouth. Nothing was thrown away that could be used to nourish a family."[77] The book served as testament to the collective's desire to ensure the livelihood of its constituents. It reflected commitment to the Confederacy. In this way, *The Confederate Receipt Book* captured the essence of communitarianism.

Unique as a period piece, *The Confederate Receipt Book* paved the way for a series of books also seeking to capitalize on the curiosity associated with "cooking Confederate." Modern-day author Patricia B. Mitchell, who has written more than twenty pamphlet-length books on southern food and foodways, notes in *Confederate Camp Cooking* (1991) that "cooking Confederate" offers an opportunity to rely on "simple whole foods" while delighting in "old-timey staples."[78] While this appeal seems to mirror those advertising the latest fad diet, the recipes included in Mitchell's *Confederate Camp Cooking* seek to foreground the aforementioned narrative of Confederate resilience.

Mitchell's pages feature an homage to "brave Southern women" who adapted their modes of food production for the sake of their families and the men who fought on their behalf. Forced to forgo traditional ingredients "thanks to the Yankee blockade," Mitchell lauds the "typical Confederate lady (and gentleman) [who] believed in the South Cause wholeheartedly."[79] Their steadfast belief in the "South Cause" was borne out, Mitchell suggests, in a people's commitment to nourishment in the face of scarcity. Women's perseverance was testament to their sacrifice.

Mitchell herself, a food writer who had been restoring the Sims-Mitchell House in Chatham, Virginia, as a contemporary bed-and-breakfast, sees a broader emotional connection with the past that also amplifies the place of women within this story of historic food cultures. Mitchell writes in *Mrs. Billy Yank's Receipt Book*, "I have been homesick enough to cry, and I have missed someone so much that the days on a calendar were just blocks to be eagerly marked off, so I can relate both to a soldier and to his lovesick lady at home."[80] With these words the contemporary writer Mitchell invokes the gendered social order in which she implicates herself. As the UDC had at the turn of the twentieth century, Mitchell foregrounds "sacrifice [as] what good Southern ladies did to maintain femininity, please Southern men, and insure their protection."[81] In writing her pamphlet-length texts, offering recipes and narrative to her readers, Mitchell enables herself to connect with history on an affective level in the present—to feel the pain of a "lovesick lady." Yet again, while feeling the lovesick lady's pain, Mitchell, too, can return to her contemporary life at will.

Imagining a "Good and Faithful Servant"

If *The Confederate Receipt Book*, its subsequent reprints, and books such as Mitchell's slim pamphlets champion the resilience of Confederate women past in the face of privation while deflecting charges of the cookbooks' political rhetoric in the present, the reprinting of books such as Mrs. M. E. Porter's *New Southern Cookery Book, and Companion for Frugal and Economical Housekeepers* (1871) in the 1970s further attempted to depoliticize food by propagating an image of a refined and elegant South, a romanticized past that could be literally consumed.[82] The *New Southern Cookery Book* was part of Cookery Americana, a reprint collection of twenty-seven cookbooks, originally published between 1837 and 1954. Gesturing to American folklore and cultural heritage, the series incorporated books from "Midwestern Home Cookery" to "Fifty Years of Prairie Cooking" to "The Indian Cook Book."[83]

Mrs. Porter's *New Southern Cookery Book* was, of course, not a unique tome. Marion Cabell Tyree's 1877 edited volume, *Housekeeping in Old Virginia*, containing contributions from some "250 ladies from Virginia and sister states," assures its collective goal of circulating an image of Virginia and its superior housekeepers—to make them marriageable and their husbands loyal as well as the "cultural forebears of southern gentility."[84]

The 530-page cookbook compiled by Patrick Henry's granddaughter included more than 1,700 recipes, among which were favorites of the so-called FFVs (First Families of Virginia).[85] The inclusion of the FFVs, Elias notes, was a "rhetorical trick that other Southern cookbook writers also used to separate their South from the South of the Civil War," making the past "part of a continuum of American culture."[86] Celebrating *Housekeeping in Old Virginia*'s historic cachet, the *News Leader* in Staunton, Virginia, grabbed the attention of its readers in 2007 by encouraging them to "Cook like it's 1877: Take a page from an old recipe book!" The article noted that while the first edition of the historic book will today cost "a bundle," it is available online through Michigan State University, enabling women across the nation to partake of the historic recipes.[87]

Like *The Confederate Receipt Book*, *Housekeeping in Old Virginia* found an audience in the 1960s. Little more than one month before Rep. Shirley Chisholm of New York, the first Black woman elected to the US Congress, would deliver her famous speech calling for "Equal Rights for Women," an April 1969 ad for the *Cookbook Collector's Library* included a cutout for interested readers to request a free copy of *Housekeeping in Old Virginia* for library members. Featuring a large photograph of an elderly white woman with spectacles in nineteenth-century period dress reading a cookbook, the ad reads, "I wish they still made cookbooks like this" (see fig. 4.1).

The appeal of the book, based on the ad, stemmed from the book's appearance: it *looked* original despite being a reprint. It "duplicates the look of the original antique, wheat-colored paper, the delicately grained leather bringing, the baroque gold decorations."[88] Located in a section of the *Honolulu Advertiser* featuring an article titled "Our Gourmet President," on Thomas Jefferson, "probably the greatest epicure and gourmet,"[89] the advertisement for *Housekeeping in Old Virginia*, like the broader food section, was marked by a disconnect from the contemporaneous moment. This was nowhere more evident than in a story on the following page about Mrs. Evelyn Whitehorn, a California mother who refused to allow her son Erik to register for the Vietnam draft.[90]

An advertisement less than two years later asked, "Why in the world would any woman want a cookbook that's 100 years behind the times?" The answer, according to the ad, was unknown. What was known was that "thousands of women from all over the country have taken us up on our offer."[91] That did not keep the *Cookbook Collector's Library* from hazarding a guess—"maybe it's because the book conjures up such a vivid picture of what life was like back in 'the good old days.' . . . Or maybe it's sim-

Figure 4.1, "I wish they still made cookbooks like this," *Housekeeping in Old Virginia* advertisement (*Honolulu Star-Advertiser*)

ply because the book is such a captivating curiosity." Platitudes like the "good old days" suggest, implicitly, that these days were an imagined past of "happy slaves" and a benevolent institution—the imagined past Paula Deen sought to re-create with a plantation wedding for her brother. It was a past in which white women conformed to the norms of historic and "excessive" southern femininity[92]—of the sort Chisholm and Betty Friedan, author of *The Feminine Mystique,* first published in 1963, sought adamantly to disrupt.

The imagined past recalled by the 1969 ad for *Housekeeping in Old Virginia* crystallized in the figure of the 1880s stereotype of Aunt Jemima, "inspired by the comic blackface routines of white vaudeville actors" and later Uncle Ben and "Rastus," the Cream of Wheat cook.[93] As food historian John Egerton writes, Aunt Jemima "sprang to life: a jolly fat black woman in a do-rag, cooking up a storm, singing while she worked. She was the dominant white majority's response to the prospect of black parity, or even superiority, in the kitchen. The image, the name, the code said it all: it had to be this way, or no way."[94] Yet Aunt Jemima was more than a jovial caricature. As historian Joan Marie Johnson argues, "The Mammy character, through her loyalty and continued service to white families long after the abolition of slavery," was necessary to maintain the fiction that the Civil War had been fought to "defend their [white men's] culture, homes, and women, rather than to defend slavery."[95]

This figure was brought to life with Blanche Elbert Moncure's collection of recipes that would eventually comprise *Emma Jane's Souvenir Cookbook* (1937). Published in Williamsburg, Virginia, Moncure's collection pays homage to the "good and faithful servant" Emma Jane Jackson Beauregard Jefferson Davis Lincoln Christian, who, according to a report, "has been in the author's family more than 50 years."[96] Written at times in the voice of Emma Jane, in "her Negro dialect," the book seeks to pay homage to the "white aproned 'Mammy.'" Presented as a beloved tribute, the book echoes Margaret Mitchell's *Gone with the Wind*'s nostalgia—the sentiment that undergirded what became the ultimately unsuccessful 1923 proposal on behalf of the UDC for a Black Mammy monument in Washington, DC.[97]

Christian's 1953 obituary, which locates her birth date "some time in 1862," states that "her parents were slaves."[98] The family's relationship to Moncure's family, however, is never stated outright. What is made clear is that Christian's lengthy name, a protracted acknowledgment of the Confederate leaders "Jackson Beauregard Jefferson Davis," was bestowed on her by "some Yankee soldiers." The *Daily Press* noted, "When only a few days old, three soldiers, who were camped in the yard, entered the little cabin where she was born and demanded that her mother show them 'the little nigger baby,' as they had never seen one before."[99] An article reporting her death later announced that Emma Jane was "always proud of her name,"[100] as if to reinforce for readers the sense that the Confederate leaders after whom she was named did not fight to keep her family enslaved. Christian is described affectionately and paternalistically. Her voice is never heard. Mrs. Moncure received credit for the book, reminding us that like the history of cooking more broadly, which was highly dependent on the labor of Black women who enabled white women to participate in social activities such as the UDC, cookbooks such as *Emma Jane's Souvenir Cookbook* foregrounded the contributions of white women to the exclusion of the enslaved women who managed the home front.[101] In so doing, white women continued to claim their central place within Confederate culture.

Community Cookbooks and Confederate Womanhood

While the aforementioned books enabled women to trade in the currency of the past, the community cookbooks I analyze below offer another dimension to the "Confederate cookbook" phenomenon. A guide, as Theophano has argued, to "demonstrate the wealth, prominence, and status of their [women's] social network,"[102] the so-called community cookbook provides an additional layer of complexity to the cookbook's interpretive possibility. Designed to raise money, community cookbooks have tended to be tethered to a cause, religious or secular. Unlike the previous cookbooks, reprinted for decades following their initial publication, the following cookbooks were published in the final years of the twentieth century, with subsequent publications in the early twenty-first century. The cookbooks discussed below exemplify a form of what Elias refers to as "Southern redemptionist writing," casting the antebellum South "as an experience of ease and pleasure with a stubborn failure to recognize that both aspects of pre–Civil War life were available only to wealthy whites and were the fruits of unfree labor."[103] This contemporary genre reasserts women's roles as arbiters of Confederate memory in the present while invoking a loosely imagined "history."

As a genre to analyze, community cookbooks are problematic due to their relative dearth of commentary. Consequently, scholar Anne Bower has dubbed the books "a subtle gap-ridden kind of artifact, that asks its reader (at least the reader who seeks more than recipes) to fill those gaps with social and culinary history, knowledge of other texts (such as commercial cookbooks), and even personal knowledge."[104] Often interpreted as celebrations of common history, which tend to connote a fairly benign effect, as political scientist Kennan Ferguson notes, "many community cookbooks were dedicated to the institution of white supremacy."[105] Ferguson cites books printed by local chapters of the UDC as examples, where recipes served to reinscribe the racialized divisions the UDC sought to enforce. The UDC, however, was certainly not alone in this endeavor.

Lynda Moreau's edited volumes, *The Confederate Cookbook* (2000) and *Sweetly Southern: Delicious Desserts from the Sons of Confederate Veterans* (2004), are two more recently published community cookbooks, the proceeds from which, at least in the case of the latter, were to go to the Sons of Confederate Veterans (SCV) for education projects.[106] Published by Pelican, "the largest independent trade book publisher in the South,"[107] these books fulfill what Ferguson describes as one of the functions of the genre: they "*intensify*. By being written, collected, sold, and passed from hand to hand, they intensify a sense of belonging and a sense of community."[108] Perhaps not traditional "community" cookbooks, Moreau's volumes speak to Pelican's "promotion of our Southern heritage, and for believing in the commercial viability of a Sons of Confederate Veterans cookbook."[109] And "promote" the SCV the books do, providing a platform for officers to share the SCV's stance with respect to memory of the Confederacy despite claims of being "non-political" and "non-sectarian." Active in the UDC, Moreau, descended from more than ten Confederate soldiers, is, she notes, "an avid collector of vintage *Gone with the Wind* memorabilia and an unabashed lover of all things Southern."[110]

As texts, Moreau's *Confederate Cookbook* and *Sweetly Southern* reflect the conservative gender ideologies underpinning the work of the women of the UDC while, as Heyse has argued with respect to the UDC in its earliest days, staking claim to women's roles as authorities of collective memory—a considerably more progressive act.[111] The books themselves render women largely passive, subverting their work and experiences to their male counterparts, yet this is precisely the point. In so doing, women position themselves as the central purveyors of Confederate memory.

The cookbooks' publication by Pelican is also significant, given Pelican's stated goal: "to give a voice to communities who might not have a national reach, along with a commitment to our own unique vision. We build our business on personal relationships and a love of books."[112] Pelican enables Moreau as editor to again locate the Confederacy as a silenced entity, voiceless and in need of a platform. Like the taxidermied Little Sorrel, the Confederate cookbook stands as testament to an entity under attack, or so neo-Confederates would have readers believe.

Providing recipes for "Appetizers and Libations," "Salads, Sauces, and Breads," "Main Dishes, Soups, and Stews," "Vegetables and Side Dishes," and "Sweets," *The Confederate Cookbook* also offers readers a foreword from Patrick J. Griffin, commander in chief of the SCV (1998–2000). By way of introduction, Griffin declares to readers, "Each household [with Confederate ancestors] is historically intertwined with the bond of a proud family heritage and the remembrance of a noble ancestral struggle for Southern independence." Beyond "time-honored family recipes," the book, in Griffin's words, is testament to "the very essence of the fabric of society, and our kitchens continue to inspire the gracious concept of 'dining in' and sharing good times with family and friends."[113] An emblem of the "fabric of society," *The Confederate Cookbook* celebrates the family as the centerpiece of community.

Praised for its "fine suggestions" for "using fresh Southern favorites," *The Confederate Cookbook*'s chapter on vegetables, as Laura Tutor wrote for the *Anniston (Alabama) Star* in May 2001, "really gives it authenticity,"[114] citing okra casserole, squash fritters, and "Confederate collard greens" as among the most noteworthy.[115] Here again, Tutor deploys "Southern" and "Confederate" as synonyms suggesting that what is being provided by *The Confederate Cookbook* is an "authentic" representation of the South. "Confederate" is thus stripped of its association with slavery and rather celebrated as a vaguely historic modifier connoting "old" and "Southern."

The publication of *Sweetly Southern*, the 2004 "sequel" to Moreau's *Confederate Cookbook*, brings with it a resolve for the twenty-first century amid public debate surrounding Confederate symbols and, in some cases, condemnation. In 2000 the state legislature of South Carolina reached a "compromise"[116]—the Confederate battle flag was removed from the top of the South Carolina State House and placed next to a thirty-foot Confederate monument on the State House grounds. That same year, a banner depicting Gen. Robert E. Lee mounted on Richmond's Canal Walk flood wall was set on fire. In 2003 "Colonel Reb," the Confederate soldier mascot at the University of Mississippi, or "Ole Miss," was retired.

Against this backdrop, historian in chief Charles Kelly Barrow, author of *Sweetly Southern*'s preface, wrote, "It will take courage, sacrifice, dedication, and devotion for the SCV to prevail in the twenty-first century. We must succeed, or the Confederate soldier's good name and this unique part of this country's cultural history and heritage will cease to exist."[117] Moreau, as editor, once again enables memory of the Confederacy to prevail through her dedication to the cause.

Despite the stakes articulated in preserving the "Confederate soldier's good name," *Sweetly Southern*'s recipes, which include banana bread, homemade vanilla ice cream, and so-called dirt cake, are hardly indigenous to the South, nor do they belong to Confederate veterans alone. *The Confederate Cookbook*, with its array of recipes, from Cheesy Rice Salsa to Grilled Peppered Beef to Heidi's Famous Fresh Tomato Pie, lays spurious claim to the past and makes no gesture to the sense of scarcity fetishized in *The Confederate Receipt Book*.

The most explicit linkages between the recipes printed in Moreau's volumes and the past are found in names that reference the Confederacy, such as Jeff Davis Dixie Pie (166) and Cassie's Confederate Cherry Pie (148) in *Sweetly Southern* and Robert E. Lee Natural Bridge Sweet Tater Pone (275)—whose name *The Confederate Cookbook* notes "is a mystery, but it sure is tasty!"—and Missouri Confederate Cake (364). Robert E. Lee Orange Pie (144) was "rumored" to have been one of the famous general's favorites, though *Sweetly Southern* offers no evidence. Jeff Davis Pudding Pie (128), readers are assured, is a "twist on a traditional Confederate confection." Other names such as Dying General Buttermilk Pie (116), whose origins the book itself notes are unknown, and Confederate Summer Punch (203) only signal southernness to the extent that the book's text encourages readers to "enjoy this on the veranda on a hot summer evening!" conjuring a trope of southern nostalgia.

Little information in Moreau's edited volumes is given to contextualize the recipes—to offer a sense of historical provenance. One of the few exceptions is the recipe for Granny Funderburk's Sweet Potato Pie (145) in *Sweetly Southern*, passed down from the wife of a "Real Son" of Confederate veteran William L. Funderburk. Honey Mammy's Jerusalem Cookies (326), included in *The Confederate Cookbook*, were passed down by Hudson Alexander's great-grandmother, Annie Lou "Honey Mammy" Miller Almon. "Honey Mammy" allegedly developed the recipe, "a true Southern treat dating back to about 1875." This text is the exception rather than the rule.

When brief context is provided, it is hardly illuminating. A recipe in *Sweetly Southern* for Never Fail Peanut Brittle (177), a "Southern favorite," is accompanied by text that states, "Boiled, roasted, and in candy, peanuts or 'Goober Peas' have an important place in Southern culture." A similar statement is used with the recipe for Louisiana Pecan Pralines (176).

Accompanying each recipe is a side panel that tells readers who submitted the recipe and the name of their Confederate ancestor, as well as a story of his regiment and death (if available). Despite this gesture to the past, the historical connection of most recipes remains fairly ambiguous.

The Hot Buttered Rum recipe (206) submitted by Bryan R. Green is a "staple" of a ceremonial tribute taking place since the year 2000 at the Confederate Hill section of Loudon Park Cemetery in Baltimore, Maryland. Used for the annual toast, the recipe, Green notes, "could not keep the troops 'hydrated' enough!" in 2003.

While readers are told that Aunt Ruby's Chocolate Cake (29), although hardly "low fat," is "still being made just like Aunt Ruby made it so many years ago," *when* Aunt Ruby lived is left unclear. There is an oblique reference to "five generations," but little more detail is offered. The recipe for Sweet Potato Cobbler (30), submitted by Harry S. Brown of Monroe, North Carolina, is his favorite—learned by his wife, whom he refused to marry "until she learned to make this dish!"

Other recipes, such as Reese's Peanut Butter Cake (46–47), submitted by Patrice J. Hardy of Saint Louis, Missouri, make no explicit connection to the past. Hardy notes beneath the recipe, "This recipe is a favorite of my daughters and granddaughters." Despite the fact that the mention of Reese's, which can be traced back to the establishment of the Reese Candy Company in 1923, bears no direct connection to the Confederacy, the format of the cookbook makes an implicit link by presenting the recipe on the left page with a historic photograph of Hardy's great-grandfather Capt. John McKim Hardy located on the right. This visual move works to authenticate the recipe through its association with the photograph, which mirrors the appearance of a historic photo: it is grainy, and the bearded Hardy looks solemn, standing in a suit. The photograph is featured in what appears to be a metal frame, giving credence to its sense of historicity.

This juxtaposition between the contemporary recipe and the old photograph highlights the slippage on which these cookbooks capitalize. These books are neither truly "Confederate" nor "southern." While invoking the past, most bear but a tenuous connection to it. Yet with each delicious dessert, the Confederacy becomes less an entity that fought to preserve the institution of slavery and more a collective of apolitical, family-loving people who value a tradition of good food. It is an image with which it is more difficult to find flaw.

Some recipes bear an even more unusual connection still. Scott L. Peeler Jr., great-great-grandson of Pvt. John Moore, submitted a recipe for Mango Cake (54). Peeler's rationale for the recipe is presented as follows: "Many of the descendants of my Confederate ancestor moved to the Miami area, where mangoes are raised commercially." While boasting a "unique, rich flavor," Peeler acknowledges that there is little historical provenance surrounding the recipe. Rather, its significance rests in its ability to gesture to the industry of the areas where Moore's Confederate descendants resided.

The cookbook's brief commentary, accompanying many of the recipes, while distancing itself from history per se, employs plays on words that seek to foreground the Confederacy in the minds of readers in a most benign way. For instance, readers are forewarned that not making enough

Peanut Butter Fingers (212) for everyone might produce a "war between the plates!" The Lexington Club Pecan Ball (202) is dubbed "a delectable confection that will make you whistle 'Dixie!'" Margaret's Southern Pecan Pie (147) is captioned "As Southern as moonlight and magnolias." Each of these names and monikers attempts to offer levity to the history to which these recipes are tethered. The Confederacy is a literal consumable—delectable and quite literally sweet.

The Confederate Cookbook and Sweetly Southern root their success in the books' ability to foster memory without history, reminding us simultaneously of women's power in forging those memories. Moreau edits the volumes as a form of public service, subordinating her identity to preserve an image of "southern manhood." Like the founding members of the UDC, who Heyse argues "re-knit[ted] the defeated and devastated Southern community with favorable collective memories,"[118] Moreau's volumes offer a vision of a united collective, bound together by a most intimate community-building ritual, consumption.

Consuming the Past

"Cooking Confederate," these books suggest, enables the contemporary chef not only to taste the past—the flavors and textures of ingredients that may not play as central a role in the twenty-first-century kitchen—but to reenact it. Cooks have the opportunity to gain a deeper appreciation for the resilience of the Confederacy in the face of food shortages and deprivation as well as the elegance and grandeur of the antebellum South—all the while retaining the capacity to return to the comforts the twenty-first century affords. It is no wonder the historic cookbooks romanticizing the Old South found themselves reprinted in the 1950s, 1960s, and 1970s, in tandem with the resurgence of Confederate symbols throughout the United States. The cookbooks celebrated the past but from a distance. They could maintain the disconnect between slavery and its more contemporary legacies, enabling a retreat from the social movements attempting to resist the culture of white supremacy that the Confederacy instantiated.

Like the Confederate battle flag, which southerners embraced as a marker of heritage, these recipes, whether anchored in history or merely in the memory of Confederate ancestors, attempt to celebrate the Confederacy as a community with shared values and principles. While celebrating the Jeffersonian values of agrarianism and individualism, such books, particularly of the community cookbook genre shaped and circulated by women, speak to the collective. What is clear from these more contemporary versions is that neo-Confederates recognize a distinct market and an opportunity to make money by walking the line between history and heritage. The books become a way to literally trade in the Confederacy by reducing it to a series of timeworn recipes that easily creep into the American home.

Paula Deen's continued success is perhaps the most powerful example of this "creep." In September 2014 Deen earned $75 million for her new company Paula Deen Ventures in a comeback campaign, proving that many fans were ready to embrace her again with open arms. The themes of her first stop in Charlotte, North Carolina, Kathleen Purvis of the *Charlotte Observer* wrote, were "reconciliation and family, with husband Groover and sons Jamie and Bobby Deen in constant attention on stage."[119] It was in many ways unsurprising for the popular southern chef. These themes have been foregrounded by Confederate women since the Civil War's end.

As I would come to realize, there were several ways in which the Confederacy could come to "creep" into one's home, regardless of heritage or region. This is a reality that neo-Confederates would recognize with particular aplomb as they debated the future of statues commemorating the Confederacy.

5 | Historical Diorama and Protecting the Confederate Habitat

With its announcement of *Morning Stroll*, acclaimed local painter John Morton Barber's homage to Monument Avenue, the *Rappahannock Record* introduced with much anticipation the Danville native and Virginia Commonwealth University (VCU) graduate's first scene of Richmond. Describing his motivation for undertaking the landscape, Barber commented, "Monument Avenue so classically captures the essence of our city. The avenue and its monuments are significant to the history of Richmond, and the beauty found in the individual architecture of those homes is magnificent."[1] While it marked a "break from the traditional Chesapeake Bay subjects" for which Barber is best known, a far cry from "watermen [and] vessels,"[2] *Morning Stroll* typifies the tranquility of the artist's corpus of works, communicating his love and appreciation for his surroundings with its soft light and cool colors (see fig. 5.1).

As one critic poetically described *Morning Stroll*, light "pours through the clouds after an early-morning shower as reflections dance across the sidewalk."[3] This characterization echoes the tone of Barber's reminiscences of his inspiration to become a painter. A childhood visit to Cape Hatteras, North Carolina, with his family led him to an encounter with a man painting a lighthouse and the sea. Mesmerized, Barber recalls "the intoxicating aroma of turpentine mingling with the salty ocean breeze while gulls wheeled all around."[4] For the next forty years, Barber would dedicate himself to his subjects, recognized for capturing "the vanishing beauty of the Chesapeake Bay and the Atlantic Coast" and ultimately devoting himself to "protect[ing] the heritage of the Chesapeake Bay."[5]

The Chesapeake Bay may not have been the focus of *Morning Stroll*, yet Barber's sense of heritage could be transposed onto the Fan district scene. While the eye is drawn to a woman pushing a baby in a stroller down the quiet, residential thoroughfare in Richmond's elite neighborhood, Jean Antonin Mercié's statue to Gen. Robert E. Lee, dedicated in 1890, stands in the distance. Amid the turn-of-the-twentieth-century mansions that developed around it, Mercié's Lee is a by-product of Lost Cause ideology, testament to a desire, articulated at the time of its creation, to display the

Figure 5.1, *Morning Stroll* (Copyright John M. Barber, Art Ltd. 1997)

general as a man of "courage and dignity,"[6] valorizing the Confederacy with the imposing equestrian statue.[7]

Without cars parked on the street to date Barber's scene, the oil painting possesses a certain timelessness with its cobbled streets and lush greenery. The painting's 1997 creation is thus all the more surprising given its disconnect from its immediate context. Barber's Monument Avenue bears none of the perceptible fault lines that characterized the fashionable thoroughfare's contemporaneous history.

During the year Barber's *Morning Stroll* was released, the controversy continued to rage surrounding the dedication of a statue roughly a mile away to philanthropist, humanitarian, and famed Black tennis star Arthur Ashe. Gov. George Allen had been successfully lobbied by the Sons of Confederate Veterans (SCV) to establish April as Confederate Heritage Month—a decision that would have undoubted implications for what has been described as "ground zero" for the Lost Cause.[8] Allen's decision came at a moment when Virginia's SCV, like chapters nationally, had grown in size to 2,700 members, "a 58 percent increase over the past four to five years," according to one SCV officer.[9] Monument Avenue's history as a "sacred road"[10] to the Lost Cause, like the thoroughfare's statue to Lee, lurked in the background.

Disruption and discord are absent from Barber's painting—forsaken for a much more sanguine, nostalgic view of the residential boulevard, with its varied architecture, including colonial, Mediterranean, Gothic, and Tudor revivals, and arts and crafts styles, and impeccable landscaping. Monument Avenue is, after all, referred to as "Richmond's Champs-Élysées," dubbed by *Southern Living* magazine as "one of the most beautiful thoroughfares in America."[11] Richmond Region Tourism notes that the site, ranked #13 of 156 things to do in Richmond on TripAdvisor and boasting more than eight hundred reviews,[12] is "a favored living area for Richmonders."[13] Of course, by "Richmonders," the modifier "white" is understood.

My "morning stroll" down Monument Avenue toward the Lee statue on September 16, 2017, weeks following the deadly violence in nearby Charlottesville, looked and felt markedly different from the scene Barber depicted. As I walked the quiet boulevard east on that warm Saturday morning toward the statue to observe the rally of the Tennessee-based neo-Confederate heritage group the CSA II: The New Confederate States of America, I was confronted with lawn signs announcing that hate would not be tolerated along the thoroughfare, a direct response to the CSA II's announcement that it would descend on the city (see fig. 5.2). The streets were peaceful, yet there was tension in the air. Observing the yellow tape that cordoned off part of the street, cautioning passersby, I was reminded of the four-by-eight-foot murals installed some five years earlier by Art 180, a local nonprofit, along Monument Avenue's grassy median. The murals, thirty-one in total, featured the artwork of local children in response to the question, "What do you stand for?" Bold and bright, the art was removed within three weeks of its installation. The city cited permit issues, but it was hard to see anything but local opposition to the life-size images painted by Black and Brown children. That morning, racism would again be made visible in the self-proclaimed heritage group's protest.[14]

The CSA II demonstration, according to the group's Facebook page, was intended to "Protect the General Robert E. Lee Monument." Declaring their mission to "raise awareness about the Confederacy and Educate the younger generation on the truth, not what the government was teaching them in school," a vow of "Heritage Not Hate," CSA II professed a desire to see "brothers and sisters from all ethnic backgrounds (Black, White, Native American, Jewish, and Mexican), banding together for the greater good."[15] Like the Confederate heritage groups I had been following for the previous four years, CSA II praised the multiculturalism of the collective as evidence that they are not, in fact, a hate group. They argue Confederate monuments should be "respect[ed], protect[ed], and save[d]." It is an argument made by another group, Americans for Richmond Monument Preservation, led by a former commander of the Virginia Division of the SCV.[16]

Figure 5.2, No H8, September 2017 (Nicole Maurantonio)

The rally was sparked by a modification in the charge of the mayor-appointed Monument Avenue Commission. The ten-member commission, composed of academics, public historians, and community leaders, was initially tasked by Mayor Levar Stoney with making recommendations for "contextualizing" Monument Avenue. This charge led the commission to hold its first public forum at the Virginia Museum of History and Culture (formerly Virginia Historical Society) on August 9, 2017, two days before hundreds of predominantly young, white men bearing tiki torches and chanting "The South will rise again!" "White Lives Matter!" and "You will not replace us!" descended onto the campus of my alma mater, the University of Virginia. In the wake of the deadly violence in Charlottesville, Mayor Stoney revised his charge, expanding the commission's purview to include the possibility of recommendations for removal or relocation—options previously unavailable.

At another historical moment, CSA II might have been written off as another passionate, but ultimately fringe and ineffectual, Confederate heritage group. Yet, with memories still raw of the chaos in Charlottesville a month earlier, the city of Richmond was committed to ensuring that it would not be defined by a similar outbreak of violence.

Days prior to the Saturday CSA II protest, I joined many neighborhood residents at First Baptist Church at the corner of Boulevard and Monument across from W. F. Sievers's Stonewall Jackson statue for a public forum led by then Richmond police chief Alfred Durham. Meant as an opportunity to display the city's preparation for the pending rally, the community discussion seemed to escalate anxieties. Who would show up? What weapons would they be wielding in this open-carry state?

As I walked down Monument Avenue that Saturday morning to witness the rally, I first encountered garbage trucks lined horizontally across Meadow Street, to be used in the event another white supremacist sought to deploy a car as a tactical weapon. On crossing the police barricades, I observed officers in riot gear, another measure that would contribute to the city's more than half-a-million-dollar expenditure in preparation for the neo-Confederate heritage group's arrival.

While the scene was neither the tranquil setting Barber envisaged nor the white supremacist horde that spewed hate in Charlottesville (only nine CSA II members showed up, much to the relief of Richmonders), what I walked to observe that morning was a neo-Confederate protest calling for something not wholly different from the oil painting John Barber produced. Members of CSA II and their supporters would call for the image that Barber immortalized: a vision of Monument Avenue as a historic habitat diorama, a beautiful landscape immobilized in the past—a landscape in need of protection.

The diorama, a museum form that rose to prominence in the early twentieth century, is infrequently seen today. However, its history as visual display maps onto broader debates surrounding the role and purpose of museums. More than a series of isolated objects, described and interpreted with label text, the diorama, with its flora, fauna, and often taxidermied animals, told a story.[17] As critic Donna Harraway notes, "each diorama presents itself as a side altar, a stage, an unspoiled garden in nature, a hearth for home and family."[18] If the taxidermied Little Sorrel provided a surrogate body for Stonewall Jackson and, by extension, the Confederacy, Monument Avenue provided the landscape—a three-dimensional setting for the display of Confederate exceptionalism.

The Confederacy in Context: Early Twenty-First-Century Richmond

In the twenty-year period between the 1997 announcement of Barber's *Morning Stroll* and the September 2017 CSA II protest, Monument Avenue shifted from a site of mere Lost Cause celebration, where annual Decoration Day parades were once held, to a site where the tensions between past and present, nostalgia and resistance, are regularly played out. This shift has been by no means linear.

Monument Avenue is where approximately 1,400 Sons of Confederate Veterans and a few women marked their hundredth anniversary in August 1996 with a parade, including Confederate flags carried by descendants of Civil War soldiers, reenactors in gray uniforms, and a Robert E. Lee impersonator, played by a Chesterfield County gun shop owner. For the Lee impersonator, "These are just a bunch of folks who are proud of their heritage. We grew up on cornbread, black-eyed peas and turnip greens."[19] Invoking food, which I argued in chapter 4 enables neo-Confederates to distance themselves from histories of racism and oppression through allegedly apolitical reenactments of "Confederate cooking," the Lee impersonator posited the parade as a display of benign "heritage." The "carnivallike" atmosphere, "complete with bugles, drums, and the occasional rebel yell,"[20] was cast by the *Richmond Times-Dispatch* as ultimately harmless. The SCV, the *Times-Dispatch* noted, asked the roughly twelve white supremacists, covered in swastika tattoos and T-shirts with white power slogans and Confederate flags, to leave. In February 2012 the *Daily Press* reported that "several hundred Civil War re-enactors and others marched down Monument Avenue" for a rally organized by the Sons of Confederate Veterans. Participants stopped at the Robert E. Lee Monument, where a small plane flew overhead carrying a banner: "Richmond, Embrace Your Confederate History."[21]

As a landmark, Monument Avenue continues to be touted among the city's walking tours, with explorations of early twentieth-century mansions advertised annually at Christmas.[22] It is, as well, the site of popular races such as the Monument Avenue 10K, bringing in tens of thousands of runners from across the world past the monuments to Confederate leaders, dedicated between 1890 and 1929. Tourists were encouraged to visit Monument Avenue during the Civil War centennial with advertisements boasting, "History *Lives* in Virginia . . . Where echoes of Civil War bugles haunt the wind on every hand."[23] While today such a description might seem overly mawkish, Monument Avenue remains, as one story acknowledged as recently as 2015, "Richmond's crown jewel."[24]

While Richmonders still turn out on Monument Avenue each year for citywide celebrations such as Easter on Parade, featuring petting zoos, clowns, and a contest of pets dressed in Easter bonnets, the space's meaning has increasingly become the subject of public debate. When the Road World Championship bike race was held in Richmond in September 2015, for instance, the route, which took racers down Monument Avenue, was dubbed "a horrific embarrassment" by Phil Wilayto of the Defenders for Freedom, Justice, and Equality, who described the thoroughfare as a shrine to the Confederacy. Wilayto announced that he would hold a press conference at the Jefferson Davis monument, the turnaround point for race participants. The Virginia Flaggers responded with a public statement that not only called the Defenders "an extremist group" but reaffirmed the race course as evidence of a broader commitment to heritage tourism. Visitors, in the Flaggers' estimation, seek out Monument Avenue "to view and admire the stately monuments and memorials to our Confederate Heroes."[25]

Amid these public disputes, Barber continued his Richmond series, painting *Evening in Shockoe Slip* (1998) with its imagining of moonlight as it "glitters over the cobblestones as a couple, hand in hand, walks up the commercial block of Cary Street." The painting features "a replica trolley car [as it] descends the hill, passing the many businesses and eclectic shops."[26] Two years later *Along the Avenue* was announced, the sixth installation in Barber's series.

Along the Avenue, which faces eastward on Monument Avenue toward the "very recognizable Jefferson Davis Monument," encourages the viewer to stroll west down "the South's most beautiful boulevard,"[27] the *Rappahannock Record* reminded readers. An article published later in June 2000 noted that color prints of *Along the Avenue* were available at $115 and in a remarqued artist's proof edition for $275.[28]

Barber's works fared so well commercially that, at a gala art sale at the Barber Gallery in Richmond in 2002, "some 66 of 70 pieces of artwork sold in one evening." It was testament, according to the artist, to the upbeat mood of the guests, "despite a sluggish economy and challenging world events,"[29] referring implicitly to the aftermath of the attacks of September 11, 2001, and the war in Afghanistan. According to Barber, however, the sale brought in more than $300,000, a more than respectable sum.

As Barber continued his Richmond series, the broader climate in the city seemed to be turning to a greater sensitivity to the city's history—and the history of Monument Avenue in particular. In 1998, one year after "Carry Me Back to Old Virginia" was declared the state song "emeritus," the Richmond Slave Trail Commission (RSTC) was established by the Richmond city council with the goal of exploring ways to preserve and commemorate the city's history of enslavement and its legacies.

The result was the city council's 2002 commissioning of a Reconciliation statue, dedicated in 2007.[30] Located at the corner of Fifteenth and Main Streets, British sculptor Stephen Broadbent's statue featuring two figures locked in an embrace linked Richmond with Liverpool and Benin, West Africa, pointing to Richmond's role within the triangular slave trade. The Virginia General Assembly voted unanimously to express "profound regret" for the state's role in slavery soon thereafter.[31] Such moves seemed to offer a rebuke to the celebration of the Confederacy characterizing Monument Avenue.

Barber's paintings romanticizing the past, particularly the Jim Crow South that had led to the monuments' construction, stood in stark contrast to the graffiti and other forms of public resistance to Confederate statues and symbols that emerged with greater frequency along the thoroughfare. In February 1998 spray paint along the base of the Lee monument proclaimed the statue a "monument to racism."[32] In January 2000 graffiti was written again on the Lee statue reading, "Kill the white devil." This act coincided with the burning of a mural of Robert E. Lee hung near the James River canal as part of the riverfront redevelopment on Lee-Jackson-King Day, a state holiday that honored Lee, Jackson, and assassinated civil rights leader Martin Luther King Jr.[33] The mural burning at the city's downtown floodwall was an act that Brag Bowling, central Virginia commander of the Sons of Confederate Veterans, argued should be treated as a hate crime against southerners. Bowling noted, "The heritage of a lot of Southerners has really been violated."[34]

This sense of violation by conservative neo-Confederate heritage groups only increased after the Richmond city council's February 14, 2000, decision to rename two historic city bridges. The bridges to Confederate generals Stonewall Jackson and J. E. B. Stuart were renamed to honor two Richmond civil rights leaders, Samuel W. Tucker and Curtis Holt Sr. In response, the Richmond–Northern Neck Council of Conservative Citizens chapter in Hanover called for a 120-day boycott of the city.[35]

When in 2003 Robert Kline, executive director of the US Historical Society, commissioned a life-size bronze sculpture of Abraham Lincoln with his son Tad to be installed at the visitor center for Tredegar Iron Works, near what is today the American Civil War Museum, neo-Confederate heritage sympathizers likened the move to "installing a bin Laden statue at the World Trade Center site or erecting a Hitler figure in Jerusalem."[36]

While Kline remained optimistic, noting that "it may take another generation or so" to move toward true reconciliation, the Sons of Confederate Veterans vowed to fight the statue's dedication. The timing was not coincidental. The resistance of the SCV came at a moment when the demographics of the city had changed dramatically. The city, at that time, was roughly 57 percent Black, with six Black council members (out of nine), including the mayor. Nearly 25 percent of businesses in the city were minority owned. Fifty years earlier, the population in the city was slightly more than 30 percent Black.[37] A proposal to rename the Boulevard, which intersects Monument Avenue at the statue of Stonewall Jackson, after Arthur Ashe was put forward by Councilman Walter Kenney Sr. in 2003. It appeared that perhaps Richmond had turned a corner.

The proposal to rename the Boulevard after Ashe, however, was defeated,[38] and the Virginia Division of the Sons of Confederate Veterans offered the American Civil War Center a $100,000 statue of Confederate president Jefferson Davis for the same site in 2008. The issue was so divisive that the city's mayoral candidates were asked their thoughts.[39] The proposed SCV donation was dubbed by King Salim Khalfani, executive director of the Virginia State Conference of the NAACP, "tit-for-tat" for the Lincoln monument dedicated in 2003.[40] Given that Monument Avenue is home to Edward Valentine's statue commemorating Davis, the SCV donation was seen as redundant, at best. The matter was eventually dropped after Christy Coleman, the museum's president, told the SCV that the museum could not guarantee how the statue, if it were to be loaned to the museum, would be used.

A little more than a year after the Lincoln statue was dedicated in 2003, the Robert E. Lee Monument was vandalized again. This time, the phrase "Happy Birthday, MLK" was spray-painted across the base. The phrase "Death to Nazis" was also written.[41] The vandalism coincided with Richmond's annual Lee-Jackson Day.

Despite the isolated graffiti, commitment to ensuring the cleanliness of the monuments remained paramount. In August 2004 the *News Leader* ran a semicomical article detailing conservator Andrew Baxter's pro bono work, courtesy of his restoration service Bronze et al. in the cleaning of the Stonewall Jackson monument. Baxter, who had seen all sorts of dirt and grime, noted that he hoped his work in cleaning the monument to Jackson atop his faithful steed, Little Sorrel, "will inspire others to contribute money to protect the other statues along Monument Avenue."[42]

The tensions between change and the status quo were further foregrounded in 2008, when Virginia went blue in the election for president of the United States, making Barack Obama the first Democratic candidate in forty years (since Lyndon B. Johnson) to win the state.[43] Obama would reprise this victory in 2012, beating the Republican candidate, Mitt Romney. Virginia would again go Democratic in 2016, throwing support behind Hillary Clinton.

On the eve of the sesquicentennial of the Civil War, a collaborative effort was formed among cultural, historical, and community organizations from the region dedicated to ensuring the anniversary recognized the histories of all affected by the war called "The Future of Richmond's Past." The collective shared a vision of a Richmond that would be "a model for the rest of the state and nation" that would not make the mistake of the centennial.[44] The vision included a series of community conversations, guided walks of the Slave Trail,[45] and a number of concluding events in April 2015, including stunning visual projections of the great Evacuation fire that began on April 3, 1865, accompanied by sounds of the fire, costumed interpreters, and a "Pop-Up Museum" at Capitol Square. Such displays and performances sought to counter the static nature of the museum diorama, projecting audio as well as video into the landscape.

Months later, the meaning of the Civil War would once again be thrust into the public arena, when photographs of the Charleston church massacre's perpetrator, Dylann Roof, embracing a Confederate battle flag began to circulate in June 2015. Little more than a week following the Charleston shooting, the words "Black Lives Matter" were sprayed in black letters along the base of the monument to Confederate president Jefferson Davis.[46] While condemning the defacement of public property, *Richmond Times-Dispatch* columnist Michael Paul Williams wrote that the statues on Monument Avenue "send the unequivocal message that our lives don't matter—not then and not now."[47] The columnist called for their removal. Virginia Flagger spokesman Barry Isenhour said in response to the graffiti, "I wouldn't have cared if it said Jefferson Davis is the best guy in the world. You don't deface a public monument."[48] The words "No-Hero" were sprayed along the base of the monument to Confederate general Robert E. Lee. Days later the Confederate Soldiers and Sailors Monument in Libby Hill Park was defaced. Gov. Terry McAuliffe announced an attempt to prohibit Confederate flag logos from vanity license places throughout the state soon thereafter.[49]

Little more than one year later, following the election of Donald J. Trump to the US presidency in November 2016, the words "Your Vote was a Hate Crime" were sprayed on the monuments to Jefferson Davis and Confederate naval commander Matthew Fontaine Maury. In the wake of the deadly violence in Charlottesville in August 2017, the base of the monument to J. E. B. Stuart was tarred.[50] Two months later, in October 2017, the word "Racist" was sprayed on the Davis monument, followed the next day by "Racist/Ban KKK," again on the Davis monument. In August 2018 several buckets of red paint were splattered along the base of the Robert E. Lee Monument, along with the sprayed letters, "BLM" (Black Lives Matter).

The speed with which the city of Richmond acts to remove such graffiti speaks to its investment in the continued whiteness of the space, thwarting attempts at disruption. It speaks to the desire for stasis and significant financial commitment. A *Richmond Times-Dispatch* story reported more than $16,000 in city funds spent in cleaning graffiti from monuments across the city.[51] In committing resources to the maintenance of the monuments' pristine appearance, the city continues to make a responsive statement that restores memory of the Lost Cause to its unvarnished material form and upholds its historic commitment to white supremacy. Despite efforts to the contrary, the diorama remains intact.

The Diorama in the Museum

When I was in the second grade, I made a diorama as part of a social studies assignment. Contained within an emptied shoebox I had placed on its side, I glued multicolored plastic figures on the interior, along with some fake trees and horses purchased at the crafts store. The assignment was to capture the "frontier."[52] It now seems somewhat counterintuitive given the frontier we were tasked with assembling was an open landscape with long vistas—basically the opposite of the old shoebox I had used. Perhaps it more accurately pointed to the limits of the diorama's capacity to represent. Yet while dioramas are no longer a mainstay of social studies classrooms, or most museums for that matter, they remain a part of historical culture.

David Ruth, superintendent of Richmond National Battlefield Park, recalled stumbling on a diorama of Chimborazo Hospital, one of the largest hospitals of the Confederacy, in the basement of the Museum of the Confederacy in the early 2000s. The exhibit had been on display at the Civil War Centennial Center in the city from 1961 to 1965. The find was, for Ruth, "one of those remarkable ways that the institutions have helped each other." He ultimately repurposed the thirty-square-foot model as "one of the great visual cocktails of the Chimborazo hospital site," enabling visitors to appreciate the building by providing a life-size rendering.[53] A similar approach has been taken at Pamplin Historical Park in Petersburg, where life-size dioramas set up with cooking scenes are among the museum showpieces.

The habitat diorama was imagined early on as a powerful pedagogical tool in natural history museums where "mounted zoological specimens [were] arranged in the foreground that replicates their native surroundings in the wild."[54] My second-grade teacher had bought into this mystique. One need only consider the later popularity of *Night at the Museum* and its sequels—Hollywood films capitalizing on childhood curiosity surrounding the liveliness of the diorama—for evidence of its continued fascination. In the first decades of the twentieth century, newspapers advertised diorama kits to "youngsters" seeking to build "their own World Museum in miniature."[55]

At the time of its emergence, the diorama included taxidermied animals as well as replicas of (and sometimes real) plant life, rocks, and soils. Dioramas were a form in which "ideally, the three-dimensional foreground merges imperceptibly into a painted background landscape, creating an illusion—if only for a moment—of atmospheric space and distance."[56] Beyond the artifacts it displayed, however, the diorama was unique in its ability to capture the attention of the viewer through the re-creation of a dramatic scene. As critic Donna Harraway notes,

> Each diorama has at least one animal that catches the viewer's gaze and holds it in communion. The animal is vigilant, ready to sound an alarm at the intrusion of man, but ready also to hold forever the gaze of meeting, the moment of truth, the original encounter. . . . The animals in the dioramas have transcended mortal life, and hold their pose forever, with muscles tensed, noses aquiver, veins in the face and delicate ankles and folds in the supple skin all prominent.[57]

More than a series of isolated objects, the diorama told a story. It was, in the words of art historian Karen Wonders, "ecological theatre."[58] The advent of film placed additional pressure on museums, and thus the diorama by extension, to narrate in a dramatic way. While expected to embrace the novelty that newer technologies afforded, dioramas also "drew on older Romantic and nationalist aesthetics of nineteenth-century landscape and animal painting," bringing with them a nostalgic look backward, revealing a past frozen in time.[59]

The diorama was distinctive for its ability to generate affective connections with viewers. It could evoke "sympathy for animals, the efficient conservation and exploitation of natural resources, successful adaptation to changing environments, and the physical processes by which life was organized and advanced"[60]—at least such was the hope. This affective connection is one of the many aspirations that drive the continued commitment to Monument Avenue's "preservation."

No one was more skilled at capitalizing on the dramatic power of the diorama than Carl Akeley. Best known for his pioneering taxidermic methods leading to his being dubbed the "Father of Taxidermy" and a story that credited the taxidermist with engaging a leopard in hand-to-hand combat,[61] Akeley revolutionized display through his combined obsession with sculpture, photography, and taxidermy. Akeley's career was launched by his charge to preserve P. T. Barnum's deceased elephant, Jumbo. Most famously associated with the Milwaukee Public Museum and later the Smithsonian, Akeley, according to Mark Alvey, was "driven by individual (psychological/scientific/artistic) forces as well as cultural (technological/historiographical) ones."[62] His obsession with verisimilitude led to the taxidermist being sought out by Theodore Roosevelt to explore and ultimately create replicas of scenes from Africa. Along with William Temple Hornaday, whose "Fight in the Treetops" (1879), which featured a contest between two orangutans in Borneo, brought national attention to the American Museum of Natural History in New York, Akeley centered both animal and nature. The result, as environmental historian Karen Jones notes, was a blurring of the lines between taxidermy as trophy, theater, and teaching tool.[63]

Despite Akeley's status as the "Father of Taxidermy," he was preceded by several colleagues.[64] While Akeley had done much to amplify the power of taxidermy and the diorama as a museum form, the fact remained: dioramas were costly and inefficient when compared to other modes of visual display. Large spaces were needed to provide the canvas for the exhibition and its attendant background art. As curators and scientists became increasingly committed to the authenticity of the production, attention was focused on the "plant communities, geomorphology, faunal habits and relationships, climate, and light" to ensure the diorama possessed the most accurate representation.[65]

In addition to their prohibitive cost, dioramas also created a rift within the museum field. For many scientists, the diorama's lack of explicit explanation left spectators confused and arguably uneducated about the scenes in question. This led to the critique that ultimately the diorama was more about the aesthetics of production than the educational value it imparted. As historians Karen Rader and Victoria Cain summarize, "Curators admired exhibit makers' capabilities in studio and field but insisted that, in the museum at least, such skills should not command the same kind of prestige as scientific expertise."[66] The diorama, it was argued, too often sacrificed empiricism for beauty, which is why they are less commonly seen outside the walls of natural history museums today. It is also why the diorama continues to elicit a certain curiosity as an antiquated yet memorable form of visual display. It was what actress Elizabeth Marvel noted when reflecting on her pleasant visits to Richmond while filming Steven Spielberg's *Lincoln* and later the popular HBO series *Homeland*: "It was a bit like living in a historical diorama."[67]

Historicizing Monument Avenue

As museum curators and scientists were debating the merits and aesthetics of the diorama as visual display at the turn of the twentieth century, Richmond was in the process of constructing Monument Avenue. From its very start, Monument Avenue was developed to pay homage to the past, Richmond's Confederate past in particular, so as to ensure the longevity of Confederate memory.

As the preparations for an expanded Monument Avenue were under way, extending the west end of Richmond, men such as historian Frederick Jackson Turner were reflecting on a larger national phenomenon: the closing of the American frontier and its significance to the American project. Reflecting on the meaning of the frontier for the development of a distinctly American consciousness, Turner commented on "that coarseness and strength combined with acuteness and inquisitiveness; that practical, inventive turn of mind, quick to find expedients; that masterful grasp of material things, lacking in the artistic but powerful to effect great ends; that restless, nervous energy, that dominant individualism, working for good and for evil, and withal that buoyancy and exuberance which comes with freedom."[68] Turner captured the sentiments and characteristics inspiring Monument Avenue. In the case of what was imagined as the residential thoroughfare, however, there was land still to conquer, to tame.

Despite its contemporary status as a site of pilgrimage for Confederate heritage sympathizers and curious tourists, who are now encouraged to see it before it's gone,[69] the fashionable block as such was not always so fashionable. Yet, never a site of commerce, Monument Avenue has, since its development, always been a residential thoroughfare, lending easily to its sense of timelessness, as captured in Barber's *Morning Stroll.*

Prior to the first monument's dedication on May 31, 1890, the tract of land formerly known as Mr. Jack Carter's vineyard had been part of a plantation. The property, adjacent to the "vast estate of the late William C. Allen," who owned more than seven hundred enslaved people, was advertised as "no speculative scheme but sale positive." In May 1873 the *Richmond Dispatch* announced "the sale of the season," which included six acres of lots west of Monroe Park. Among the selling points of the land was its proximity to Richmond College (the University of Richmond before the university's 1914 move to the west end) "and other most substantial and first-class improvements, and in the very pathway of Richmond's present growth and future expansion."[70]

Part of the land's appeal rested with the whiteness of the space and its inherently exclusionary nature. An advertisement published in the April 17, 1913, *Richmond Dispatch* specifies under the heading "Restrictions" that no land within Monument Avenue Park would be sold to persons of African descent.[71] While certainly the back alleys of the grand mansions being built along Monument Avenue were designed for the Black workers hired to maintain the stately homes, their presence was to be rendered invisible.

The area surrounding Monument Avenue would eventually be cast as "among the most desirable lots in this delightful section, and present opportunities for securing choice home sites, or a handsome speculation in the near future."[72] In June 1898 the land was advertised as "what must soon become the most fashionable and attractive section of the city, will, doubtless, command a much higher price than is now expected for it."[73] Investors were advised to put their money in Monument Avenue. The land, they were assured, would be worth the investment. It was.

With the dedication of each successive Confederate monument, Monument Avenue reiterated Richmond's commitment to the Lost Cause. The first unveiling, of French sculptor Antonin Mercié's Lee, brought more than a hundred thousand onlookers to the area for an event that had garnered much discussion and anticipation in the months leading up to it.[74] In February 1890 the *Richmond Dispatch* included a printed page of suggestions, ranging from fireworks to a "Colonial Ball" to a "sham-battle."[75] The list went on. Days before the Lee monument's unveiling, the *Richmond Dispatch* announced to readers that it would be offering "souvenir" issues coinciding with the public event. Such editions, the newspaper promised, would be "handsomely illustrated,"[76] intended as collectibles. As historian Robert Cook notes, former Rebel officers embraced the Confederate celebration or "spirit," as William H. Payne, one such officer, called it.[77] The pomp and circumstance only amplified a sense of the unveiling's significance. A photograph of a piece of the rope allegedly used to pull the Lee monument into place is today owned by the Library of Virginia, the state library.[78]

Similar fanfare accompanied the dedications of the Stuart (1907), Davis (1907), and Jackson (1919) monuments, with photographs of the events resold as postcards (see fig. 5.3).

Yet, as early as the unveiling of the Lee monument in 1890, John Mitchell, Richmond's leading Black editor, warned, "The South may revere the memory of its chieftains. It takes the wrong steps in so doing, and proceeds to go too far in every similar celebration. It serves to retard its progress in the country and forges heavier chains with which to be bound."[79] Mitchell's words proved more prescient than he could have ever known.

The decision to dedicate a monument to Robert E. Lee in Richmond had been made long before the statue's 1890 dedication in what would become known as Lee Circle. Richmond's Lee monument would be qualitatively different from native son Edward Valentine's recumbent Lee located in the Lee Chapel on the grounds of Washington and Lee University.[80] Richmond's Lee would stand one foot six and ⅞ inches higher than the monument to George Washington in Capitol Square.[81] The equestrian Lee would literally tower over his surroundings, and as art historian Kirk Savage has argued, he would serve as "at once a retrospective image of the benevolent master, good to his inferiors, and a prospective image of a postwar white government claiming to know what is best."[82] Lee's stature was intended to align with the general's impact on Virginia. His statue, like his memory, loomed large.

Mercié's Lee was designed to display the dignity of the general, although, as the *Richmond Dispatch* noted, he was not the Lee Mercié himself originally envisioned. Mercié, the *Dispatch* reported, "wished to represent General Lee as he passed among his dying troops on the field of Gettysburg—the horse rearing, the dying stretching for a last affectionate

Figure 5.3, Postcard of the dedication of the Jefferson Davis Monument, 1907 (Library of Virginia)

glance of their leader." Yet, much to the French sculptor's initial chagrin, the Confederate troops deemed the design too "dramatic." The *Dispatch* recounted Mercié's response: "they [the Confederate troops] were artists, *true* artists. They did not wish to revive the past."[83] The *Dispatch* framed Mercié's comment as a sympathetic assessment of the reconciliationist commitment of the Confederacy—or at least the Confederacy's desire not to wallow in defeat.

There were efforts, particularly in the post–civil rights era of the 1960s, to add further works of public art to Monument Avenue, namely, to include Maggie Walker, to whom a statue was dedicated near her home in Jackson Ward in July 2017, and, in a more bizarre turn, Confederate captain Sally Tompkins, proposed by surrealist artist Salvador Dalí.[84] But such efforts failed. Despite Dalí's desire to commemorate a woman associated with the Confederacy, his design was too avant-garde for the otherwise architecturally conservative neighborhood. Tompkins is, however, among the twelve women from four hundred years of Virginia history chosen to be represented in bronze as part of the Virginia Women's Monument on Capitol Square. Ground for the project broke in December 2017.[85] Joining women such as Elizabeth Keckley,[86] an enslaved woman who became a successful dressmaker and confidante of Mary Todd Lincoln, and suffragist Adèle Goodman Clark, Tompkins's place among the honorees was not itself without controversy.[87]

The one "successful" attempt to change Monument Avenue occurred in 1996, with the dedication of Paul DiPasquale's statue to Arthur Ashe.[88] While the dedication of the Ashe statue enabled "at least some ghosts of our past" to be exorcised, in the words of *Richmond Times-Dispatch* columnist Michael Paul Williams,[89] the process of deciding to include Ashe among the Lost Cause's revered generals and leaders was far from peaceful.[90] Resistance to the dedication of the Ashe monument, which "integrated" Monument Avenue, made the statue a powerful backdrop for former Ku Klux Klan leader David Duke, who declared in 1999, in response to the decision to remove the aforementioned mural of Gen. Robert E. Lee from the floodwall, that whites must stand up against "an assault on 'our European-American heritage.'"[91]

Monument Avenue Postcards

Monument Avenue's status as a site to relive the past through diorama can be seen most visibly in popularly circulating picture postcards, which date to the early decades of the twentieth century. I focus on postcards not only due to their status as "a rich cultural reservoir of popular perceptions of peoples and places"[92] but also because of their place, as geographers Gordon Waitt and Lesley Head argue in their analysis of contemporary postcards of the Kimberley in Australia, within the "'time machine' of the tourism industry. They provide tourists with the illusion of traveling back in time to a disjunctive moment, when history is just about to begin, through discovery, conquest, and civilization."[93] The picture postcard is, as anthropologist Elizabeth Edwards stated, "a multi-faceted icon of the tourist experience."[94] They "can use the power of imagery to place the recipient figuratively in the picture. They may trigger a long subdued vacation need and following information search and purchase behaviors. Picture postcards not only present the product (i.e., destination) but also can communicate attributes, characteristics, concepts, values, and ideas."[95]

While the postcard's status as a fairly ephemeral object might make it appear an unusual choice for sustained analysis, this is precisely, as Waitt and Head argue, why postcards should be subjected to scrutiny. The postcard, as anthropologists Patricia Albers and William James note, "has been used to advertise and anticipate travel, to keep as a personal memento of the sights encountered on a vacation, and to validate the tourist's trip to friends and family at home."[96] Waitt and Head note, "Places depicted in postcards . . . are also more about myths than about substance. Picture postcards are endowed with symbolic meanings. Postcard imagery is one mechanism by which tourism places are reinvented in the image of particular tourism motivations and desires."[97] Monument Avenue is one such place.

Postcards are widely available, mass-produced, and fairly inexpensive. The rationales deployed by the purchasers, whether for souvenir or testimony, the most common logics for consumption, are unknown. In the former case, for souvenir purposes, the postcard functions to satisfy "the purchaser's demand for nostalgia," an opportunity to reconnect with longing. In this way, the postcard can also serve as a relic, "becoming a prop around which the actuality of travel can be convincingly told to those left behind."[98] Both logics are nonetheless critical to our understanding of the postcard broadly and postcards of Monument Avenue in particular.

All of the postcards I explore are tethered to photographs, which makes their presence significant for their negotiation of space and time. As cultural geographer Marion Markwick notes, "The photograph can also decontextualize that which is depicted by transposing it to other contexts."[99] It works to subtly "institutionalize what tourists see and how they see it" as well as "how they know and understand what they see."[100] When hundreds of children gathered at the Lee monument during the unveiling of the Stuart monument in 1907, forming a human Confederate battle flag, little did they know that the black-and-white image would be suffused with the bright colors of the Confederacy and circulated in postcard form, making the Confederacy an entity that could be consumed and circulated as well as a destination (see figs. 5.4 and 5.5).

Part of the "Beautiful and Historical Richmond, VA." series, several of the postcards identifying the monuments lining Monument Avenue characterize the area as "the heart of the handsome residential section of Richmond."[101] Created by the Southern Bargain House, one of the most popular wholesalers in the South, these postcards share a visual symmetry: in each, the monument, whether to Lee, Jackson, Davis, or Stuart, occupies the center of the frame. When there are exceptions, such as "Stewart's [sic] Monument," which is slightly left of center, and "Lee Monument & Monument Avenue," the angle enables the outline of another Confederate monument, the Lee monument in the former case and the Davis monument in the latter, to remain visible in the distance.

Often highlighted with warm colors, the postcards foreground the settings' timelessness. The front of each postcard includes a sense of place: Jackson Monument (Boulevard and Monument Avenues), Richmond, VA; Lee Circle (Monument Ave.), Richmond, VA; Stewart's Monument, Richmond, VA. No time period is annotated. That no additional caption is provided suggests that the postcard is to speak for itself. Other than place,

Figure 5.4, Photograph of the Lee monument during the unveiling of the Stuart monument, May 1907 (The Valentine)

HUMAN CONFEDERATE FLAG   "And 'Twill Live in Song and Story Though Its Folds Are in the Dust"

Figure 5.5, Human Confederate flag postcard (Library of Virginia)

Figure 5.6, Robert E. Lee Monument, Monument Avenue postcard montage (Library of Virginia)

little additional information is offered. In few cases is even the general's full name offered. Rather, the icons of the Confederacy are identified by last name only, as if to assume a collective familiarity with the men being commemorated.

Many postcards of the statue of Gen. Robert E. Lee, dated between roughly 1900 and the 1930s, share a common point of perspective (see fig. 5.6).[102] Where persons are visible in the postcards' imagery, the people are visible only as a reference point, providing viewers with a sense of the massive scale of the monument. They do little to date the postcard as such. The individuals depicted rarely bear markers of dress linking them to a particular historical moment.

When dates are mentioned, they say little about the postcard itself. In the case of Jackson, the general's birth (1824), death (1863), and the dedication of the monument (1919) are listed. For Lee, the date of the monument's unveiling (1890) is provided, an event, the postcard notes, for "the greatest reunion of the Confederate Veterans ever held"—a reunion that is unpictured. There is little sense of the site itself but rather the tradition surrounding it.

Another postcard notes that at the unveiling, which occurred "north of the monument (now covered by handsome residences)[,] a great sham battle was fought." Yet another, also mentioning the unveiling before a crowd of a hundred thousand, notes that the statue was "drawn by ropes by citizens to this spot." A Jackson postcard points to the statue's unveiling address as well, delivered by Gen. Robert E. Lee's grandson.

With their references to the "handsome"-ness of the monument to the "Confederate chieftain" (Jackson) and the "Idol of the South" (Lee), the postcards depict a Monument Avenue of relative peace. The quiet boulevard is settled but not overbuilt. It is residential and not commercial, with few passersby. While there is undoubtedly a sense of the postcards' "historicity," at least to the contemporary consumer, who observes 1920s cars and women adorned in period clothing in one example, there is also something atemporal about the postcards. In describing a contemporary postcard of "traditional" Malta, Markwick writes, "The past which is drawn upon in such postcard imagery is not a historical past but rather one which stands in opposition to now and is nostalgically defined as somehow better."[103] These postcards of Monument Avenue are testament to this nostalgia, privileging the timeless beauty of the landscape, home to spectacular monuments.

The Monument Avenue featured in each of these postcards is static, virtually unchanging from the point of dedication through the time the postcard was created. Each postcard emphasizes the "artistic beauty" of the monuments, a phrase used specifically to describe Edward Valentine's Jefferson Davis monument. The most laden with imagery and text, standing in sharp contrast to the largely equestrian monuments that define the thoroughfare, the Jefferson Davis monument is, in fact, explained with text on the back. "His right hand is outstretched in eloquent appeal to the Future, while his left hand rests upon the open book of history. . . . In the center rises a lofty column, surmounted by an allegorical figure, representing the 'Spirit of the South,' at the feet of which is the inscription, 'Deo Vindice' (God will vindicate)." It is likely that the explanation for Davis stems from its less immediate legibility. While the equestrian monuments specifically invoke the generals' honor and gallantry, the Confederate president's monument is discernible by its scale. Its symbolism and iconography, such as the presence of Vindicatrix atop the structure, is less transparent.[104]

While featuring the monuments along Richmond's most fashionable block, such postcards emphasize the unrivaled beauty of the area. Monument Avenue, according to one postcard created by the Richmond chamber of commerce, was credited with "perpetuating the names of the Southern heroes." The back of the postcard, reserved for correspondence, included a printed statement: "Richmond's hospitality and charming beauty make one's visit a pure delight."[105] Featuring four of the five current Confederate statues visible along Monument Avenue, the postcard frames the monuments centrally, cropped so that few of the surrounding structures, notably homes and churches, can be seen. The postcard fails to mention that the fifth statue depicted on the postcard is not in fact from Monument Avenue. Rather, it is a monument to George Washington visible outside the Virginia state capitol. Although it would be easy to dismiss this factual error as a careless mistake, it speaks more broadly to a connection forged between Washington and the Confederacy, as described by American studies scholar Maurie McInnis.[106] The postcard implicitly underscores the belief that Confederates were fighting for the principles of 1776, on which the nation was founded.

Invoking Washington, distanced by more than half a century from the Confederacy, the postcard elides space and time. The postcard focuses the reader instead on Richmond's "hospitality" and "charming beauty." This is all the more significant because the postcard was sponsored by the chamber of commerce. It was not created by a German company, as had been credited with printing many of the cards I analyzed. This slippage between the American Revolution and the Confederacy, the sense of nationhood that Washington evokes and the division the Confederacy wrought, gestures to the ways the postcards sell Monument Avenue as a testament to triumphs of American history.

The Richmond chamber of commerce's lack of care in identifying the Washington monument as part of Capitol Square and not a part of Monument Avenue suggests that historical context was malleable. What Richmond sought to champion was the city's "beauty"—in celebrating "southern heroes." Deemphasizing the Confederacy, the postcard signaled how the monuments were sold as a part of a site anchored to a particular identity, "southern," suspended in time and divorced from the history of Jim Crow. It was not an anomaly. Largely devoid of people, these early twentieth-century picture postcards offered a comfortable remove from the lived experiences of Richmonders and the structures shaping them.

Several community members seeking to preserve the statues, in situ, on Monument Avenue articulated this stance during the Monument Avenue Commission's first public forum on August 9, 2017. One speaker noted, "If you tear down these statues you're not discussing, you're suppressing a side, ending conversation. . . . I'm not sure if those statues need any context." Another speaker noted, "The Lee monument it's nice and long, and nowhere in there does it say slavery, racism, or white supremacy. . . . There's an entire rest of the city to add statues to whatever you choose to do. Monument Avenue is a Confederate memorial in itself."[107] For these individuals, the setting spoke for itself. No explanation needed. The diorama as an apolitical, antiracial backdrop would be the ideal setting for performances on both the physical stage of Monument Avenue and a virtual one online, further complicating the sense of time and timelessness. As the virtual world would demonstrate, old and new forms of commemoration would come into sharp and ultimately violent collision.

6 | Heroes, Villains, and the Digital Confederacy

On the night of August 11, 2017, images went viral of white men in polo shirts and khakis storming the iconic Lawn at the University of Virginia with Polynesian tiki torches aflame. The haunting videos of the hate-spewing horde chanting, "The South will rise again! White lives matter! You will not replace us! Jews will not replace us!" continued to replay online (see fig. 6.1).

Depicted in those images was hardly the picturesque college town and "progressive enclave" that I remembered from my college years at UVA.[1] Led by self-professed "white advocate" Jason Kessler, the Unite the Right rally, which drew neo-Nazis and members of the Ku Klux Klan (KKK), crystallized bigotry and white rage.[2] There had been blood, a critic would later write, "on the streets of Mr. Jefferson's town."[3] With graphic poignancy, the myth of the peaceful, liberal college community nestled in the foothills of the Blue Ridge Mountains shattered. That embattled symbol, the Confederate battle flag, had been embraced alongside Nazi flags by white supremacist protesters—obliterating neo-Confederate hopes for maintaining distance from the hatred the Confederate battle flag signified.

Several days after the deadly violence ceased, the Virginia Flaggers posted an article to Twitter, linked from the conservative website Life-Zette. Titled "Left Conflates Southern Heritage with Hate in Wake of Charlottesville," the article discussed the "target[ing]" of Confederate statues and monuments "in states across the Old South, [by] left-wing protesters." Quoting Dr. Lee Cheek, dean of the School of Social Sciences at East Georgia College and senior fellow of the Alexander Hamilton Institute in New York, the article described the violence in Charlottesville as an incident deployed by "the American Left and opportunistic politicos in America . . . attempting to use these events throughout the South to advance their political agenda." Cheek stated, "The extreme ideological activists on the Left and Right—both in Charlottesville and on the national scene—purposefully conflate recent events with any defense of the South. These activists and their financial and academic supporters do not want to engage in a free and uninhibited discussion of the issue." The article's

Figure 6.1, White supremacists march with torches in Charlottesville (Photo by Samuel Corum/Anadolu Agency/Getty Images)

author, Kathryn Blackhurst, left "the issue" unstated. Conspicuously absent was any discussion of racism in the days following progressive activist Heather Heyer's murder by a white nationalist. Dr. Marshall L. DeRosa, a professor of political science at Florida Atlantic University and a former Salvatori Fellow with the Heritage Foundation, largely reiterated Cheek's stance, claiming, "there are provocateurs on both sides." "Violence is the name of the game," he noted, "for the progressive Left in particular."[4]

Echoing President Trump's tweet a few days prior, in which he condemned "this egregious display of hatred, bigotry, and violence on many sides,"[5] spurring the hashtag #manysides, the article made little distinction among the alt-right, "Black-clad Antifa protesters," and Black Lives Matter activists. Citing DeRosa, Blackhurst's article concluded by noting, "These are just small skirmishes, but the people of southern heritage are outnumbered, they're outflanked, and they're just walking into a trap."[6]

Casting the "people of southern heritage" as victims of a left-wing setup, Blackhurst's article maintained a separation between Confederate heritage advocates who enjoyed the delectable desserts of *Sweetly Southern*, listened to the music of Lynyrd Skynyrd, and nostalgically watched *Dukes of Hazzard*, and the likes of David Duke, who would call the rally in Charlottesville a "turning point for the people of this country." The former grand wizard of the Ku Klux Klan stated, "We are determined to take our country back, we're going to fulfill the promises of Donald Trump, and that's what we believed in, that's why we voted for Donald Trump, because he said he's going to take our country back."[7] Those advocating on behalf of Confederate symbols were not the Jason Kesslers of the world, Blackhurst's article suggested. They were not racists.

This distinction between Confederate heritage advocates and the alt-right[8] in the wake of thirty-two-year-old Heather Heyer's murder in Charlottesville seemed not only out of touch but disconnected from the frightening reality. The tiki-torch parade of white supremacists at UVA did not emerge spontaneously. Several months earlier, in May 2017, several dozen protesters, led by white supremacist Richard Spencer, convened in Lee Park in Charlottesville to protest plans to remove the monument to Robert E. Lee. While the protest was quickly dispersed, Charlottesville's mayor, Michael Signer, claimed, "This event . . . was either profoundly ignorant or was designed to instill fear in our minority populations in a way that hearkens back to the days of the K.K.K."[9] In July 2017 approximately fifty members of the Ku Klux Klan, some donning hooded white robes, shouted "white power" in Justice Park, formerly Lee Park. Following the demonstration, city spokeswoman Miriam Dickler acknowledged the plan for another white nationalist rally on August 12.[10]

The events in Charlottesville in mid-August 2017 raised the stakes in the battle over Confederate memory. Dylann Roof, the perpetrator of the massacre of nine Black congregants at Emanuel AME Church in Charleston, South Carolina, in June 2015, had been openly condemned by the Virginia Flaggers and other neo-Confederate heritage organizations on social media. They marked Roof as a loner, a crazed individual. As hashtags such as #takedownthatflag, #takeitdown, and #ConfederateTakeDown gained national traction, Michael Givens, former commander in chief of the Sons of Confederate Veterans (SCV), likened Roof to Charles Manson, men who were "obviously insane."[11] It was a statement with which few could disagree.

In a post-Charleston world, neo-Confederates—the likes of the SCV, United Daughters of the Confederacy (UDC), and the Virginia Flaggers—were, in Givens's words "maligned," unfairly victimized.[12] The Flaggers posted Givens's public talk to Facebook to bolster claims that their supporters were heroes fighting for the restoration of the honor of the "southern people." Such a move implicitly aligned the preservation of Confederate memory with fighting "hate and misinformation." Within this framework, the Virginia Flaggers and their supporters were the consummate American heroes. If such a stance was problematic then, it was untenable in Charlottesville little more than two years later. The crowd of white nationalists, embracing the Confederate battle flag, demonstrated the impossibility of clinging to a narrative of individual bad apples. Contrary to the hashtag circulating on Twitter #ThisIsNotUS, popularized by celebrity musician Lady Gaga, Charlottesville was America.

However, what I had seen of Charlottesville in mid-August 2017 and read in the Flaggers' posted article were two radically different versions of America. I had witnessed national fracture stemming from an unresolved past—a collective, willful amnesia of the history of American race relations and the legacies of slavery.[13] For Blackhurst and the Virginia Flaggers, the violence in Charlottesville signaled an attack on the most American of rights by members of the Black Lives Matter and antifascist movements. They had witnessed a rebellion against Confederate exceptionalism—resistance to the very version of Americanness they viewed as exemplary. It was a sentiment echoed almost a year later by Virginia senate candidate Corey Stewart, who, sitting in his restored plantation home outside Washington, DC, would "insist that black Virginians were against removing statues of Confederate leaders." Pointing out a room where George and Martha Washington had allegedly stayed as guests, Stewart spoke with pride about "history." Stewart claimed, "To take history away from a Virginian is like taking a beach away from a Floridian."[14] It was thus little wonder that the battle over Confederate memory flared. In Stewart's eyes, Virginians had their history taken away, much like the song "Carry Me Back to Old Virginia" had been "taken away" from Susan Hathaway and the Virginia Flaggers.

Corey Stewart, the man who would be dubbed a "neo-Confederate poster boy," assumes particular significance in this story of Confederate exceptionalism. A native of Duluth, Minnesota, about "as far from the South as could be," Stewart hails from a state that today boasts its commitment to the Union. Minnesotans captured the Confederate flag at Gettysburg, a historical fact they are loath to let anyone forget.[15] Stewart, who has claimed to be a "proud Southerner," has also claimed that the Confederate flag "is our heritage, it's what makes us Virginia, and if you take that away, we lose our identity." He analogized the removal of Confederate statues to actions undertaken by the terror group ISIS and, in the wake of the Unite the Right rally, called his fellow Republicans "weak" for "play[ing] right into the hands of the left wing." After being publicly criticized for endorsing Wisconsin Republican House candidate Paul Nehlen, a man eventually banned from Twitter for posting racist images, Stewart's campaign replied, "Sadly, it's unsurprising to see the establishment Republicans continue to play the race card against President Trump's most vocal supporters."[16] The "race card," according to Stewart's campaign, translated into the mere mention of racism.

As the violence in Charlottesville reached its climax on August 12, 2017—as white supremacists protested the loss of their "history" with racist harangues and violence—members of the Virginia Flaggers stood outside the Virginia Museum of Fine Arts (VMFA) in Richmond with their Confederate battle flags, much like that first time I formally encountered Barry Isenhour, spokesman for the group. A photograph of a small group of Flaggers was posted to Facebook and Twitter that afternoon, captioned, "Virginia Flaggers on the ground this afternoon, forwarding the colors at the #vmfa Virginia Museum of Fine Arts. Museum officials desecrated the Confederate Memorial Chapel when they forced the removal of Confederate Battle Flags."[17]

As protesters and counterprotesters came to blows in the streets of Charlottesville, as Heather Heyer was killed on the Downtown Mall, mowed down by a car driven by a white supremacist, a small group of Flaggers stood outside the VMFA as if nothing had changed. They had reconnected with their original cause for protest—tethering it to the local removal of the Confederate battle flag outside Pelham Memorial Chapel on VMFA grounds. It was an implicit call to antiracialism, which is, as critical race theorist David Theo Goldberg posits, "always a *local* call, in a word, the reduction of the global to the local."[18] At that moment, the national chaos in the streets some seventy miles east on I-64 did not even constitute a backdrop. The Flaggers stood, frozen in time—that is, to the events that had first spurred their protest seven years earlier.

The Virginia Flaggers would continue to act as if suspended in time—seeking to normalize their stance on social media not only by distancing themselves from their contemporaneous context but also by reducing political contests over the meaning of the past to a series of fictional fantasies, hallmarks of American popular culture. The Flaggers' use of memes and hashtags via Facebook and Twitter to respond to the aftermath of Charlottesville, a popular tactic of the alt-right during a national moment of rupture, points to their efforts to simultaneously disconnect from the virulent racism unfolding in the streets as well as recast themselves, and the broader neo-Confederate movement, as heroic victims.[19]

The twenty-first-century turn to the "new museum," with its emphasis on "new media and an interactive-participatory agenda," offers, as communication scholar Chaim Noy has explained, "unprecedented opportunities for audience participation." While Noy considered the participatory possibilities within the museum's physical spaces, I suggest in this chapter that social media offer powerful platforms for neo-Confederates to similarly "establish a *shared* discourse" by fostering a "speech community."[20] These opportunities for expression, however, come with consequences. As communication scholars Adrienne Massanari and Shira Chess argue, "We are at a moment where eliminationist rhetoric that was once regional or ideologically specific can spread rapidly, now, due to the ubiquity of the Internet and the movement of memes online. Memes, in this way, are the new frontline of hate speech."[21] Within this chapter, I examine a series of memes circulated by the Virginia Flaggers, exposing the dangers of this digital Confederacy,[22] an entity that, while it exists and persists within the virtual realm, continues to be enacted in real life to disastrous effect.

Beginning with a few diehards, the Virginia Flaggers have grown their social network to include a number of like-minded Confederate "heritage" protectors. Their Twitter account, which enables considerably less latitude where verbiage is concerned, describes the group as "Citizens of the Commonwealth who stand AGAINST those who would desecrate our Confederate Monuments and memorials, and FOR our Confederate Veterans." The account has approximately three thousand followers.

Composed of men, women, and children, the Flaggers are willing to stand with a Confederate battle flag, either in person on the sidewalk or online. They emphasize the lack of place required to be a Flagger. One can ostensibly flag *anywhere*, which is why the digital platform is so appealing as a mechanism of communication. Separated by space, the Virginia Flaggers do not need to be physically co-present.

While their stated mission to "educate and inform" hardly sounds heroic, let alone *super*heroic, the Flaggers claim to "speak for those who have no voice." Portraying themselves as modern-day Robin Hoods, attending to those who lie on the margins of society, the Flaggers define their work as follows:

> We relay a message of Honor, Dignity, Respect, and Heritage to those who never knew, or to those who have forgotten, and to attempt to reach those who refuse to hear. Our weapon is the Confederate Battle Flag. Our enemies are those who worship ignorance, historical revisionism, and Political Correctness. . . . The Va Flaggers reject any person or group whose actions tarnish or bring dishonor upon the Confederate soldier or his reason for fighting, including those groups and persons using our cherished flag as a symbol for their own dishonorable purposes.[23]

In this way, their work is cast like their cause: noble and thus worth fighting against their "enemies," however ill defined.

The Flaggers' mission is deeply rooted in the sense of not only their ideology (defined in opposition to these "enemies") but also their bodies falling under attack. They locate themselves as a group pushed to the margins and silenced. I see the Flaggers' digital presence functioning akin to the "cyber-Confederacy" explored by media studies scholar Tara McPherson: "a very sincere attempt to make 'self' in the world and to articulate a very particular (and racially naturalized) presence."[24] While the Flaggers do not cite a specific foe, the "enemy" is one who seeks to "tarnish or bring dishonor upon the Confederate soldier or his reason for fighting." In keeping with Lost Cause ideology, this is a thinly veiled reference to those who cite slavery as the cause of the American Civil War. Deeply rooted in memory of the past, the Flaggers' cause is larger than themselves. Like so many superheroes, they see themselves fighting for the "greater good" amid a landscape descending into chaos.

Waging the #TarpWars

Among the most discernable signs of the Flaggers' retreat into a fantastical world suspended in time came some six months following the violence in Charlottesville. By this time, Charlottesville's statues to Robert E. Lee and Stonewall Jackson in Emancipation and Justice Parks, respectively,[25] had been shrouded in large black tarps for nearly as long, following a unanimous decision by the city council. It was an unpopular response among neo-Confederates, several of whom were arrested multiple times over the following months for removing the tarps, often under the cover of night. The tarps were promptly refashioned over the statues, a process that was then repeated, sometimes on the same night—that is, until a judge ordered the city to remove the tarps permanently on February 28, 2018. However, weeks prior to the tarps' permanent removal, as the cycle of removal and refashioning was at its height, the Virginia Flaggers began to circulate what would become the "Tarp Wars" meme. Mocking Charlottesville city council's order to shroud the statues and keep them covered, the Virginia Flaggers posted an announcement to their Facebook group that read:

A short time ago, in a city not too far away . . .
A Valiant Effort
A small band of Rebel tarp warriors struck yet again this
evening against the evil Charlottesville empire.
They were able to free Jackson but were thwarted
in their efforts to free Lee.
Two of our Rebels were questioned by representatives

of the empire, but were able to make their escape and
rendezvous with the excursionary forces and withdraw to safety.[26]

Mimicking the fonts and colors of George Lucas's famous *Star Wars* franchise, the post elicited more than 150 responses, including "likes" as well as "loves" and emojis connoting laughter.

More than a week after the Tarp Wars announcement, a more elaborate Facebook announcement deployed the same trope. It read: "Now Playing in Charlottesville. . . . It's a time of darkness, as the rebellion fights against the police state and leftist villains of hate, art censorship and the dishonoring of our veterans."[27] In this post, the Flaggers once again harked back to the format of promotional materials for George Lucas's "lavish space opera."[28] The meme, which emphasized the title with the hashtag #TarpWars, received more than 180 responses, from "likes" to emojis of anger. Based on the commentary, the "anger" was not directed at the Virginia Flaggers but rather at the leaders of Charlottesville, the "villains" in the saga.

With this meme, Charlottesville transformed from a site of crisis and national upheaval into a fantasy world, divorced from the present and operating on a wholly different temporal plane. It served as a convenient distraction in the wake of the early February 2018 news story that "rising white supremacist leader" Elliott Kline (aka Eli Mosley), who was an organizer of the deadly Unite the Right rally, had lied about his service in Iraq.[29] Emphasis on the Tarp Wars assured distance from a thorny present of untruths and denial. The popularity of *Star Wars* and its lexical congruity made for an easy substitution in terms ("tarp" for "star"). While this might at once explain the Flaggers' reference, the cultural allusion was more than mere coincidence. Declaring themselves "Rebels," a term that gestures to Confederate history as well as to *Star Wars'* freedom-fighting resistance, the Flaggers position themselves squarely as the "good guys" fighting against a tyrannical dictatorship rooted in hate. The invocation of *Star Wars* conjured nostalgia and nationalism, two inextricable elements of Confederate exceptionalist mythology.

Described by one film critic in 1977 as "straight out of 'Buck Rogers' and 'Flash Gordon' by way of Tolkien, 'Prince Valiant, 'The Wizard of Oz,' 'Boy's Life' and about every great western movie ever made,"[30] *Star Wars* is a veritable pastiche of American cultural forms: science fiction, fantasy, superhero, and the western. Not only did these forms capture Lucas's sense of imagination and wonder, conveyed, as Lucas would note, with "a sort of effervescent giddiness,"[31] they each conformed neatly to a series of archetypal characters: "reluctant young hero, warrior-wizard,

brave and beautiful princess, and monstrous black villain."[32] While conformity to a preordained set of scripts might have generated a stale story,
Star Wars managed to repackage the past in a way that in fact, as scholar
Andrew Gordon would write, "rework[ed] a multitude of old stories, and
yet creat[ed] a complete and self-sufficient world of its own."[33]

The story of *Star Wars* animated the American public at a particular
cultural moment—the late 1970s. As critic Michael Wood wrote reflecting
on the space fantasy's popularity, the story wielded the ability to "clean
up the world of our imagination, resurrect the good old values in snappy
contemporary form."[34] It was a public response to the political upheaval
that characterized the 1970s with opposition to the Vietnam War and the
Watergate scandal. Lucas's film signaled an attempt at "renewal of faith
in ourselves as Americans, as good guys on the world scene, as men and
women" and did so by drawing liberally from "20th century popular mythology—old movies, science fiction, television, and comic books"[35]—all
pieces of popular culture that tend to be inscribed nostalgically in American culture.

At a moment of national fracture and unrest, backlash to the American civil rights movement, and the rise of the New Right, *Star Wars* offered
solace. The world of "plucky, cheerful fellow-robot, Artoo-Detoo" and See
Threepio, "a gilded cross between Jeeves and Noel Coward," in addition,
of course, to "the stalwart, fair-skinned human hero . . . who rescues a
princess"[36] was a welcome respite from the economic malaise and political
crisis that characterized the period. The 1970s, historian Bruce Schulman
notes, saw "Americans develop[ing] a deeper, more thorough suspicion
of the instruments of public life and a more profound disillusionment
with the corruption and inefficiency of public institutions."[37] *Stars Wars*
was the antidote to that.

George Lucas's world was one of difference, including nonhuman
creatures speaking in invented languages that fused, according to Lucas,
"a combination of exotic languages—partly Zulu, partly Swahili—that
would serve as pidgin English." It was a world where such difference was
strange yet also eminently "believable"[38]—where the main nonhuman
characters were also strikingly human in their emotions. The film depicts
fantasy and fiction in a way, however, that blurs the lines of the real. This
is critical to the Flaggers' presentation of their narrative and cause.

It would be easy to see "Tarp Wars" as harmless parody, not unlike
Mel Brooks's *Spaceballs* or *Sesame Street*'s "Star S'mores," a universe centered around desserts.[39] As they attempt to draw out what they see as the
absurdity of their continued battle against "the leftist villains of hate,"
the Flaggers' use of these intertextual references works to normalize the

Confederacy, presenting it as part of the American cultural mainstream while marginalizing its more progressive critics. In this way, the Tarp Wars meme functions not unlike the invocation of the Confederate battle flag and song "Dixie" in the popular action-comedy television series *Dukes of Hazzard*, which ran from 1979 to 1985. However, in the case of Charlottesville, the stakes were considerably higher, and on August 12, 2017, they were a matter of life and death.

The Flaggers' continued focus on the Tarp Wars reduced the issue to the material tarps themselves, which, as the *Cavalier Daily*, the University of Virginia's student newspaper, wrote in early February 2018, served to "place Charlottesville law enforcement in a cat-and-mouse game of constantly attempting to secure the tarps."[40] The *Cavalier Daily*'s editorial board called the tarps a distraction, keeping the city from preparing for the possible return of white supremacists, who had gathered in October 2017, led by UVA alumnus and white nationalist Richard Spencer,[41] to reprise their rally, dubbing it "Charlottesville 3.0."

Events in Charlottesville remained tense and the aftershocks continued to reverberate across the country. In early February 2018 Arthur Jones, an unabashed white supremacist who dubbed the Confederate battle flag "a symbol of White pride and White resistance" and who blamed "Radical Leftists" for Heather Heyer's death,[42] was announced as an unopposed Republican candidate for Congress in Illinois. That same week South Carolina gubernatorial candidate Catherine Templeton reaffirmed her pride in her Confederate ancestors who fought "because the federal government was trying to tell us how to live."[43] The Anti-Defamation League released a report that "instances of white supremacist propaganda on college campuses more than tripled in 2017,"[44] coinciding with the announcement that Matthew Heimbach, cofounder of the Traditionalist Worker Party, a hate group, planned to speak at the University of Tennessee–Knoxville.

The Flaggers' use of *Star Wars* as the reference for the meme deployed a familiar trope in popular culture—that of a community under attack. In *Star Wars* "the entire Universe is in peril from the tyrannical Galactic Empire; the quest is to rescue the beautiful Princess Leia from the clutches of the villainous Darth Vader and transport to the rebel forces the secret plans of the Death Star." In an unsurprising conclusion, "the good guys save the universe." Simply, "the pure of heart are able to defeat the forces of wickedness."[45]

The narrative crafted by the Virginia Flaggers in the wake of violence in Charlottesville offered a substitution in terms: Charlottesville was the "tyrannical empire," "leftist villains" were the contemporary Darth Vaders, the functional "equivalent of the Red Baron or the leader of the Nazi Luft-waffe,"[46] depicted with photographs of a red-eyed city councilman Wes Bellamy and Mayor Michael Signer. In the Flaggers' narrative "darkness" loomed. The universe teetered on the brink of destruction. Within this frame, the "beautiful Princess Leia" is the Confederate monuments and in earlier conversations the Confederate battle flag, the icons of honor and valor in need of protection by contemporary neo-Confederates such as the Virginia Flaggers. Linked narratively to the historic construction of the southern lady, typically an elite, white wife of a plantation owner, Confederate monuments were dependent on men's protection.[47] The heroes, the Flaggers, were tasked with "saving" the damsel, Confederate memory. The substitution was neat, but unlike the *Star Wars* franchise, real lives were at risk.

While the Virginia Flaggers' Tarp Wars meme used popular culture to reiterate the myth of the neo-Confederate superhero through allusions to form and narrative, Facebook posts, too, begged inquiry into the super-hero himself as what literature scholar Joseph Campbell termed "mono-myth," the arc whereby the "hero of epic myth is a dream-figure who stands in for the entire culture."[48] According to Campbell, the "mono-myth" is divided into three stages—departure, initiation, and return. The Flaggers' mythology departs little from Campbell's construction, with its conformity to a narrative divorced from history.

The hero, Gordon notes, is typically "the orphaned son of royalty."[49] Exiled to a life of drudgery, he must, if he is to fulfill his fate, overcome his guardians. The Flaggers follow a similar formula. They narrate their origins as follows: "What began with just a few dedicated Southerners, has now grown to include hundreds of people, from all over the country, who have joined us in protesting against Heritage offenses in Richmond, and Virginia . . . and beyond!"[50] What is described is something of an awaken-ing, a call to action, as the Flaggers mobilize an incensed populace. There might not be a formal Obi-Wan Kenobi to protect the hero as such; how-ever, the Flaggers' inspiration and mentorship derives from their memo-ries of Robert E. Lee and Stonewall Jackson, the venerated Confederate leaders who, despite their passing more than a century ago, loom large. Their fairy tale of the Confederate hero materialized in the expression of monuments to the generals—the source of Charlottesville's explosive protests.

Like *Star Wars*' Luke Skywalker, the Flaggers' destiny, at least as they present it, is preordained. Like *Star Wars*' hero, they are "provided with a readymade excuse for rebellion in the political situation."[51] As they ven-ture into the next stage of the myth, initiation, they are forced to endure a set of "tests" and "ordeals." The Flaggers present this "ordeal" publicly on Facebook. Like the heroes they invoke, the Flaggers rely on the "trope of superheroic justice as opposed to state law."[52]

This is a trope they returned to months after the Tarp Wars had ended. To draw on another superhero story, *Batman*, the Flaggers' Facebook posts emphasized the "atemporal and cartoonish qualities of Gotham City."[53] Charlottesville was cast by the Flaggers as a modern-day Gotham City, under siege by what one commenter noted was a "Liberal and Yankee invasion."[54] Another Facebook post featured an image of a Confederate flag as a "bat signal," set against a screenshot of Batman and Robin from the popular 1960s television show. Robin exclaims, as seen in a word bubble, "Holy Heritage Batman! The Virginia Flaggers are fighting political correctness again!"[55] The invocation of the "dynamic duo" recalled that the Flaggers' fight was a historic one, but also one that was being continuously reenacted. Like *Star Wars*, which boasts an original trilogy, a prequel trilogy, a sequel trilogy, and anthology films, spanning 1977 through the forthcoming *The Rise of Skywalker* in 2019, *Batman*, too, has been adapted to film and television, spanning more than half a century. These referents, gesturing to historical films and genres, were far from culturally distant. While present, these films and programs remind us of a fantastical world that was both commercially viable and easily reduced to clearly defined heroes and villains.

Tarp Warriors

The flaring Tarp Wars announced on Facebook were part of a broader attempt to make sense of what the Flaggers had witnessed on the ground in Charlottesville. On August 15, 2017, days following Heather Heyer's murder, the Flaggers posted a story to their Facebook page that received more than five thousand comments, which shared the tale of a "young man" who "traveled to Charlottesville today to stand guard at the LEE monument in LEE Park." Throughout the story, the "young man's" identity is never revealed, enabling him to stand in for *any* protester. The emphasis on his youth is equally significant as it invokes his alleged "innocence." The story is narrated as follows:

> He [the young man] was immediately approached by leftist activists who demanded to know why he was there and if he was a "white supremacist." After he assured them he had nothing to do with the weekend rally or white supremacy and that he was there to honor his ancestor and Robert E. Lee, the

"oh so tolerant" citizens of Charlottesville proceeded to spend the next hour shouting obscenities and displaying obscene gestures inches from his face. To his credit, and in the spirit of the man he was there to honor, the young man never responded in kind or flinched . . . imagine what this man endured for a solid hour. THIS . . . is Wes Bellamy's Charlottesville.[56]

By encouraging visitors to "imagine what this man endured," the Flaggers situated the young man as a victim of virulent "leftist" slander. Called a white supremacist, the young man was, the Flaggers assured, simply standing guard, protecting his "heritage," minding his own business. He had not goaded the activists on. Rather, the young man was engaged in an apolitical action that could be summarized as a mere paying of respect to an ancestor and historic general. It was an act divorced from the hatred evidenced in the Unite the Right rally, they assured. The young man had been targeted but responded in a way speaking to his honor, internalizing the gallantry of his ancestors. He had neither "responded in kind [n]or flinched." He bravely withstood the onslaught of "obscenities" and "obscene gestures." Enduring rants for a "solid hour," the "young man" in question was held up as a martyr, sacrificing his body on behalf of the cause—in this case the "protection" of Charlottesville's Robert E. Lee Monument. At a moment when the nation recoiled in horror at the site of hooded Klansmen in the streets of Charlottesville, the Flaggers used social media to champion the protest of a single young man seeking to protect the statues that had led to loss of life. Such a rhetorical move demonstrated that the Flaggers had transitioned past nostalgia. No longer were they reflecting wistfully on their ancestors' past. They were using a romanticized history to legitimate continued confrontation in the present.

The Flaggers' commentary on the young man's endurance and tolerance evokes popular memory of the verbal and physical assaults sustained by Black students and activists who worked to desegregate schools and other public spaces in the 1950s and 1960s—men and women who endured *for a cause*—in these cases the desegregation of public spaces such as schools and retail establishments. For the Virginia Flaggers, in 2017, the "young man" called a white supremacist for standing with a Confederate battle flag next to the Robert E. Lee statue in Charlottesville had been forced to similarly "endure." In this way, the Flaggers attempt to forge a narrative linkage between protesters for civil rights and their "activist" efforts, as they are similarly compelled to defend their rights.[57]

Like the civil rights activists of the 1950s and 1960s, the Flaggers and sympathizers in the 2010s were forced to sustain verbal harangues. This temporal slippage, the corollary between some sixty years ago and the present, evidences their anachronistic uses of the past much like the conservative rendering of the Rev. Martin Luther King Jr., who, as historian Thomas Sugrue noted, has been deployed as "an icon of racial conservatism" by those who have drawn King's words out of context.[58] The Flaggers' narration of the "young man's" endurance displays a similar lack of context, particularly neglect of the history of American race relations. This historical neglect was crystallized in a comment by Eddie Zipperer, an assistant professor of political science at Georgia Military College, who, while acknowledging the Civil War was about slavery, noted, "The Democratic party tore our country apart when they refused to accept Republican Abraham Lincoln's election as legitimate, and they formed their own union for the sole purpose of protecting slavery. When I see a Confederate flag, all I see is the Democrat traitor flag."[59] Zipperer makes no note of the fact that the historic "Democratic party" to which he referred is in fact the modern-day Republican Party.

The "hatred" purportedly sustained by the Flaggers and other "heritage" groups only amplified in their online statements attempting to reassert themselves as the "true" protectors of history in the wake of the "young man's" experience in Charlottesville. The "young man" was a hero in the Flaggers' telling, protecting the "victims"—the Robert E. Lee and Stonewall Jackson statues. On August 19, 2017, less than a week after Heather Heyer's murder, the Virginia Flaggers posted a meme that included a photo of Tom Hanks as Forrest Gump that said, "And just like that people were mad at statues." Making light of the deadly violence, not unlike the later Tarp Wars meme, the post received 290 likes.[60] The use of Forrest Gump, the titular character in Robert Zemeckis's film based on the novel by Winston Groom, points to the Flaggers' sense that their stance is obvious even to the most simpleminded. The absurdity, however, rested with the Flaggers' use of yet another fictionalized underdog character, whose story was predicated on a fortuitous coincidence of events, to capture their sentiments. Critiqued for its "rearticulation of a traditional version of the American story," *Forrest Gump*, film scholars have argued, is a politically conservative film.[61] The Flaggers' invocation of a character who validated the right but was unaware of the gravity of his surroundings thus seemed especially apropos.

Commenters on the Flaggers' post were similarly unwilling to engage the immediate context in Charlottesville directly. One commenter noted, "It really boggles the mind. The world is full of injustice and terrible things like modern slavery, torture, sex trafficking of children. . . . But omigosh statues are the most easy . . . Ooops evil . . . to attack."[62] Like the Flaggers, the commenter suggested that debate surrounding Confederate monuments was, in comparison to the ills confronting the world, a trivial issue. There were, in the commenter's estimation, more dire problems to be addressed in the city of Charlottesville. The larger, structural debate surrounding slavery and its legacies was a discussion in which they were unwilling to engage.

Beyond giving meaning to the violence perpetrated in Charlottesville, the story of the victim as told by the Virginia Flaggers did what myths do—it invited identification. As communication scholar Jack Lule argued in his analysis of news coverage of the 1985 murder of Leon Klinghoffer by the Palestine Liberation Organization (PLO), "The terror—as opposed to disgust over the slaughter or grief over the loss—resides in a personal, primarily unconscious understanding that the victim is a symbol of the self: It could have been me."[63] In forging identification with the victims of violence in Charlottesville, victimhood that was about "hate" broadly but never about racism specifically, the Flaggers redrew what appeared to be the neat lines of victims and villains. They had invited a public audience, watching the unfolding events across the world, to identify with them as a fundamentally misunderstood organization seeking to honor their ancestors alone. Unlike the members of the KKK and neo-Nazis, they were not motivated by hate. It was the same point they made more than two years earlier in the wake of Dylann Roof's violent massacre in Charleston. The Flaggers' actions were not born from hate but were rather a labor of love, they noted.

If the Flaggers publicly demonstrated their "departure" and "initiation" through efforts to combat "evil," they were also to embark on the final stage: the return. The hero's role, according to Campbell, "is the destruction of the status quo in order to permit renewal and restoration."[64] Within a post-Charlottesville context, the "status quo" to be destroyed was an insistence that the monuments represent white supremacy—to foreground race and racism in discussions of the American Civil War, its causes, and its memory. Destroying the status quo, in this framework, is equivalent in the discourse of neo-Confederates to taking up arms to vanquish an evil foe.

Prevalent throughout the Flaggers' posts and memes, this language of an "evil" foe was also used by Ronald Reagan during his first term as US president as a way to rally national support for his policies and spur a greater sense of nationalism. Reagan undertook three addresses during the early 1980s that worked to help advance US nuclear arms buildup: the "Zero Option," "Evil Empire," and "Star Wars" speeches. As rhetorician G. Thomas Goodnight notes, the latter two speeches, capitalizing on the widespread circulation of the superhero myth, "affirmed and extended the position by envisioning nuclear war as part of an age-old struggle between good and evil, a conflict beyond strict rational assessment, and advancing the idea that the power of science and technology can be channeled in such a way as to control nuclear war."[65]

Ronald Reagan's "Evil Empire" speech, delivered before a meeting of the National Association of Evangelicals in the early 1980s, is now considered a seminal example of such rhetoric. As Goodnight argued, "festooned with stories, jokes, biblical quotations, and personal revelations, which together create an ahistorical, dream-like vision of American and world destiny,"[66] Reagan's speech created a sense of Americanism around which a collective could coalesce—a conservative collective. In a Facebook post on February 24, 2018, the Flaggers noted pointedly, "The long-standing lack of opposition to the left's jihad against Confederate history and heritage is coming to an end."[67] Much like references to the "Evil Empire" of the 1980s necessitating nuclear armaments, the violence in Charlottesville simultaneously necessitated action, specifically the protection of the monuments. And the Flaggers noted, there was no one better equipped to take up the mantle of the Confederacy than the collective itself. Like the stakes in the early 1980s as the United States feared nuclear war with the Soviet Union, the climate in 2018 was one of heightened anxiety and an uncertain future.

#SouthernAvenger: The Man, the Myth, the Meme

If the Tarp Wars meme communicated the Flaggers' dissociation from reality and distance from the contemporary moment, the emergence of the "Southern Avenger" as hashtag and meme, often used in tandem with #TarpWars, magnified this distance. Initially referred to as #ConfederateAvenger, a moniker quickly forsaken for #SouthernAvenger, the character brought the superhero metaphor to life. While #TarpWars invoked both a franchise and a genre, the Southern Avenger ensured that the referent was more than metaphor. The superhero Southern Avenger was not only a symbol; he was a man, myth, and meme.[68]

The Flaggers' circulation of the Tarp Wars meme little more than two and a half years after the Charleston massacre and some six months following the violence in Charlottesville showed the Virginia Flaggers as a neo-Confederate heritage group that continued to position itself as heroic; the meme more overtly connected that heroism to the superhero genre in particular. The superhero, as gender studies scholar Rebecca Wanzo notes, "is an indelibly American invention connoting ideal citizenship through white muscular force."[69] Since its emergence in the late 1930s with the character of Superman, there has been little to disrupt the white superhero's preeminence.[70] Superheroes, Wanzo notes, are "routinely represented as models of right action and feeling."[71] The Tarp Wars meme made abundantly clear the identities of the villains and heroic models of right.

Beyond the Tarp Wars meme, the Virginia Flaggers' self-positioning as heroes is evidenced in their Facebook group's "About" tab, where they share their origin story, a hallmark of the superhero genre. As film scholar Federico Pagello notes, "*The 'origin story' remains the only 'real' narrative in the superhero fiction,* precisely because it is the *exact* moment this break away from the temporal world takes place."[72]

While the superhero wields virtually limitless strength, a feature of myths far and wide, he is to be differentiated from the heroic figures of classical or Nordic mythologies or of Messianic religions, notes Umberto Eco. Whereas the traditional figures were of human or divine origin, "whose image had immutable characteristics and an irreversible destiny," the mythical superhero in contrast, due to the necessity of being "a man like anyone else," must assume an "'aesthetic universality,' a capacity to serve as a reference point for behavior and feelings which belong to us all." In sum, "the mythological character of comic strips finds himself in this singular situation: he must be an archetype, the totality of certain collective aspirations, and therefore, he must necessarily become immobilized in an emblematic and fixed nature which renders him easily recognizable . . . but . . . he must be subjected to a development which is typical . . . of novelistic characters."[73] Lee and Jackson fit this mold as men immortalized in bronze seated atop gallant horses, featured across the American landscape, though concentrated within the South.

What this attention to character has meant for the superhero genre is "endless variations on the same fundamental elements made possible by replacing a linear, temporal narrative with a proliferation of co-existing parallel universes." A postmodern product employing a cyclical structure, superhero stories "are thus located in a *space* outside of time, strategically placed in-between an origin and an end that are never to be experienced except via the memories of an irretrievable past . . . or through the anticipations of a future never to come." For neo-Confederates, this episodic quality takes on particular strategic significance, as they locate themselves within the context of a setting divorced from history yet besieged by villains—in a city, Charlottesville in this case, constantly and predictably in need of a hero. This world is not dissimilar to that depicted by Tim Burton in later Batman films—an "entirely mediatized, consumerist and corrupted society lacking in historicity."[74] Charlottesville became the setting where the forces of good and evil came into conflict—a setting remediated through social media in which the neo-Confederacy was positioned as the fearless hero, the surrogate American, fighting on behalf of a virtuous cause—memory of a Confederate past.

The #SouthernAvenger referenced in the Flaggers' posts was both local and national. Locally, the phrase referenced the work of Christopher James Wayne, a white, thirty-four-year-old Richmond resident whose removal of the tarps from the statues in Charlottesville on more than one occasion led to Wayne being barred from the parks and charged with trespassing and vandalism.[75] During previous arrests, Wayne was given a summons, a response not dissimilar to a parking ticket.[76] Nationally, "Southern Avenger" conjured Charleston, South Carolina–based conservative radio personality Jack Hunter, who had become famous for donning a Confederate flag wrestling mask as his personality's costume. This play between the local and the national amplified the stakes in the debate surrounding Confederate monuments. #SouthernAvenger evoked a national battle—one made visible in Charlottesville and Charleston.

In the wake of the city of Charlottesville's decision to shroud the Lee and Jackson monuments in tarps, the Flaggers used Facebook as a space to rally support for Wayne, known in posts only as the "Southern Avenger." His name was identified in public news broadcasts and articles but never used by the Flaggers online, contributing to the mystique—that is, until local news outlets featured a photograph of the Confederate heritage sympathizer.

The Flaggers kept their online community informed of Wayne's efforts, offering regular updates and announcing that they had "covered the bond, but many of you have asked how you can help." The Flaggers specified, "Any amount above $1,000 [his bond] raised will go toward legal expenses for his defense. Any amount left after legal defense expenses will be used for Charlottesville heritage defense projects." The Flaggers included a P.O. box address and PayPal link.[77] An announcement earlier that night to the Facebook page of Wayne's arrest in Justice Park queried as to whether a GoFundMe account could be created, following a strategy used by the neo-Confederate group CSA II: The New Confederate States of America, whose failed rally in Richmond in September 2017 led to the small group seeking funds through online means in order to leave town.

Despite the fact that #SouthernAvenger was most often used to reference Wayne indirectly, the Flaggers used the phrase more capaciously. They claimed "God bless the Southern Avengers" on the eve of the ruling regarding the legality of the tarps covering the statues in Charlottesville.[78]

The post acknowledged that, while perhaps the most visible perpetrator, Wayne was not the only one committed to the removal of the tarps, which had been removed seven times during the month of February alone. The Flaggers' "blessing" of the Southern Avengers once again drew a line of false equivalency between those repeatedly removing the tarps and civil rights activists. The action, they noted, was a collective one attempting to restore the honor and dignity of their ancestors.

While Wayne's identity as the Southern Avenger was tethered to his commitment to removing the tarps from the Lee and Jackson statues in Charlottesville, the Flaggers propagated the myth of neo-Confederate heroism even more explicitly through a visual representation of the so-called Southern Avenger. A white man whose build mirrors the "typical" superhero, with muscular arms and legs, the Southern Avenger dons a gray suit and red cape, the colors of the Confederate soldiers' uniforms. He wears a gray mask over his eyes (see fig. 6.2).

The Southern Avenger was fashioned into comic form, standing to the side of the Lee monument in Charlottesville, accompanied by #TarpWars and #winning.[79] While the creator of the meme is unknown, its references were not lost on the Flaggers' Twitter followers. The use of #winning referred to the meme made famous in 2011 by actor Charlie Sheen. After Sheen's appearance on conservative talk radio's *Alex Jones Show,* during which the actor, who had recently completed rehab, boasted of his sobriety and was therefore "winning" at life, the hashtag gained momentum. It continues to be used and applied to a variety of non-Confederate contexts. The legacy of #winning, as journalist Nick Carbone notes, is that the term "became a part of our growing vernacular for use in those situations that demand arrogance."[80] In referencing Sheen's meme, the Flaggers projected a certain hubris, associated with what they believe to be the moral high ground, thwarting their liberal foe. It also signaled their awkward embrace of a popular cultural icon, Charlie Sheen, whose claim to "winning" made him the butt of a national joke.

While the Flaggers invoked the famous actor Charlie Sheen through #winning, their use of #SouthernAvenger speaks to the personality of Jack Hunter, who made a career for himself by defending the Confederate battle flag as "heritage" and with such claims as whites lost "the right to celebrate their own cultural identity" and John Wilkes Booth's heart was "in the right place."[81] Hunter's public identity might seem a logical tie for the Flaggers to make, yet Hunter publicly recanted his outrageous claims in the wake of Dylann Roof's 2015 rampage. Writing in the *Daily Beast,* the ideologue admitted that the Confederate battle flag, contrary to earlier statements, was "always about race." He concluded, "The Confederate flag

Figure 6.2, #SouthernAvenger Facebook post (Virginia Flaggers Facebook group)

will always be a roadblock to the betterment of our natures. Let's take it down so that we might all rise up."[82] It was a public announcement that was not received well within alt-right circles, with Breitbart lambasting the former Rand Paul staffer and more liberal-leaning individuals expressing skepticism on Twitter that Hunter's public mea culpa was sincere.[83]

Given Hunter's public 180, it might seem strange that the Virginia Flaggers would embrace the moniker "Southern Avenger" in the Tarp Wars saga. As Jim Ehlen tweeted on June 25, 2015, the action left him to wonder "what he [Hunter] was avenging in the first place."[84] Yet this rhetorical move was precisely the point—consistent with the Flaggers' invocations of popular culture across social media. In appropriating the identity of the white masculinist Southern Avenger, the Flaggers attempted to flip the narrative once again. Embracing Hunter's original claims regarding the Confederate flag's allegedly benign, yet honorific, symbolism, the Virginia Flaggers attempted to invert the statement Hunter made regarding the Confederate battle flag's meaning post-Charleston. Never explicitly mentioning Hunter, the Flaggers continued to use the hashtag, suggesting there was no past with which to engage.

While openly denouncing neo-Nazis and members of the KKK who descended on Charlottesville in August 2017, the Flaggers and other likeminded Confederate heritage sympathizers were explicit in their denunciation of those who disagreed with their stance. Days after images of an embattled Charlottesville circulated internationally, the Virginia Flaggers retweeted a story from WCSC Live 5 news. The story showed a photograph of a white man and Black woman embracing, titled, "Viral photo shows peace in Lynchburg, 'If I were KKK would I hold you like this?'"[85] Echoing the arguments of the living historians I discussed in chapter 3, the story seeks to deflect critiques of the Confederacy's racism by invoking stories of interracial friendships. The Flaggers sought to demonstrate that they were not the racists who advocated hate. They were not the Klan. They were "peaceful Southern American Patriots"—men and women whom all should aspire to emulate.

Alongside the Facebook posts attempting to assure readers of the Southern Avenger's heroism, commenters on the Virginia Flaggers' page continued to lambast their opponents. One, receiving more than 1,500 emoticons, noted, "What a bunch of uneducated dumbasses . . . they [liberals] have No idea what that Flag Stands for . . . WoW! This Country sure ain't what it use [sic] to be."[86] Another commenter stated, "They act the way they do [because] for the last 8 years it was allowed."[87] The commenters cast the counterprotesters as ignorant of history yet also, at least in the case of the latter comment, the product of a permissive culture cultivated during Barack Obama's tenure as president of the United States. Although not stated explicitly, the sense that the country "ain't what it use to be" echoed President Trump's campaign slogan, "Make America Great Again." Those who opposed the work of the Southern Avenger were deemed ignorant and stupid. They needed an education that the social media platform, in the absence of in-person conversation, could provide.

Remembering the Confederacy Online

The Flaggers' use of memes and hashtags invoking heroes and villains, fantasies and the genre of science fiction provided a public articulation of the Flaggers' sense of self in the midst of public unrest. However, when tarps are not being removed or protesters arrested, the Flaggers continue to locate themselves and their dearest symbols, the Confederate battle flag and monuments in particular, as ordinary and familiar—part of American popular culture—seeking to further normalize the Confederacy through not only genre and narrative but also material culture.

The Flaggers post Facebook photos of the Confederate flag being paraded about at football games such as the historic 1960 Sugar Bowl matchup between Louisiana State University and the University of Mississippi.[88] The photograph had more than four hundred responses, mostly "likes" and "loves." They repost stories from mainstream news outlets posing questions of the contemporary audience such as, "Why do Italian soccer fans and other foreigners fly the Confederate flag?"[89] alongside clips from films from the neo-Confederate favorite *Gone with the Wind* to the more recent *Gods and Generals*.[90] They post photographs of Flaggers selling T-shirts supporting Confederate heritage at the Hanover Tomato Festival, a local favorite.

The Flaggers' Facebook feed features art created by famous painters, such as *The Generals Were Brought to Tears* (1992) by Brooklyn native Mort Kunstler. Known widely as "America's Artist" and the "Kinkade of Civil War art" due to his penchant for historical scenes, Kunstler captures the heart of "Lost Cause orthodoxy," as historian Gary Gallagher has written.[91] While the Flaggers' deep appreciation for Kunstler's work is unsurprising, his solemn portrayal of the two Confederate generals, Lee and Jackson, bowing in prayer next to two children, bears a Norman Rockwell–like quality that evidences not simply a romanticization of the Confederacy but also a distinctly American aesthetic that transcends scenes of battle. Kunstler's work is timeless; it is sympathetic and human. It is also displayed at many of the historic sites I visited throughout my work on this project, including the VMI Museum.

As they reiterate the Confederacy's transcendence through popular culture circulated online, they post videos of musicians such as southern rock band Lynyrd Skynyrd and singer Tom Petty, who sang in front of a Confederate battle flag in 1985 as part of his "Southern Accents" tour. They regularly retweet popular quizzes romanticizing southern "dialect" such as "Are you Southern Enough to Finish All These Southern Phrases?"[92] and "listicles" such as "20 quotes that'll make you fall in love with being Southern all over again."[93] They post "stories" with such headlines as "Obvious poll says that Southern accents are the sexiest in America"[94] and "Here's why southerners refer to all soft drinks as 'coke.'"[95] Each of these posts and tweets, while harmless in isolation, gestures to a larger effort to at once conflate "the South" with the Confederacy, a trend I discussed at length in chapter 4 when considering the "Confederate cookbook" genre and its attempts to normalize the Confederacy. Drawing on mainstream popular culture such as the 2011 film *The Help*, featuring Oscar-winning actress Emma Stone, and A-list actors such as Reese Witherspoon, whose southernness is very much a part of her public identity, the Flaggers position themselves as similarly "mainstream" and harmless, their ideology as American as rock music and Hollywood.

The Flaggers have circulated other memes such as "Confederate Lives Matter," printed on pins, and "Straight Outta Danville," appropriating the rhetoric of Black liberation movements. Like their invocation of Forrest Gump, the Flaggers' appropriation of *Straight Outta Compton* seeks to highlight an absurdity to their opposition. Yet in so doing, they underscore their neglect of either the issues or the stakes involved—race and white supremacy, life and death.

The Flaggers publicly discouraged followers on social media from participating in what would become the ill-fated CSA II rally in September and later December 2017, and, like the members of the Sons of Confederate Veterans, they would publicly denounce the hatred and racism that had manifested on the streets in Charlottesville.[96] But they also poked fun at the continuing conversation surrounding Confederate monuments, refusing to acknowledge their presence as continued violence, symbolic as well as physical.

The Virginia Flaggers' direct attacks on their ideological opposition are consonant with the actions of alt-right groups across the United States. The Flaggers' use of the hashtags #TarpWars and #SouthernAvenger, alongside others, reiterate, however, not only the power of their rhetoric but also how, through invocations of popular culture, they attempt to normalize their stance by reducing political contests over the meaning of the past to a series of mostly fictional fantasies.

When read through the lens of the Tarp Wars, the violence in Charlottesville and its aftermath were both a grave harbinger of what could come as well as a reminder that "good" Americans will triumph over "evil" ones—at least within the story as they had narrated it. As the city of Richmond considered the future of its historic Monument Avenue, this fantastical Confederate saga, with its heroes and villains, would once again alternately move into and out of focus as the future of Confederate exceptionalism was located on the public docket and the sanctity of the neo-Confederate museum debated.

Conclusion
The Future of the Neo-Confederate Museum

On August 9, 2017, Jamie Bosket, the president and CEO of the Virginia Museum of History and Culture (then the Virginia Historical Society), introduced the first public forum of Mayor Levar Stoney's appointed Monument Avenue Commission as "an important community conversation."[1] Bosket's remarks took particular note of the institution's mission of "telling a story and telling it to the largest possible audience."[2] Bosket had not been speaking only about the audience in attendance that summer evening. However, it was a large audience. The packed auditorium, whose capacity was set at five hundred, was left with standing room only. The line to get into the much-anticipated forum snaked around the building, with interested parties lining up more than an hour in advance and many turned away at the door due to lack of space.

As I walked past the front of the building to the side entrance to find my place in line, I paused at Tessa Pullan's monument to the horses and mules of the Civil War, dedicated some twenty years earlier. Staring at the emaciated bronze horse, I thought about the questions of context that I knew the Monument Avenue Commission would be most interested in engaging with that evening. I wondered why I was standing in front of a cast of an animal whose wartime sacrifice was championed in a city where one is hard-pressed to find statues commemorating the work and contributions of Black people. The statues commemorating Arthur Ashe, Maggie Walker, and Bill "Bojangles" Robinson, along with the Virginia Civil Rights Memorial, and the forthcoming Emancipation Proclamation and Freedom Monument,[3] scheduled to be installed by December 2019, were the only ones that came to mind.[4]

Two blocks from the Stonewall Jackson statue on Monument Avenue, the Virginia Museum of History and Culture sits between past and present, on grounds deemed sacred or profane depending on whom one speaks to. An entity founded on the notion that the history of Virginia is the history of America,[5] the Virginia Museum of History and Culture houses a permanent exhibit titled "The Story of Virginia" whose subtitle proclaims, "An American Experience." The Museum was thus more than a venue. It was a cultural touchstone, an embattled site of memory to which the myth of Confederate exceptionalism was intimately tied. As I stood before Pullan's horse, the Confederacy seemed hardly "a ghost" haunting the South, as Charles Stafford had written for the Associated Press in 1961.[6] Rather than some phantomlike apparition, the Confederacy is embodied, material, performed, *present*. One need not walk down Monument Avenue or wait for Lee-Jackson Day to engage with it.

Built as the Confederate Memorial Institute, or the Battle Abbey, in 1913, the neoclassical structure was designed to house the archives and portraits the institute acquired.[7] It was imagined "by the Confederate Memorial Association as a shrine to the Confederate dead and as a repository for the records of the Lost Cause."[8] This mission was captured in a time capsule hidden in the cornerstone of the Battle Abbey on May 20, 1912. One hundred years later, the copper box's contents were unearthed to much amazement. Inside were "newspapers, photographs, architectural drawings, construction contracts, Civil War signatures and records, a 5-by-5-inch Confederate battle flag, a delegate's pin for the 1912 United Confederate Veterans reunion and even a lawsuit over fundraising."[9] It was, at least for archivists, an embarrassment of riches.

Located next to what had once been the R. E. Lee Camp No. 1 for Confederate veterans, the grounds where I had first met Virginia Flagger spokesman Barry Isenhour, the Virginia Historical Society merged with the Confederate Memorial Association in 1946, occupying the structure today called the Virginia Museum of History and Culture, plus the extensions added in the years since.[10] No longer a reliquary for the Lost Cause, the Virginia Museum of History and Culture is home to a comprehensive collection of Virginia history, which has enabled it to display broad exhibitions such as "The Story of Virginia" as well as a series of traveling exhibitions, including "American Turning Point: The Civil War in Virginia" (cosponsored by the Virginia Sesquicentennial of the American Civil War Commission) and "Lee and Grant."

Before entering the building on that warm August evening, I stood between the building and the headquarters of the United Daughters of the Confederacy, where I had taken my predominantly white students, hailing mostly from the Northeast, several months earlier to observe enactments of Confederate memory in the twenty-first century. They had been shocked and, in many cases, appalled. For my students who were Richmond natives, their response was subtler, nodding in solemn acknowledgment that what we had seen was, in fact, a part of life in Richmond, particularly if you are a white person of a certain socioeconomic class.

On the other side of the UDC headquarters was the Virginia Museum of Fine Arts, ground zero for the Virginia Flaggers. It was also where I had first seen Richmond-based artist Sonya Clark's *Black Hair Flag* (2010) on display in the modern art gallery overlooking the UDC. As the *Boston Globe* described it, Clark's piece "stitched through a painted Confederate flag with black thread . . . then cornrowed the thread and used it to represent the stripes of the American flag while Bantu-knotting the stars."[11] Clark's *Black Hair Flag* invoked the labor of Black people implicated in forging the nation—men, women, and children whose presence was denied on Monument Avenue. I had taken my American studies students to see *Black Hair Flag* years earlier. Offering a sharp contrast to my students' experiences at the UDC, my students were inspired by Clark's piece. They took pride in her art as an act of cultural resistance, recognizing the careful and laborious work of producing not only the flag but also the nation. Clark reminded us that while indeed Confederate history was a part of American history, histories of race and of slavery in the United States were just as much a part of the Confederacy. It was a powerful critique of racial neoliberalism. The centrality of race, and by extension racism, Clark suggested, could not be denied in understanding national heritage.

As I took my seat toward the front left of the crowded auditorium, I looked around a sea of familiar faces. Several rows in front of me, surrounded by members of the Virginia Flaggers and other local Confederate heritage organizations, sat Susan Hathaway, the neo-Confederate Jeremiah whom I had seen make an impassioned call to protect Confederate heritage at Gus and George's Spaghetti and Steak House in Virginia Beach four years earlier. This time, rather than decrying the loss of "Carry Me Back to Old Virginia," she was holding a sign, like many around her, professing "No Context, No Compromise." The sign shared her resistance to the suggestion of any form of context added to Monument Avenue. Nearby sat Virginia Flaggers' photographer Judy Smith, who captured the photograph of me that had been captioned "Changing Hearts and Minds" on Facebook. In the years since that photograph was taken, neither my heart nor my mind had been changed. However, in undertaking this project, considering over time how neo-Confederates navigated national tragedy and disaster, articulations of virulent racism and hatred amid calls for change, I had come to realize that the Confederate past was not simply being relived but constantly reappropriated, reinterpreted, and reimagined as the consummate American project.

I looked behind me toward the other side of the room to see Teresa Roane, the archivist at the United Daughters of the Confederacy headquarters, as the living embodiment of this reappropriated and subsequently performed past. And I saw my colleagues, historians Ed Ayers, Julian Hayter, and Lauranett Lee, seated on stage as members of the

Monument Avenue Commission, along with commission cochair Gregg Kimball, director of education and outreach at the Library of Virginia, whom I would later meet while a Virginia Humanities Fellow at the Library the coming year.

Kimball began the event by asking audience members the questions directing the commission's charge. More than forty attendees were given the opportunity to speak, sharing their thoughts in two minutes or less, or so was the directive. The remaining audience was to listen. What materialized in practice over the next two hours was hardly so coordinated.

The tense scene, a *Richmond Times-Dispatch* article later noted, "border[ed] on chaotic." The article's author began, "So much for civility." The article captured my experiences in the audience. Impassioned participants voiced their responses. They ranged widely. One man approached the podium shouting, "You lost, get over it already, get rid of your participation trophies!"[12] It was a sentiment captured by a protest sign, "Fuck these statues," displayed weeks later by a counterprotester at the failed CSA II rally.

The side supporting the monuments, in situ, was just as adamant. As one woman claimed during the forum, "removing or changing the monument statues on Monument Avenue would be removing or changing history."[13] The crowd cheered and heckled, alternately clapped and booed. At various points, Kimball attempted to step in and quiet the raucous crowd but to little effect. It was, in the words of one community member, "theater of the absurd."[14] The day following the forum, Twitter exploded with commentary, including graphics of boxers coming to blows,[15] mock examples of "context,"[16] and the retweeted suggestion by *Richmond Times-Dispatch* columnist Michael Paul Williams that the panel was "veering toward dead end."[17] Shawn Cox, *Richmond Times-Dispatch* deputy news editor, retweeted Williams's column, noting, "[Mayor] Stoney tried to straddle fence on Monument Avenue, but the fence is now on fire #RVAmonuments."[18] Little did he know, fire would be more than a metaphor in nearby Charlottesville the next day as the tiki-torch march of white supremacists proceeded down the Lawn at "Mr. Jefferson's University."

As I anxiously looked around the auditorium listening to the polarized responses, my eyes were drawn to the flyer in the hands of the older white man sitting next to me. It was titled "Save Monument Avenue: Why We Oppose Any and ALL Attempts to Add Context to RVA's Confederate Monuments." The flyer, signed by the Virginia Flaggers, called its readers to entreat Mayor Stoney to invest city resources in schools and not to spend "thousands in taxpayer dollars on an unnecessary commission, and subsequent unnecessary signage."[19] While the plea to invest in underfunded city schools could hardly be disputed, the Flaggers' call offered, in the words of Michael Paul Williams, a "false dichotomy." Williams summarized, "It took decades for the schools to get this way, and ameliorating this situation is a long-term fix. And yet we hear constant talk that seems to suggest that the schools' fate will be sealed by statue removal."[20] As I read the Virginia Flaggers' flyer, I was confronted again with an argument that elided Richmond's history of racism and segregation. The flyer concluded, "True diversity is NOT achieved by destroying the history and heritage of one group of people in order to pacify another."[21] The perspective was summed up by the "No Context, No Compromise" signs held by Hathaway and others. Before it even began, the "conversation" was destined to fail. "No Context, No Compromise" was a nonstarter.

The Flaggers' flyer echoed the words that would be spoken weeks later at the failed CSA II rally. At once protesting for the "protection" of Monument Avenue, a call for the maintenance of the famous thoroughfare as a habitat diorama, members of CSA II situated themselves as part of a silenced minority, an irony that became only more pronounced as one member displayed a cardboard sign draped around his neck that stated "I Support Trump." The protester was not claiming kinship with some fringe ideologue but rather with the president of the United States. While the "protection" of the Lee monument was the immediate stated motivation for the rally, CSA II's arrival in Richmond was about more than Confederate statues. It was about the future of the neo-Confederate museum and the principles underpinning it.

This rhetoric of white victimhood, however, has nonetheless found purchase in the contemporary political landscape. It is an appeal similarly seized by neo-Confederate sweetheart Corey Stewart, who ran for the governorship of Virginia in 2017, narrowly losing the Republican nomination to Ed Gillespie. Stewart later went on to win the Republican primary for senate—to face off unsuccessfully with incumbent Democrat Tim Kaine in November 2018. Stewart is the chair of the Prince William County Board of Supervisors and previously served on President Trump's campaign team, a post from which he was later fired.

Stewart's passionate speech regarding the necessity of preserving Confederate history, made during an "Old South" ball hosted by a secessionist in April 2017, placed the Minnesota native on the Tea Party map, garnering him the support of the neo-Confederate group Save Southern Heritage.[22] Standing before a crowd of Confederate heritage supporters in period dress, Stewart made a gamble in an attempt to raise funds readily accessible to his wealthier opponents.[23] Stewart sought to represent the "average" American by appealing to a romanticized past. Following

Stewart's public display, he was endorsed as a viable candidate from the Virginia Flaggers' Twitter account. Stewart's gamble paid off, at least to a point. After winning the Republican primary in Virginia, he continued to declare his pride in Virginia's "history"—the state of not only founding fathers George Washington and Thomas Jefferson but also of Confederate leaders Robert E. Lee and Stonewall Jackson. For Stewart, Virginians "think for ourselves. And if the established order is wrong, we rebel. We did it in the Revolution, we did it in the Civil War, and we're doing it today. We're doing it today because they're trying to rob us of everything that we hold dear: our history, our heritage, our culture."[24] One month after his sixteen-point defeat by Tim Kaine, however, Stewart announced he would step back from statewide politics for "a couple of years at least."[25] By January 2019 the brash Virginia Republican told the *Washington Post*, "Politics sucks" and said he was "leaving politics 'until and unless the Commonwealth is ready' for his views."[26]

The neo-Confederate museum, which political leaders such as Corey Stewart seek so desperately to preserve, enacts a particular script, costuming, and performance, whether part of the CSA II protest in September 2017 (and then later in December 2017, May 2018, and August 2018), a Sons of Confederate veterans parade, or the Virginia Flaggers on the streets.

While trading in a sense of southern gentility, of kindness and hospitality, neo-Confederates tie their legitimacy to what they claim is an apolitical version of history. This history is devoid of "liberal" politics and vilifies talk of race and racism, anchoring itself to calls for "truth" and "education." It is a constructed historical memory rooted in more fiction than fact—one that celebrates Black Confederates while it forsakes race as a concept structuring experience. The familiar script is articulated in speech as well as materially on the body. The members of CSA II held a Confederate battle flag with the words "Learn the Truth and You Will Not Be Offended" written on the front during the September 16, 2017, rally. A T-shirt worn by a CSA II protester stated those same words. At face value, the statement is not inherently problematic or inflammatory. Yet the "truth" to which they refer is not a truth grounded in empirical fact. Rather, it is a constructed "truth" communicated ritually.

Neo-Confederates make no claim to formal education. In fact, it is this education that they shun, claiming it seeks to dilute history with political correctness. It is, I assume, why I was received initially by the Virginia Flaggers with such disdain. I work for an institution, the University of Richmond, seen as part of the liberal machine, populated by academics who have sought to ensure that history acknowledges the centrality of slavery to the story of the American Civil War. This is a point that has drawn the continued ire of neo-Confederates.

This hostility to formalized education was articulated boldly during the Monument Avenue Commission forum. One speaker noted, "I will request . . . [that] commission not be run by African American 101 class but be run with all opinions from all sides." Not only did this comment foreshadow what would be President Trump's response to the violence in Charlottesville days later; it also mocked a sense that knowledge was tethered to a course—specifically an African American history course. A curriculum, and in particular a curriculum that foregrounded histories of race, did not qualify as "true" history from the speaker's perspective. Another speaker, quoting Proverbs 22:28, said, "Who are you to publicly contextualize or judge Maury, Lee, Stuart, Jackson and President Davis monuments?"[27] In this way, speakers criticized the commission members, whose authority was intimately connected to their training as historians, for not wielding "true" knowledge, born from experience living Confederate memory.

Yet if neo-Confederate authority was not derived from scholarly knowledge, it was knowledge gained through culture. It may or may not be gained through birth—through Confederate ancestry and, as many shared with me, oral traditions. As the visible case of Corey Stewart demonstrates, this knowledge could be embraced rhetorically, whether by inscribing Confederate icons on the body or by espousing the necessity of preserving "heritage" as marked by symbols (i.e., Confederate battle flag, monuments).

During the Monument Avenue Commission forum, speakers appealed not as "experts" but rather as individuals with familial connections to the Confederacy or as Monument Avenue residents fearing the decline in property values should the monuments be removed. The neo-Confederate commenters were not trained historians but rather positioned themselves as outsiders whose perspectives were tainted by neither political correctness nor the agendas of liberals.

This perspective was crystallized by Henry Kidd, a lifelong Colonial Heights resident and former Virginia Division Commander of the Sons of Confederate Veterans. Kidd stated before the Monument Avenue Commission, "When it comes to Confederates, all I hear is discrimination. I look up here at this council now, and I see you have no moral guidance, no heart. I see a bunch of historians and people that are picking and choosing history, not telling a full history."[28] Kidd's critique, echoing the arguments made in each of the contexts I have explored within this book, locates neo-Confederates as victims, discriminated against and marginalized. Despite their status as a moral compass, at least according to Kidd, they are repeatedly shunned in public—at least by their more politically progressive counterparts. This "discrimination," in his words, is borne out in calls for the contextualization of Monument Avenue.

When I spoke with Karen Cooper, the infamous Black Flagger, in 2014 regarding her claim that the Confederacy did not fight to preserve slavery,[29] she replied, "I didn't do too much research. I used my brain, the brain that God gave me . . . I just thought wow. Did the South really fight to keep their slaves? And I was like well . . . most of the South didn't even have slaves."[30] For Cooper, education need not be learned in the classroom. Knowledge is something one can intuit.

Such performances have earned neo-Confederates ridicule from their opposition. Several weeks after the handful of CSA II members descended on Monument Avenue in September 2017, Richmond's "local provocateur" Goad KC[31] used Facebook to plan a semisatirical event titled "Yell at the Lee Statue While Drinking Out of a Container in a Brown Bag." It was to be precisely what the event's title suggested.

On Monday, October 23, 2017, at 2 p.m., when about thirty protesters joined Goad at the Lee Circle, where the monument stands tall, the mood was considerably lighter than it had been the morning of the September CSA II rally. Citing the city's lack of action—and specifically the postponement of Mayor Stoney's Monument Avenue Commission's second public forum to discuss the future of Richmond's Confederate monuments, Goad stated, "We are completely powerless over this right now, and it's really frustrating! Which is why I held an event, it's about yelling at it."[32]

Using public space in order to protest the promotion of so-called Confederate heritage was not a new tactic for Goad, orchestrator of the anti-Flagger protest outside the Virginia Museum of Fine Arts, otherwise known as the Anti-Confederate Rap Battle.[33]

The Limits of the Neo-Confederate Museum

While those who advocate to preserve Monument Avenue in situ (without context) claim to hail from a variety of political perspectives, I suggest here that there is a fundamental thread connecting such claims: a sense that the meaning of the monuments is, at present, transparent and readily accessible to the public. Like the museum curators who assumed the diorama's meanings were readily visible to visitors, neo-Confederates presume a certain legibility to Monument Avenue that stands divorced from the period and politics of its construction, a contemporary diorama. The "history" neo-Confederates invoke pays no attention to the Jim Crow era or the implications of this period in the disenfranchisement and terrorism of Black people. It is a past and present that continue to celebrate Little Sorrel and Traveller with children's books narrating the story of the horses' contributions to a cause bigger than themselves.[34]

The monuments lining Monument Avenue memorializing the Lost Cause are imposing, towering over passersby. They communicate reverence for the Confederacy and those who fought on its behalf. Those advocating for the status quo know this, of course, and claim that efforts to add context to the stretch of land evidences a broader silencing of history—of attempts to marginalize their voices. These advocates claim, like members of the Tea Party, that they are made outsiders by the dominant political culture.

For neo-Confederates, the goal is really not to upset the status quo but rather to reinforce it. While situating themselves as victims, claiming the Confederacy as an endangered species and its habitat, in Monument Avenue, in need of protection, neo-Confederates attack the very political system they support and that ultimately continues to support them. They are the embodiment of the exceptionalist frame and its concomitant nostalgia. Despite their commitment to a vanquished entity, neo-Confederates continue to assert not only the Confederacy's continued relevance but also its superiority. The Confederacy, in this cast, is the truest version of Americanism.

This frame of Confederate exceptionalism, as this book has argued, persists both on and in the landscape—the neo-Confederate museum. It is at times grandiose and in other cases fairly unobtrusive, nonetheless capitalizing on the expectations surrounding the museum to which we have been socialized. As historian Susan Crane notes, "We learn how to behave in museums, what to expect from them, what to buy, and how to remember the occasion." The museum "instill[s] the value of art, the past, and science."[35] It serves to create a set of shared understandings, of collective memory.

From my office at the Library of Virginia, I was able to walk two blocks into the Medical College of Virginia (MCV) to observe the Jefferson Davis Memorial Chapel on the seventeenth floor. The chapel was "dedicated with affection and reverence by the United Daughters of the Confederacy" in 1960.[36] A plaque commemorating the "American patriot and president of the Confederate states, a virtuous and resolute man whose creed was exemplified in his life of duty, honor, sacrifice" praises Davis as "a possession of the entire nation and the immortal future, a valiant figure for youth to emulate."[37] While there is a Move On petition to "Rename the Jefferson Davis Memorial Chapel at VCUHS/MCV," the chapel is one of the lesser-known commemorative sites of Confederate memory in the city.[38] Monument Avenue has attracted far and away the greatest attention.

At the same time, Richmond seems to be turning a corner, suggesting that the existing myth might be undergoing revision. In November 2018 voters elected Democrat Ralph Northam as Virginia's governor in a contest against Republican Ed Gillespie. Among Northam voters, 62 percent supported removing Confederate monuments from public spaces.[39] While 86 percent of Ed Gillespie's supporters opposed removing Confederate monuments, Northam's victory suggests that perhaps Virginians are willing to come to grips, at least in part, with the history inscribed on the landscape. This was borne out in the data supplied by the report of the Monument Avenue Commission, released in July 2018. Overwhelmingly, Richmonders were supportive of *some* action that moved beyond leaving the monuments on Monument Avenue in situ.[40] This willingness to engage with the past was also affirmed with broad calls for Northam's resignation in early February 2019 after his medical school yearbook surfaced. The governor's yearbook page featured a photograph of two men, one dressed in a KKK robe and the other in blackface, along with Northam's racist nickname. While Northam remained in office, one week following news of the yearbook scandal the Richmond city council voted to rename the Boulevard, home of the UDC, VMFA, and Virginia Museum of History and Culture, after Arthur Ashe. Progress is neither linear nor absolute.

Despite public acknowledgment that histories of racism should be not only identified but also addressed in the present, how this reckoning is to take place remains a point of contest. The announcement by popular amusement park Kings Dominion of the renaming of the historic roller coaster "The Rebel Yell" in February 2018 elicited strong responses. While the park's public relations staff were circumspect about the reasons for the name change, the announcement drew more than 150 comments on the Kings Dominion Facebook page. Edwin Ray, an officer of the Virginia Division of the Sons of Confederate Veterans stated in response, "We're disappointed that they are falling in step with the political correctness bandwagon."[41] Memory of the Confederacy continues to divide.

This was seen in responses to the July 2018 report of the Monument Avenue Commission. While recommending removal of the Jefferson Davis statue, the monument that most explicitly asserts Lost Cause ideology, the commission acknowledged the legal difficulties likely to ensue. Concerns were immediately expressed that the statues, as war memorials, would be protected by the state. Context remains the most viable option at present along with alternate ways of reimagining the space through public art.[42]

Following the first anniversary of the deadly violence in Charlottesville, ignited by a white supremacist Unite the Right rally, I recalled my experience, standing outside Mixed Greens Gallery in the Chelsea neighborhood of New York City, staring at a Confederate battle flag made visible from the street. The sight of the iconic and embattled emblem would have been jarring on a New York sidewalk even had it not been days following Dylann Roof's deadly rampage. Yet this particular flag had a story. Part of artist Sonya Clark's latest installation, the Confederate battle flag in question was in the process of *Unraveling*, as Clark and volunteers pulled apart the flag's cotton threads.

An active and arduous process of the radical historical deconstruction of a racist past, "a perfect metaphor for the project of combatting white supremacy,"[43] as Emily Elizabeth Goodman wrote for the art website Hyperallergic, the piece visualized the necessary labor involved in loosening the tightly woven stitches. Accompanying *Unraveling* was *Unraveled*, visible inside the Chelsea gallery, featuring three tidy piles of red, white, and blue thread—piles that once were woven into the aforementioned symbol of the Confederacy. On June 20, 2015, they sat peacefully on a shelf.

Amid the quiet of the New York art gallery, I considered the possibility of those red, white, and blue piles of thread. Stripped of their historical association with the Confederacy, the fibers could be woven into a new pattern. Yet, just as easily, those piles could be woven to resurrect the contested symbol they had once composed—the very symbol the men and women I had been studying across Virginia sought desperately to valorize. Unraveling the myth of Confederate exceptionalism is more than a metaphor. Clark's work reminds us of the physical, emotional, and symbolic labor involved in such an extensive task.

In January 2019 a book appeared in my mailbox at the University of Richmond. Sent to me by H. V. Traywick Jr., a graduate of Virginia Military Institute, member of the Sons of Confederate Veterans, and the book's author, *The Monumental Truth: Five Essays on Confederate Monuments in the Age of Progressive Identity Politics* was intended to offer "some perspective" on my "support of vandalism."[44] The book attempts to correct the historical record by claiming that "the [American Civil] war was not the South's war to defend slavery . . . but Lincoln's war to prevent Confederate independence."[45]

At first glance, Traywick's slim book might seem to suggest a simple reinvigoration of late nineteenth-century Lost Cause mythology, reiterating the adage, often quoted by neo-Confederates, that the victors write history. Traywick argues that what we have seen in recent years are "attacks on Confederate monuments honoring men who defended our homeland against invasion, conquest, and a coerced political allegiance—just as their fathers had done in 1776 when the thirteen slave-holding Colonies—from Georgia to Massachusetts—seceded from the British empire."[46] Such a claim could just as easily be cited as evidence of American exceptionalism's alignment with the Lost Cause's validation of the Confederacy as a movement for liberation.

Beyond merely invoking two dominant strands of American ideology, the book updates them by taking aim at a twenty-first-century target—so-called progressives. For Traywick, the "monumental truth" is that "these attacks [on Confederate monuments] have nothing to do with the truth and everything to do with Progressive virtue-posting and their divide-and-rule identity politics."[47] Invoking "identity politics" as a pejorative substitute for discourses of race and racism, Traywick articulates Confederate exceptionalism's call to antiracialism and its efforts to engage in a form of historical amnesia. His book propagates the myth of the Confederacy as an entity under attack and whiteness its unspoken victim. While Traywick is correct that the removal of monuments will not "fix" national racial division, the "monumental truth" is that the legacies of racial oppression require more than a neoliberal claim that race is a threat in twenty-first-century America.

Richmond's new and long-awaited American Civil War Museum is envisioned as the antidote to this Confederate exceptionalist frame. The product of the 2013 merger between the American Civil War Center and the Museum of the Confederacy, the museum, which opened to the general public on May 4, 2019, is already being heralded for its work in "redefin[ing] the war's legacy as perpetually bound to our always-fraught present." Focusing on a truthful rendering of history, the museum seeks to distance itself from the tradition of mythmaking with which the Civil War is intimately connected. Critics have praised the museum's bold move to "reflect a divided, fragmented nation that altogether qualifies as a kind of conceptual artwork"[48] along with "surprising" choices like the colorization of historic photographs.[49]

The museum deploys history in an attempt to disrupt deep-seated myths—to trouble expectations—or at least that is its goal.[50] This is, of course, a great risk with profound implications for the future of the neo-Confederate museum. As I walked through the crowded galleries on opening day, I observed as visitors navigated the space's emotional pull, peering intently into exhibit cases at eye level and beneath ground, engaging with men and women in period clothing, and touching the many interactive screens available to curious tourists. I wondered about the stories with which these experiences would collide and how visitors would respond. Days following the museum's grand opening, it is too soon to tell, but given the life-and-death stakes, the work of educating minds and changing hearts could not be more imperative.

May 2019

Notes

A Note on Language Usage

1. See Kimberlé Crenshaw, "Mapping the Margins: Intersectionality, Identity Politics, and Violence against Women of Color," *Stanford Law Review* 43, no. 6 (1991): 1244n6 for Crenshaw's explanation of why she capitalizes "Black." See also Lori L. Tharps, "The Case for Black with a Capital B," *New York Times*, November 18, 2014, https://www.nytimes.com/2014/11/19/opinion/the-case-for-black-with-a-capital -b.html?gwh=E0361179FB2DC6C09F9C64D85954AAEF&gwt=pay&assetType=opi nion.

2. See the "Note on Usage" in Martha Biondi, *To Stand and Fight: The Struggle for Civil Rights in Postwar New York City* (Cambridge, MA: Harvard University Press, 2003).

3. Merrill Perlman, "Black and White: Why Capitalization Matters," *Columbia Journalism Review*, June 23, 2015, https://www.cjr.org/analysis/language_corner_1 .php.

4. P. Gabrielle Foreman et al., "Writing about Slavery/Teaching about Slavery: This Might Help," community-sourced document, May 2, 2019, https://docs .google.com/document/d/1A4TEdDgYslX-hlKezLodMIM71My3KTNozxRvoIQ TOQs/mobilebasic.

5. I refrain from using the term "blacks" in favor of "Black people," following the style guide of the National Association of Black Journalists. See "African, African American, black," https://www.nabj.org/page/styleguideA.

Preface: Confederates on My Corner

1. According to the University of Virginia website, "Grounds" is "the term used by generations of students, faculty, and alumni to refer to the University, rather than 'Campus.'" "Students & Traditions," https://odos.virginia.edu/students-traditions.

2. For more on massive resistance, see James H. Hershman Jr., "Massive Resistance," *Encyclopedia Virginia*, last modified June 29, 2011, https://www.encyclope diavirginia.org/massive_resistance.

3. On the formulation of these images, described, in part, as the "moonlight and magnolias" tradition, see Tara McPherson, *Reconstructing Dixie: Race, Gender, and Nostalgia in the Imagined South* (Durham, NC: Duke University Press, 2003), and Karen L. Cox, *Dreaming of Dixie: How the South Was Created in American Popular Culture* (Chapel Hill: University of North Carolina Press, 2011).

4. On these images of the South internalized predominantly by middle- and upper-class northerners, see Nina Silber, *The Romance of Reunion: Northerners and the South, 1865–1900* (Chapel Hill: University of North Carolina Press, 1993).

5. Tony Horwitz, *Confederates in the Attic: Dispatches from the Unfinished Civil War* (New York: Pantheon, 1998).

6. "Who Are the VA Flaggers?" Virginia Flaggers, http://vaflaggers.blogspot.com/.

7. See Annette Gordon-Reed's important work on this topic in *Thomas Jefferson and Sally Hemings: An American Controversy* (Charlottesville: University of Virginia Press, 1997).

8. Goad Gatsby is also known as "Goad KC" on social media.

9. Harmeet Kaur, "Kanye West Just Said 400 Years of Slavery Was a Choice," *CNN*, May 4, 2018, https://www.cnn.com/2018/05/01/entertainment/kanye -west-slavery-choice-trnd/index.html.

10. I will call the association with President Obama "liberalism," though surveys of neo-Confederate literature would suggest that the term "socialism" would be the term used by the Flaggers.

11. See Michelle Alexander, *The New Jim Crow: Mass Incarceration in the Age of Colorblindness* (New York: New Press, 2010).

12. Langston Hughes, "One-Way Ticket," accessed March 31, 2019, http:// nationalhumanitiescenter.org/ows/seminars/tcentury/gmigration/Hughes_One WayTicket.pdf.

13. Matthew D. Lassiter and Joseph Crespino, "Introduction," in *The Myth of Southern Exceptionalism*, ed. Matthew D. Lassiter and Joseph Crespino (New York: Oxford University Press, 2010), 5.

14. C. Vann Woodward, *The Burden of Southern History* (Baton Rouge: Louisiana State University Press, 1960), 3–26, 167–191, summarized in James M. McPherson, "Antebellum Southern Exceptionalism: A New Look at an Old Question," *Civil War History* 50, no. 4 (2004): 431. On southern identity and the contests surrounding the concept of southern exceptionalism, see James C. Cobb, *Away Down South: A History of Southern Identity* (New York: Oxford University Press, 2005), and McPherson, "Antebellum Southern Exceptionalism," 418–433. A more recent attempt to deconstruct the concept of southern exceptionalism can be seen in Lassiter and Crespino, *Myth of Southern Exceptionalism*.

15. This is a point made as well in Lassiter and Crespino, *Myth of Southern Exceptionalism*, 29–30.

16. Robert Sullivan, "It's Hard to Get Rid of a Confederate Memorial in New York City," *New Yorker*, August 23, 2017, https://www.newyorker.com/culture/cul ture-desk/its-hard-to-get-rid-of-a-confederate-memorial-in-new-york-city.

17. Karen L. Cox defines "Confederate culture" as "those ideas and symbols that Lost Cause devotees associated with the former Confederacy" in *Dixie's Daughters: The United Daughters of the Confederacy and the Preservation of Confederate Culture* (Tallahassee: University of Florida Press, 2003), 1.

18. Lisa A. Flores and Christy-Dale L. Sims, "The Zero-Sum Game of Race and the Familiar Strangeness of President Obama," *Southern Communication Journal* 81, no. 4 (2016): 209, italics in original.

19. This is a point made in Peter Ehrenhaus, "Silence and Symbolic Expression," *Communication Monographs* 55, no. 1 (1988): 41–57.

20. Monique Calello, "As Richmond's Confederate Statues Go, So Might the South's," *USA Today*, February 11, 2018, https://www.usatoday.com/story/news /nation-now/2018/02/11/black-history-month-richmond-confederate-statues /1001960001/.

Introduction: History, the Museum, and Confederate Exceptionalism

1. These were the three participant groups identified by the center. See "Exhibits at Historic Tredegar: In the Cause of Liberty," American Civil War Center, accessed January 23, 2014, https://acwm.org/visit-us/exhibits/historic-tredegar-exhibits.

2. Emory Thomas, "American Civil War Center Tells Stories from All Sides," *Richmond Times-Dispatch*, October 1, 2006, E-1; John Motley, "U.S. Citizens Can Learn from Nation's Prior Struggles," *Richmond Times-Dispatch*, October 1, 2006, E-1.

3. The American Civil War Center at Historic Tredegar, The Center, accessed January 23, 2014, http://www.tredegar.org. This link is no longer publicly accessible.

4. Editorial, "Reconciliation," *Richmond Times-Dispatch*, October 7, 2006, A-10.

5. Associated Press, "James Alex Fields' Trial in Deadly Charlottesville White Nationalist Rally Set to Begin," NBC News, November 26, 2018, https://www.nbcnews .com/news/us-news/james-alex-fields-trial-deadly-charlottesville-white-nationalist -rally-set-n939991.

6. Matt Thompson, "The Hoods Are Off," *Atlantic*, August 12, 2017, https:// www.theatlantic.com/national/archive/2017/08/the-hoods-are-off/536694/.

7. Virginia Flaggers, "Message from Michael Givens Scv," Facebook, June 21, 2015, https://www.facebook.com/The-Virginia-Flaggers-378823865585630/.

8. The phrase "confederate exceptionalism" has been previously used by historian Kevin Levin in a May 2015 blog post which describes the conflation of Confederate camp servants and soldiers. See Kevin Levin, "Camp Servants and Confederate Exceptionalism," *Civil War Memory*, May 31, 2015, http://cwmemory .com/2015/05/31/camp-servants-and-confederate-exceptionalism/.

9. Alan T. Nolan provides an excellent overview of the Lost Cause in "The Anatomy of the Myth," in *The Myth of the Lost Cause and Civil War History*, ed. Gary W. Gallagher and Alan T. Nolan (Bloomington: Indiana University Press, 2000), 11–34.

10. Darrel Enck-Wanzer, "Barack Obama, the Tea Party, and the Threat of Race: On Racial Neoliberalism and Born Again Racism," *Communication, Culture and Critique* 4, no. 1 (2011): 24.

11. Lisa A. Flores and Christy-Dale L. Sims, "The Zero-Sum Game of Race and the Familiar Strangeness of President Obama," *Southern Communication Journal* 81, no. 4 (2016): 209.

12. David Theo Goldberg, *The Threat of Race: Reflections on Racial Neoliberalism* (Malden, MA: Blackwell Publishing, 2009), 21.

13. Goldberg, *Threat of Race*, 5, 10, 21, 360, 22.

14. Euan Hague, Edward H. Sebesta, and Heidi Beirich, "Introduction: Neo-Confederacy and the New Dixie Manifesto," in *Neo-Confederacy: A Critical Introduction*, ed. Euan Hague, Heidi Beirich, and Edward H. Sebesta with foreword by James W. Loewen (Austin: University of Texas Press, 2008), 9.

15. "Neo-Confederate," Southern Poverty Law Center, n.d., accessed March

31, 2019, https://www.splcenter.org/fighting-hate/extremist-files/ideology/neo -confederate.

16. This point is made in Hague et al., "Introduction," 1–2.

17. Michael Hill and Thomas Fleming, "The New Dixie Manifesto: States' Rights Shall Rise Again," *Washington Post*, October 29, 1995, C3.

18. "Neo-Confederate," SPLC.

19. On the status of the "culture wars," see Andrew Hartman, "The Culture Wars Are Dead," Baffler, May 2018, https://thebaffler.com/outbursts/culture-wars-are -dead-hartman.

20. Billig argues that "in the established nations, there is a continual 'flagging,' or reminding, of nationhood" that fosters "banal nationalism." Particularly important to this study is Billig's claim that "the metonymic image of banal nationalism is not a flag which is being consciously waved with fervent passion; it is the flag hanging unnoticed on the public building." Michael Billig, *Banal Nationalism* (London: Sage, 1995), 8.

21. On the historic antagonism between history and memory, see, for instance, Pierre Nora, "Between Memory and History: Les Lieux de Mémoire," *Representations* 26 (Spring 1989): 7–24.

22. David W. Blight, "If You Don't Tell It Like It Was, It Can Never Be as It Ought to Be," in *Slavery and Public History: The Tough Stuff of American Memory*, ed. James Oliver Horton and Lois E. Horton (Chapel Hill: University of North Carolina Press, 2006), 24.

23. See Barbara A. Gannon, *Americans Remember Their Civil War* (Santa Barbara: Praeger, 2017), xiii–xv; Edward S. Casey, "Public Memory in Place and Time," in *Framing Public Memory*, ed. Kendall Philipps (Tuscaloosa: University of Alabama Press, 2004), 20–32. For more on the concept of collective memory, see Maurice Halbwachs, *On Collective Memory*, trans. Louis A. Coser (Chicago: University of Chicago Press, 1992).

24. For Kitch's discussion of the term and rationale for employing it, see Carolyn Kitch, *Pennsylvania in Public Memory: Reclaiming the Industrial Past* (University Park: Pennsylvania State University Press, 2012), 7–12.

25. Casey, "Public Memory," 37.

26. On myth, see Bronislaw Malinowski, *Magic, Science and Religion and Other Essays* (Prospect Heights, IL: Waveland, 1942/1992); Jack Lule, *Daily News, Eternal Stories: The Mythological Role of Journalism* (New York: Guilford, 2001); Donald Pease, *The New American Exceptionalism* (Minneapolis: University of Minnesota Press, 2009), 5.

27. Lule, *Daily News*, 18.

28. Lule, *Daily News*, 21–25.

29. Marie Tyler-McGraw, "Southern Comfort Levels: Race, Heritage Tourism, and the Civil War in Richmond," in Horton and Horton, *Slavery and Public History*, 153.

30. Cynthia Mills, "Introduction," in *Monuments to the Lost Cause: Women, Arts, and the Landscapes of Southern Memory*, ed. Cynthia Mills and Pamela H. Simpson (Knoxville: University of Tennessee Press, 2003), xvii.

31. Gary W. Gallagher, "Introduction," in Gallagher and Nolan, *Myth of the Lost Cause*, 4.

32. David W. Blight, *Race and Reunion: The Civil War in American Memory* (Cambridge, MA: Harvard University Press, 2002), 284.

33. Blight, *Race and Reunion*, 284.

34. "Gray Warriors Extolled by Grandson of Leader," *Atlanta Constitution*, April 27, 1911, quoted in Blight, *Race and Reunion*, 283.

35. Blight, *Race and Reunion*, 283.

36. See Karen L. Cox, *Dixie's Daughters: The United Daughters of the Confederacy and the Preservation of Confederate Culture* (Tallahassee: University of Florida Press, 2003); Amy Heyse, "Women's Rhetorical Authority and Collective Memory: The United Daughters of the Confederacy Remember the South," *Women and Language* 33, no. 2 (2010): 31–53; Caroline E. Janney, *Burying the Dead but Not the Past: Ladies' Memorial Associations and the Lost Cause* (Chapel Hill: University of North Carolina Press, 2008).

37. Gallagher, "Introduction," 44.

38. Pease, *New American Exceptionalism*, 7.

39. Donald E. Pease, "Exceptionalism," in *Keywords for American Cultural Studies*, ed. Bruce Burgett and Glenn Hendler (New York: New York University Press, 2007), 109, 111.

40. Pease, *New American Exceptionalism*, 8.

41. Pease, *New American Exceptionalism*, 8.

42. Pease, "Exceptionalism," 110, 111.

43. Pease, *New American Exceptionalism*, 9.

44. Roberts and Mahtani cited in Flores and Sims, "Zero-Sum Game," 209.

45. Monroe Billington, ed. *The South: A Central Theme?* (Huntington, NY: Krieger, 1978), 1, quoted in James McPherson, "Antebellum Southern Exceptionalism: A New Look at an Old Question," *Civil War History* 1, no. 4 (2004): 418–419.

46. W. J. Cash, *The Mind of the South* (New York: A. A. Knopf, 1941), ix.

47. Dwight Garner, "Pulp Valentine: Erskine Caldwell's Lurid Vision of the American South," *Slate*, May 24, 2006, http://www.slate.com/articles/news_and _politics/pulp_fiction/2006/05/pulp_valentine_2.html.

48. "Poor Whites," *Photos in Black and White: Margaret Bourke-White and the Dawn of Apartheid in South Africa*, https://bourkewhite.wordpress.com/galleries/afrikaners /poor-whites/.

49. Franklin Delano Roosevelt Message, Franklin Delano Roosevelt Library, OF 788, Box 3, italics added, quoted in William E. Leuchtenburg, *The White House Looks South: Franklin D. Roosevelt, Harry S. Truman, Lyndon B. Johnson* (Baton Rouge: Louisiana State University Press, 2005), 104.

50. Robert Penn Warren, *The Legacy of the Civil War* (Lincoln: UNP–Bison Books, 1998), ProQuest Ebook Central, 28.

51. Peter Applebome, *Dixie Rising: How the South Is Shaping American Values, Politics, and Culture* (New York: Times Books, 1996), 10.

52. Lochlainn Seabrook, *Give This Book to a Yankee: A Southern Guide to the Civil War for Northerners* (Spring Hill, TN: Sea Raven Press, 2014), 12.

53. Seabrook, *Give This Book to a Yankee*, 12.

54. Seabrook, *Give This Book to a Yankee*, 8.

55. On the history of the Confederate battle flag, see John M. Coski, *The Confederate Battle Flag: America's Most Embattled Emblem* (Cambridge, MA: Harvard University Press, 2005); Robert E. Bonner, *Colors and Blood: Flag Passions of the Confederate South* (Princeton, NJ: Princeton University Press, 2002). On the contests surrounding the flag in South Carolina specifically, see K. Michael Prince, *Rally 'Round the Flag, Boys!*

South Carolina and the Confederate Flag (Columbia: University of South Carolina Press, 2004).

56. Rick Hampson, "Confederate Monuments, More than 700 across USA, Aren't Budging," *USA Today*, May 22, 2017, https://www.usatoday.com/story/news /politics/2017/05/22/confederate-monuments-new-orleans-charlottesville-re moval-race-civil-war/101870418/.

57. Gannon, *Americans Remember Their Civil War*, xvi.

58. See, for instance, Blight, *Race and Reunion*; W. Fitzhugh Brundage, *The Southern Past: A Clash of Race and Memory* (Cambridge, MA: Harvard University Press, 2008); Cox, *Dixie's Daughters*; William C. Davis, *The Cause Lost: Myths and Realities of the Confederacy* (Lawrence: University Press of Kansas, 1996); Gaines M. Foster, *Ghosts of the Confederacy: Defeat, the Lost Cause, and the Emergence of the New South, 1865–1913* (New York: Oxford University Press, 1988); Gallagher and Nolan, *Myth of the Lost Cause*; Janney, *Burying the Dead*; Mills and Simpson, *Monuments to the Lost Cause*; Charles Reagan Wilson, *Baptized in Blood: The Religion of the Lost Cause, 1865–1920* (Athens: University of Georgia Press, 2009).

59. Caroline E. Janney, *Remembering the Civil War: Reunion and the Limits of Reconciliation* (Chapel Hill: University of North Carolina Press, 2013), 10. Here Janney draws on Blight's framework in *Race and Reunion*.

60. See, for instance, Robert J. Cook, *Troubled Commemoration: The American Civil War Centennial, 1961–1965* (Baton Rouge: Louisiana State University Press, 2007); Karen L. Cox, *Dreaming of Dixie: How the South Was Created in American Popular Culture* (Chapel Hill: University of North Carolina Press, 2011); Gary W. Gallagher, *Causes Won, Lost, and Forgotten: How Hollywood and Popular Art Shape What We Know About the Civil War* (Chapel Hill: University of North Carolina Press, 2008); Carol Sheriff, "Virginia's Embattled Textbooks: Lessons (Learned and Not) from the Centennial Era," *Civil War History* 58, no. 1 (2012): 37–74.

61. For a national visualization of these trends, see Southern Poverty Law Center (SPLC) Report, "Whose Heritage? Public Symbols of the Confederacy," April 21, 2016, https://www.splcenter.org/20160421/whose-heritage-public-symbols-confed eracy#findings.

62. According to the Southern Poverty Law Center, at least 39 of the 109 public schools named after prominent Confederates were built or dedicated between 1950 and 1970. "Whose Heritage? Public Symbols of the Confederacy," April 21, 2016, 10, https://www.splcenter.org/sites/default/files/com_whose_heritage.pdf.

63. Eugene Scott, "Nikki Haley: Confederate Flag 'Should Have Never Been There,'" CNN, July 10, 2015, http://www.cnn.com/2015/07/10/politics/nikki -haley-confederate-flag-removal/index.html.

64. Mitch Landrieu, "'We Can't Walk Away from This Truth,'" *Atlantic*, May 23, 2017, https://www.theatlantic.com/politics/archive/2017/05/we-cant-walk-away -from-this-truth/527721/.

65. See, for instance, Fenit Nirappil, "Baltimore Hauls Away Four Confederate Monuments after Overnight Removal," *Washington Post*, August 16, 2017, https:// www.washingtonpost.com/local/md-politics/baltimore-begins-taking-down-con federate-statues/2017/08/16/f32aa26e-8265-11e7-b359-15a3617c767b_story .html?noredirect=on&utm_term=.961efca114dd; Chris Perez, "Robert E. Lee Me-

morial in Brooklyn to Be Taken Down," *New York Post*, August 15, 2017, http://nypost.com/2017/08/15/robert-e-lee-memorial-in-brooklyn-to-be-taken-down/.

66. See "All School Name Changes by State and Year," Southern Poverty Law Center, n.d., accessed March 31, 2019, https://www.splcenter.org/20180604/whose-heritage-public-symbols-confederacy.

67. See, for instance, Steven Hoelscher, "'Where the Old South Still Lives': Displaying Heritage in Natchez, Mississippi," in *Southern Heritage on Display: Public Ritual and Ethnic Diversity Within Southern Regionalism*, ed. Celeste Ray (Tuscaloosa: University of Alabama Press, 2003), 218–250.

68. "Teen Sues School District over Confederate Flag Prom Dress," Wave3 News, December 21, 2004, http://www.wave3.com/story/2719135/teen-sues-school-district-over-confederate-flag-prom-dress.

69. "Student Settles over Confederate dress," *USA Today*, February 28, 2006, https://usatoday30.usatoday.com/news/nation/2006-02-28-confederate-dress_x.htm.

70. Ed Mazza, "Confederate Flag Prom Photo with Gun-Toting High Schoolers Backfires," HuffPost, May 6, 2015, http://www.huffingtonpost.com/2015/05/06/confederate-flag-prom-photo_n_7219802.html.

71. Halle Kiefer, "HBO Issues a Statement Addressing #NoConfederate Protest Against Upcoming Drama," Vulture, July 30, 2017, https://www.vulture.com/2017/07/hbo-issues-statement-addressing-noconfederate-protest.html.

72. Halle Kiefer, "HBO's *Confederate* Delay Allegedly not Due to Controversy, but Rather Extreme Busyness," Vulture, February 8, 2019, https://www.vulture.com/2019/02/hbos-confederate-delay-reportedly-not-due-to-controversy.html.

73. John V. Moeser, "Introduction," in *A Virginia Profile, 1960–2000*, ed. John V. Moeser (Palisades Park, NJ: Commonwealth Books, 1981), ix.

74. David Treadwell, "SYMBOLS: Battle Still Rages over Confederate Flag and Song 'Dixie,'" *Los Angeles Times*, March 9, 1987, 12.

75. Christopher Silver and John V. Moeser, *The Separate City: Black Communities in the Urban South, 1940–1968* (Lexington: University Press of Kentucky, 1995), x.

76. Lewis A. Randolph and Gayle T. Tate, *Rights for a Season: The Politics of Race, Class, and Gender in Richmond, Virginia* (Knoxville: University of Tennessee Press, 2003), 2. For more on the politics of the 1977 decision, see Julian Maxwell Hayter, "From Intent to Effect: Richmond, Virginia, and the Protracted Struggle for Voting Rights, 1965–1977," *Journal of Policy History* 26, no. 4 (2014): 534–567.

77. Randolph and Tate, *Rights for a Season*, 3.

78. Randolph and Tate, *Rights for a Season*, xii–xiii.

79. Attributed to *Richmond News Leader* editor Douglas Southall Freeman, the "Virginia Way" refers to a form of white paternalism marked by an overt rejection of racial segregation and the simultaneous belief among whites that separation was in the best interests of African Americans. See Julian Maxwell Hayter, *The Dream Is Lost: Voting Rights and the Politics of Race in Richmond, Virginia* (Lexington: University Press of Kentucky, 2017), 25. The "Virginia Way" and so-called genteel paternalism is also discussed in J. Douglas Smith, *Managing White Supremacy: Race, Politics, and Citizenship in Jim Crow Virginia* (Chapel Hill: University of North Carolina Press, 2002), 3–17.

80. Parke Rouse, "Richmond Keeps 'Cult of Confederacy' Alive," *Daily Press* (Newport News, VA), June 3, 1990, J3.

81. On these historical developments, see Benjamin Campbell, *Richmond's Un-healed History* (Richmond: Brandylane, 2012); Cook, *Troubled Commemoration*; Julian Maxwell Hayter, *City Profile of Richmond: Thriving Cities* (Richmond: Institute for Advanced Studies in Culture, University of Virginia, 2015); Hayter, "From Intent to Effect," 534–567; Hayter, *Dream Is Lost*; John V. Moeser and Rutledge Dennis, *The Politics of Annexation: Oligarchic Power in a Southern City* (Cambridge, MA: Schenkman, 1982); Randolph and Tate, *Rights for a Season*; Smith, *Managing White Supremacy*. On memory, history, and Arthur Ashe, see Matthew Mace Barbee, *Race and Masculinity in Southern Memory: History of Richmond, Virginia's Monument Avenue, 1948–1996* (Lanham, MD: Lexington Books, 2014).

82. "Future of Richmond's Past," American Civil War Museum, https://acwm .org/richmonds-journey/future.

83. Jackie Kruszewski, "Mayor Stoney Announces a Commission on Monument Avenue Statues," *Style Weekly*, June 22, 2017, https://www.styleweekly.com/richmond /mayor-stoney-announces-a-commission-on-monument-avenue-statues/Content ?oid=3720059. The commission's initial charge was to propose recommendations for the addition of "context." That charge was later amended, following the deadly violence in Charlottesville, to include possible recommendations for monument removal. See Mark Robinson, "Mayor Stoney: Commission to Consider Removal of Confederate Statues on Richmond's Monument Ave.," *Richmond Times-Dispatch*, August 16, 2017, https://www.richmond.com/news/local/city-of-rich mond/mayor-stoney-commission-to-consider-removal-of-confederate-statues-on /article_0120e8e9-d3f8-5b9e-8343-69902df255a6.html.

84. Mark Robinson, "'It's Theater of the Absurd': Monument Avenue Commission's First Public Hearing Borders on Chaotic," *Richmond Times-Dispatch*, August 9, 2017, https://www.richmond.com/news/local/city-of-richmond/it-s-theater-of -the-absurd-monument-avenue-commission-s/article_48b3cf9d-9d87-5bd9-9405 -ce20b4111dbf.html.

85. Katherine D. Walker, "United, Regardless, and a Bit Regretful: Confederate History Month, the Slavery Apology, and the Failure of Commemoration," *American Nineteenth Century History* 9, no. 3 (2008): 316–318.

86. *Richmond Free Press*, "Gilmore Breaks with Allen on Rebels, but . . ." April 2–4, 1998, A1, quoted in Walker, "United, Regardless," 318.

87. Olympia Meola, "McDonnell Recognizes April as Confederate History Month," *Richmond Times-Dispatch*, April 6, 2010, https://www.richmond.com/news /article_7a699c1f-f533-52bf-af52-d64d79a15722.html.

88. CNN Wire Staff, "Gov. McDonnell Apologizes for Omitting Slavery in Confederacy Proclamation," *CNN*, April 9, 2010, http://www.cnn.com/2010/POLI TICS/04/07/virginia.confederate.history/index.html.

89. Brent Tarter, "Lee-Jackson-King Day in Virginia," VA-Hist Listserv, January 15, 2014, accessed April 9, 2019, http://listlva.lib.va.us/scripts/wa.exe?A2=ind1401&L =VA-HIST&F=&S=&P=7926.

90. On the role of the United Daughters of the Confederacy in advancing Lost Cause education, see Cox, *Dixie's Daughters*, 120–134. For more on the textbooks, see Rex Springston, "Happy Slaves? The Peculiar Story of Three Virginia School Textbooks," *Richmond Times-Dispatch*, April 14, 2018, https://www.richmond.com /discover-richmond/happy-slaves-the-peculiar-story-of-three-virginia-school-text

books/article_47e79d49-eac8-575d-ac9d-1c6fce52328f.html; Adam Wesley Dean, "'Who Controls the Past Controls the Future': The Virginia History Textbook Controversy," *Virginia Magazine of History and Biography* 117, no. 4 (2009): 318–355.

91. For more on the playing of "Dixie" at the University of Richmond, see Victoria Charles, "The 'Dixie' Question," *Race & Racism at the University of Richmond* blog, September 14, 2016, https://blog.richmond.edu/memory/2016/09/14/the-dixie-question/.

92. Melanie L. Buffington and Erin Waldner, "Human Rights, Collective Memory, and Counter Memory: Unpacking the Meaning of Monument Avenue in Richmond, Virginia," *Journal of Cultural Research in Art Education* (2011): 98. See also Sheriff, "Virginia's Embattled Textbooks," and Tracy Thompson, "The South Still Lies About the Civil War," *Salon*, March 16, 2013, http://www.salon.com/2013/03/16/the_south_still_lies_about_the_civil_war/.

93. This is the subject of a forthcoming book by historian Kevin Levin, *Searching for Black Confederates: The Civil War's Most Persistent Myth* (Chapel Hill: University of North Carolina Press, 2019).

94. Bruce C. Levine, *Confederate Emancipation: Southern Plans to Free and Arm Slaves during the Civil War* (New York: Oxford University Press, 2006). For more on this discussion, see *Back Story*, "Coming Home: A History of War Veterans," November 6, 2015, https://www.backstoryradio.org/shows/coming-home-3/.

95. Tyler-McGraw, "Southern Comfort Levels," 165.

96. Colleen Curran, "Beard Wars: The Ultimate Salute to Civil War Facial Hair," *Richmond Times-Dispatch*, March 23, 2015, https://www.richmond.com/entertainment/art/beard-wars-the-ultimate-salute-to-civil-war-facial-hair/article_ef2577a9-7b8e-55b3-87cc-e277f1101c77.html.

97. Katherine Calos, "Steven Spielberg Reflects on His Experiences with Richmond and 'Lincoln,'" *Richmond Times-Dispatch*, November 11, 2012, http://www.richmond.com/entertainment/movies/steven-spielberg-reflects-on-his-experiences-with-richmond-and-lincoln/article_12d08888-2176-529c-b93d-caf2580cc4e7.html.

98. For more on the bill to allow a Sons of Confederate Veterans Virginia state license plate, see Graham Moomaw, "Va. Lawmaker Files Bill to Bring Back License Plates with Confederate Flag," *Richmond Times-Dispatch*, December 16, 2015, http://www.richmond.com/news/virginia/government-politics/article_fb7d694d-0702-5b19-8a57-7477ab9d2e51.html. On the Confederate battle flag in northern Virginia, see Susan Svriuga, "A Confederate Flag Divides a Virginia Community," *Washington Post*, August 1, 2014, https://www.washingtonpost.com/local/a-confederate-flag-divides-a-virginia-community/2014/08/01/118792ae-18e6-11e4-9349-84d4a85be981_story.html.

99. On this point, see Nicole Maurantonio, "Material Rhetoric, Public Memory, and the Post-It Note," *Southern Communication Journal* 82, no. 2 (2015): 83–101.

100. Nora, "Between Memory and History," 7–24.

101. Susan A. Crane, "Introduction: Of Museums and Memory," in *Museums and Memory*, ed. Susan A. Crane (Stanford, CA: Stanford University Press, 2000), 12.

102. For more on this experience, see Susan A. Crane, "Memory, Distortion, and History in the Museum," *History and Theory* 36, no. 4 (1997): 44–63.

103. See Edward Linenthal, "Anatomy of a Controversy," in *History Wars: The*

Enola Gay and Other Battles for the American Past, ed. Edward Linenthal and Tom Engelhardt (New York: Henry Holt, 1996), and Edward T. Linenthal, *Preserving Memory: The Struggle to Create America's Holocaust Museum* (New York: Viking Penguin, 1995).

104. Michel Foucault, *Discipline and Punish: The Birth of the Prison* (New York: Vintage, 1979). Historian Steven Conn credits cultural studies scholar Tony Bennett for being among the first to draw on the work of Foucault, in a "nuanced, thoughtful, and provocative" way. Conn argues the same cannot be said more broadly. See Steven Conn, *Do Museums Still Need Objects?* (Philadelphia: University of Pennsylvania Press, 2010), 3, and Tony Bennett, *The Birth of the Museum: History, Theory, Politics* (London: Routledge, 1995).

105. Conn, *Do Museums Still Need Objects?*, 3.

106. Historian Charles Reagan Wilson cited in Jonathan I. Leib, "Separate Times, Shared Spaces: Arthur Ashe, Monument Avenue and the Politics of Richmond, Virginia's Symbolic Landscape," *Cultural Geographies* 9 (2002): 286.

1. "Carry Me Back to Old Virginny" and the Neo-Confederate Jeremiad

1. Anthony Jackson, "Engaging the Audience: Negotiating Performance in the Museum," in *Performing Heritage: Research, Practice, and Innovation in Museum Theatre and Live Interpretation,* ed. Anthony Jackson and Jenny Kidd (Manchester, UK: Manchester University Press, 2012), 18–19.

2. Susan Hathaway, "Address to Sons of Confederate Veterans," Virginia Beach, VA, July 28, 2014.

3. Hathaway would ultimately come to sing the song so often that by July 28, 2015, Civil War historian and critic of the neo-Confederacy Brooks D. Simpson would title a post on his blog *Crossroads,* "(Don't) Sing Along with Susan Hathaway," https://cwcrossroads.wordpress.com/2015/07/28/dont-sing-along-with-susan-hathaway/.

4. Hathaway, "Address to Sons of Confederate Veterans."

5. David A. Jasen and Gene Jones, *Spreadin' Rhythm Around: Black Popular Songwriters, 1880–1930* (New York: Schirmer, 1998), 8.

6. Scott Dance and Michael Dresser, "Senators Pass Bill Stripping 'Maryland, My Maryland' of 'Official' Status," *Baltimore Sun,* March 16, 2018, https://www.baltimoresun.com/news/maryland/politics/bs-md-state-song-senate-20180316-story.html. The song was subsequently rebranded as Maryland's "historical" tune.

7. Laurajane Smith, "The 'Doing' of Heritage: Heritage as Performance," in *Performing Heritage: Research, Practice, and Innovation in Museum Theatre and Live Interpretation,* ed. Anthony Jackson and Jenny Kidd (Manchester, UK: Manchester University Press, 2012), 69.

8. Smith, "'Doing' of Heritage," 69.

9. See, for instance, John M. Murphy, "'A Time of Shame and Sorrow': Robert F. Kennedy and the American Jeremiad," *Quarterly Journal of Speech* 76 (1990): 401–414; Daniel O. Buehler, "Permanence and Change in Theodore Roosevelt's Conservation Jeremiad," *Western Journal of Communication* 62, no. 4 (1998): 439–458; Katherine Henry, "'Slaves to a Debt': Race, Shame, and the Anti-Obama Jeremiad," *Quarterly Journal of Speech* 11, no. 3 (August 2014): 303–322; John M.

Jones and Robert C. Rowland, "A Covenant-Affirming Jeremiad: The Post-Presidential Ideological Appeals of Ronald Wilson Reagan," *Communication Studies* 56, no. 2 (2005): 157–174; N. E. Mitchell and K. S. Phipps, "The Jeremiad in Contemporary Fundamentalism: Jerry Falwell's Listen America," *Religious Communication Today* (1985): 54–62.

10. Henry, "'Slaves to a Debt,'" 304.

11. Denise M. Bostdorff, "George W. Bush's Post-September 11 Rhetoric of Covenant Renewal: Upholding the Faith of the Greatest Generation," *Quarterly Journal of Speech* 89, no. 4 (2003): 294–295.

12. Andrew R. Murphy, "Longing, Nostalgia, and Golden Age Politics: The American Jeremiad and the Power of the Past," *Perspectives on Politics* 7, no. 1 (2009): 126.

13. Henry, "'Slaves to a Debt,'" 306.

14. Hathaway, "Address to Sons of Confederate Veterans."

15. Sacvan Bercovitch, *The American Jeremiad* (Madison: University of Wisconsin Press, 1980), 62.

16. Jasen and Jones, *Spreadin' Rhythm Around*, 9.

17. Andrew Petkofsky, "Senate Committee Approves Panel to Improve State Song," *Richmond Times-Dispatch*, February 21, 1987, 13. This is a point also made in John Hix, "Strange As It Seems," *Honolulu Advertiser*, May 1, 1940, 14.

18. "Hail to 'Carry Me Back,'" *Highland (VA) Recorder*, March 8, 1940, 1. Will Ruebush's "Old Virginia" was advocated as an alternative to "Carry Me Back to Old Virginny." Yet, as the *Recorder* notes, while the Shenandoah College professor's composition was considered, ultimately the "better-known ballad" won the day.

19. Dr. Kelly Miller's article on Bland points to this discrepancy firsthand, noting, "One writer says that he was of Virginia slave parentage; another that the ballad expresses the lament of a Virginia Negro slave who was sold in New Orleans in 1811; another tells us that his father, Allen M. Bland, was a graduate from Oberlin College, with high honor, and still another that the son graduated from Howard University with high honors." All, Dr. Miller notes, "are purely legendary and fictitious." Dr. Kelly Miller, "Black 'Stephen Foster,'" *Pittsburgh Courier*, August 5, 1939, 24.

20. Robert C. Toll, *Blacking Up: The Minstrel Show in Nineteenth-Century America* (New York: Oxford University Press, 1974), 216.

21. William R. Hullfish, "James A. Bland: Pioneer Black Songwriter," *Black Music Research Journal* 7 (1987): 1.

22. "James A. Bland Historical Marker," Explore PA History.com, n.d., accessed March 31, 2019, http://explorepahistory.com/hmarker.php?markerId=1-A-26A. For more on the Mummers, see Patricia Anne Masters, *The Philadelphia Mummers: Building Community through Play* (Philadelphia: Temple University Press, 2007).

23. While news articles suggest that Bland composed more than seven hundred works (see Miller, "Black 'Stephen Foster,'" 24), historians have challenged this number. See Jasen and Jones, *Spreadin' Rhythm Around*, 14.

24. Cited in Hullfish, "James A. Bland," 2.

25. Hullfish, "James A. Bland," 8, 17.

26. In 1890 Bland reportedly purchased a 4¾ carat diamond—"the largest ever worn by an African-American entertainer." "James A. Bland Historical Marker."

27. Jasen and Jones, *Spreadin' Rhythm Around*, 14.

28. "Bland Music Scholarships Honor Composer of the Former State Song," *Rappahannock (VA) Record*, January 15, 1998, A7.

29. The Virginia Conservation Commission was abolished in 1948 and became part of the Virginia Department of Conservation and Development, which assumed not only the function of the Virginia Conservation Commission but the State Port Authority and State Planning Authority as well. http://ead.lib.virginia.edu/vivaxtf /view?docId=lva/vi00960.xml.

30. "Official State Song," *Rappahannock (VA) Record*, February 29, 1940, 4.

31. "Hail to 'Carry Me Back,'" 1.

32. "Hail to 'Carry Me Back,'" 1.

33. Guy Friddell, "Some Things in Life, Such as State Songs, Are Best Left Alone," *Richmond Times-Dispatch*, February 11, 1991, 13.

34. Douglas Southall Freeman cited in Brent Tarter, *The Grandees of Government: The Origins and Persistence of Undemocratic Politics in Virginia* (Charlottesville: University of Virginia Press, 2013), 340.

35. Tarter, *Grandees of Government*, 340.

36. J. Douglas Smith, *Managing White Supremacy: Race, Politics, and Citizenship in Jim Crow Virginia* (Chapel Hill: University of North Carolina Press, 2002), 4.

37. Smith, *Managing White Supremacy*, 4.

38. "America's Favorite Songs: Carry Me Back to Old Virginny," *Star-Gazette (Elmira, NY)*, November 7, 1923, 5.

39. "President of Ireland Will Plead Cause Here," *Richmond Times-Dispatch*, August 26, 1919, 1.

40. "League Adherents Turn Out to Honor President," *Richmond Times-Dispatch*, November 5, 1920, 8.

41. "America's Favorite Songs: Carry Me Back to Old Virginny," 5.

42. Brendan Wolfe, "Buck v. Bell (1927)," *Encyclopedia Virginia*, n.d., accessed March 31, 2019, https://www.encyclopediavirginia.org/Buck_v_Bell_1927. In a public talk at Virginia Humanities on December 5, 2017, Lulu Miller shared this history of eugenic sterilization, drawn from a chapter from her forthcoming book, *Why Fish Don't Exist* (Simon & Schuster).

43. Wolfe, "Buck v. Bell (1927)."

44. Tarter, *Grandees of Government*, 342.

45. Smith, *Managing White Supremacy*, 50.

46. "New Travel Booklet Contains 100 Pages," *Rappahannock (VA) Record*, September 17, 1964, 8.

47. "'Carry Me Back to Ole Virginny' Proposed Anthem," *Highland (VA) Recorder*, October 14, 1938, 4.

48. "Lions Honor Composer on Parley Eve," *Philadelphia Inquirer*, July 16, 1946, 17; "James A. Bland Historical Marker." See also Dean Levi, "Songwriter, Educator, Both Black, Honored in 1946," *Richmond Times-Dispatch*, July 17, 1986, 17. For more on Governor Tuck, see William B. Crawley Jr., "William M. Tuck (1896–1983)," *Encyclopedia Virginia*, n.d., accessed March 31, 2019, https://www.encyclopediavirginia .org/Tuck_William_M_1896-1983.

49. "Lions Honor Composer on Parley Eve."

50. Levi, "Songwriter, Educator," 17.

51. "Lions Honor Composer on Parley Eve."

52. William Bryan Crawley Jr., *Bill Tuck: A Political Life in Harry Byrd's Virginia* (Charlottesville: University of Virginia Press, 1978), 138–139.

53. Betty Booker, "The Day's Top Story," *Richmond Times-Dispatch*, February 21, 1987, A-8.

54. Mary Washington Ball, "Pageant Will Depict History of Old Virginia; 3000 Actors," *Morning Call (Allentown, PA)*, May 14, 1922, 4.

55. W. B. Cridlin, "The Virginia Historical Pageant," *Virginia Magazine of History and Biography* 30, no. 2 (April 1922): 120.

56. "Miss Cooper, of Cherrydale, Named Sponsor," *Washington Times*, May 7, 1922, 4; "Virginians Depict Early Days of U.S. under G. Washington," *Palatka (FL) Daily News*, May 24, 1922, 1; "Virginia Historical Pageant Draws 22,000 to Huge Coliseum," *Tampa Tribune*, May 24, 1922, 4; "Virginia Historical Pageant: Richmond, Va., May 22 to 28" (advertisement), *Twin City Sentinel (NC)*, May 16, 1922, 11.

57. "Virginia Historical Pageant: May 22–28th 1922" (advertisement), *Richmond Times-Dispatch*, April 16, 1922, 5.

58. Cridlin, "The Virginia Historical Pageant," 119; Ball, "Pageant Will Depict History," 4.

59. Ball, "Pageant Will Depict History," 4.

60. "Depict Confederate Era in Great Parade Today," *Richmond Times-Dispatch*, May 25, 1922, 3.

61. While the *Times-Dispatch* referred to the "Confederate Memorial Society," the reference was likely a gesture to the Confederate Memorial Association, which sought to preserve the records and artifacts of the Confederacy.

62. "Depict Confederate Era in Great Parade Today," 3.

63. "War Heroes Pass in Pageant Line," *Richmond Times-Dispatch*, May 27, 1922, 3.

64. "War Heroes Pass in Pageant Line," 3.

65. "The Virginia Pageant: A Series of Great Moments in ye History of ye State" (advertisement), *Richmond Times-Dispatch*, April 21, 1922, 7.

66. "Tragles: The Department Drug Store" (advertisement), *Richmond Times-Dispatch*, May 21, 1922, 9.

67. "Miller & Rhoads: The Shopping Center" (advertisement), *Richmond Times-Dispatch*, April 18, 1922, 12.

68. "Miller & Rhoads: The Shopping Center" (advertisement), 1922, 5.

69. E. J. Conway, "Employment Bulletin" [issued monthly by public employment bureau], *Richmond Planet*, May 6, 1922, 4.

70. "Pageant Facts," *Richmond Times-Dispatch*, May 27, 1922, 3.

71. "The Virginia Historical Pageant . . ." *Richmond Planet*, May 27, 1922, 4.

72. "The Virginia Historical Pageant."

73. Editorial, "Why Not Larger Crowds?" *Richmond Planet*, June 3, 1922, 4.

74. "Living Klansmen Add Big Thrill at Exhibit of 'Birth of a Nation,'" *Times Dispatch*, February 12, 1922, 1, 2. This is a point made in Melissa Ooten, *Race, Gender, and Film Censorship in Virginia, 1922–1965* (Lanham, MD: Lexington Books, 2014).

75. Virginia Conservation Commission, "Virginians in the Struggle for Freedom," *Carry Me Back to Old Virginia*, pamphlet, 1941, 1, Library of Virginia, Richmond (hereafter LVA).

76. "Virginians in the Struggle for Freedom," 1.

77. *Equal Justice Initiative: A History of Racial Injustice*, https://racialinjustice.eji .org/timeline/1950s/. See also James H. Hershman Jr., "Massive Resistance," last modified June 29, 2011, https://www.encyclopediavirginia.org/massive_resistance.

78. "Virginians in the Struggle for Freedom," 1.

79. Virginia Department of Conservation and Development, "South of the James," *Carry Me Back to Old Virginia*, pamphlet, 1953, 20, LVA.

80. "Virginians in the Struggle for Freedom," 1.

81. Virginia Conservation Commission, "Historic Shrines and Gardens: Richmond," *Carry Me Back to Old Virginia*, pamphlet, 1941, 15–18, LVA.

82. Virginia Department of Conservation and Development, *Enchanting Virginia*, pamphlet, 1952, LVA.

83. Virginia Department of Conservation and Development, Division of Public Relations and Advertising, "A Virginia Population Trend," *Moving to Virginia*, pamphlet, 1966, 4, LVA.

84. "A Virginia Population Trend," 4, italics in original.

85. Virginia State Travel Service, "The Magic of Virginia," *Carry Me Back to Old Virginia*, pamphlet, 1971, 1, LVA.

86. "Magic of Virginia," 1.

87. Virginia State Travel Service, "Richmond," *Carry Me Back to Old Virginia*, pamphlet, 1971, 33, LVA.

88. "You haven't seen America until you see Historic Virginia: 1607," Virginia Department of Conservation and Development [between 1976 and 1985], pamphlet, LVA.

89. Andrew Petkofsky, "Senate Committee Approves Panel to Improve State Song," *Richmond Times-Dispatch*, February 21, 1987, 13.

90. Editorial, "The Godwin Factor," *Richmond Times-Dispatch*, September 26, 1985, A-1.

91. See James R. Sweeney and the *Dictionary of Virginia Biography*, Mills E. Godwin (1914–1999), *Encyclopedia Virginia*, last modified December 19, 2016, http://www .EncyclopediaVirginia.org/Godwin_Mills_E_1914-1999.

92. "State Song Hearings to Be Held," *Richmond Times-Dispatch*, June 5, 1987, 20.

93. "SCLC Chapter Wants State to Scrap Song," *Richmond Times-Dispatch*, November 12, 1987, 17.

94. Editorial, "Designing a Camel," *Richmond Times-Dispatch*, January 24, 1988, F-6.

95. "UDC Chapter, Others Urged to Comment on State Song," *Rappahannock (VA) Record*, January 28, 1988, 28.

96. "What to Do with the State Song," *Smithfield (VA) Times*, January 13, 1988, 2.

97. Olivia Winslow, "Capitol Hill Is Alive with the Sound of Music," *Richmond Times-Dispatch*, February 4, 1988, B-1.

98. "Michie Bill Would Retire State Song," *Richmond Times-Dispatch*, January 15, 1988, 4.

99. Winslow, "Capitol Hill Is Alive," B-1.

100. Editorial, "Whitewashing 'Virginia,'" *Richmond Times-Dispatch*, January 30, 1991, 14.

101. The House Joint Resolution No. 179, 1994 Session, accessed March 31, 2019, http://www.netstate.com/states/symb/song/va_carry_me_back.htm.

102. Senate Bill No. 231, 1994, n.d., accessed March 31, 2019, http://www
.netstate.com/states/symb/song/va_carry_me_back.htm.

103. "Lawmakers Debate Wish Lists, Change in State Song," *Daily News (Staunton, VA) Leader*, February 3, 1994, 2.

104. David Lerman, "Racist State Song Being Rewritten," *Republic (Columbus, IN)*, February 11, 1994, 12.

105. Michael Hardy, "House Rejects State Song Revisions," *Richmond Times-Dispatch*, March 4, 1994, A-12.

106. Cited in Michael Paul Williams, "A Group's Song and Dance over 'Carry Me Back,'" *Richmond Times-Dispatch*, March 7, 1994, B-1.

107. Mary Wakefield Buxton, "One Woman's Opinion," *Southside (Urbanna, VA) Sentinel*, March 10, 1994, 2.

108. Buxton, "One Woman's Opinion," 2.

109. Buxton, "One Woman's Opinion," 2.

110. Cited in Williams, "Group's Song and Dance," B-1.

111. Hardy, "House Rejects State Song Revisions."

112. Robert Mason Jr., "Fiction or Fact," *Rappahannock (VA) Record*, February 6, 1997, 4.

113. "Our Great Virginia," March 26, 2015, http://www.netstate.com/states /symb/songs/va_our_great_virginia.htm.

114. "Sweet Virginia Breeze," n.d., accessed March 31, 2019, https://statesym bolsusa.org/symbol-official-item/virginia/songs/sweet-virginia-breeze.

115. For more on the history of the Confederate battle flag, see John M. Coski, *The Confederate Battle Flag: America's Most Embattled Emblem* (Cambridge, MA: Harvard University Press, 2005); Robert E. Bonner, *Colors and Blood: Flag Passions of the Confederate South* (Princeton, NJ: Princeton University Press, 2002).

116. Hathaway, "Address to Sons of Confederate Veterans."

117. Hathaway, "Address to Sons of Confederate Veterans."

118. John M. Murphy, "'Time of Shame and Sorrow,'" 402.

119. Hathaway, "Address to Sons of Confederate Veterans."

120. Comment by Maeve Magdalen (August 7, 2017), to Susan Hathaway, "Fight Like Forrest, Not Sherman," Virginia Flaggers (blog), September 11, 2013, http:// vaflaggers.blogspot.com/2013/09/fight-like-forrest-not-sherman.html.

2. Stonewall Jackson and Sacred Relics

1. T. L. Marr, "Years Ago at V.M.I.," *VMI Cadet*, April 25, 1949, 2.

2. While legend has it that Stonewall Jackson had an affinity for lemons, the VMI archive notes that "he [Jackson] had no special fondness for lemons; in fact, peaches were his favorite." VMI further cites the work of Civil War historian and Jackson biographer James I. Robertson Jr., who calls this claim the "lemon myth." "Stonewall Jackson FAQ," VMI Archives, n.d., accessed March 31, 2019, https://www.vmi.edu /archives/stonewall-jackson-resources/stonewall-jackson-faq/.

3. "The Legacy of Great Leaders," Lexington: Visitor's Guide, n.d., accessed March 31, 2019, https://lexingtonvirginia.com/history-buffs/the-legacy-of-great -leaders.

4. Michael Bedsworth, "The Packet Boat Marshall," Carriage House Inn Bed and Breakfast, May 13, 2014, https://www.thecarriagehouseinnbandb.com/packet-boat-marshall/. I thank Earl Swift for drawing this to my attention.

5. Jason Harding, "Jackson Memorial Hall: The Untold History," *The Cadet*, January 20, 1995, 6.

6. Lori Stevens, "Museum Exhibits Take Up Permanent Residence JM Hall," *Institute Report*, October 2008, 1, 5.

7. Philippa Strum, *Women in the Barracks: The VMI Case and Equal Rights* (Lawrence: University Press of Kansas, 2002), 4–5.

8. Historian Drew Gilpin Faust notes that Little Sorrel, like other famous warhorses of the time, was considered a relic to many late nineteenth-century Americans. Drew Gilpin Faust, "Equine Relics of the Civil War," in *Southern Cultures: The Fifteenth Anniversary Reader*, ed. Harry L. Watson and Larry G. Griffin with Lisa Eveleigh, Dave Shaw, Ayse Erginer, and Paul Quigley (Chapel Hill: University of North Carolina Press, 2008), 393. The point that the arm of Stonewall Jackson can be interpreted as "a reliquary for a secular saint" has also been made by Kenneth E. Hall, *Stonewall Jackson and Religious Faith in Military Command* (Jefferson, NC: McFarland, 2005), 42–44.

9. Teresa Barnett, *Sacred Relics: Pieces of the Past in Nineteenth-Century America* (Chicago: University of Chicago Press, 2013), 23.

10. Joe Nickell, *Relics of the Christ* (Lexington: University Press of Kentucky, 2007), 13.

11. Barnett, *Sacred Relics*, 23–24.

12. Barnett, *Sacred Relics*, 25, 8.

13. See Barnett, *Sacred Relics*, chap. 7. On the historic relationships between museums and objects, see Steven Conn, *Do Museums Still Need Objects?* (Philadelphia: University of Pennsylvania Press, 2010), chap. 1.

14. Barnett, *Sacred Relics*, 195.

15. Gordon Waitt and Lesley Head make this argument with respect to picture postcards in their study "Postcards and Frontier Mythologies: Sustaining Views of the Kimberley as Timeless," *Environment and Planning D: Society and Space* 20 (2002): 323.

16. Wallace Hettle, *Inventing Stonewall Jackson: A Civil War Hero in History and Memory* (Baton Rouge: Louisiana State University Press, 2011), 38–40, quotation on 3.

17. Faust, "Equine Relics of the Civil War," 393.

18. "Lexington Historic District (Lexington, Virginia)," Wikipedia, last modified January 7, 2018, https://en.wikipedia.org/wiki/Lexington_Historic_District_(Lexington,_Virginia).

19. "Legacy of Great Leaders."

20. Rick Killmeyer, "Self-Knowledge through History," *The Cadet*, March 3, 1995, 2.

21. Strum, *Women in the Barracks*, 4–5.

22. "VMI Museum," n.d., accessed March 31, 2019, http://www.vmi.edu/museums-and-archives/vmi-museum/.

23. Strum, *Women in the Barracks*, 21.

24. "Battle of New Market," VMI Archives, n.d., accessed March 31, 2019, https://www.vmi.edu/archives/civil-war-and-new-market/battle-of-new-market/.

25. "New Market Ceremony History: The 19th Century Commemorations," VMI Archives, n.d., accessed March 31, 2019, https://www.vmi.edu/archives/civil-war-and-new-market/battle-of-new-market/new-market-ceremony-history/.

26. Monument Avenue is additionally home to the statue of Arthur Ashe. See chapter 5, as well as Matthew Mace Barbee, *Race and Masculinity in Southern Memory: History of Richmond, Virginia's Monument Avenue, 1948–1996* (Lanham, MD: Lexington Books, 2014), and Jonathan I. Leib, "Separate Times, Shared Spaces: Arthur Ashe, Monument Avenue and the Politics of Richmond, Virginia's Symbolic Landscape," *Cultural Geographies* 9 (2002): 286–312.

27. Little Sorrel earned the name "little" not because of his size relative to other horses but rather because he was comparatively smaller than Jackson's *other* sorrel-colored horse, named Big Sorrel. While initially dubbed Fancy, Little Sorrel was anything but. The horse appeared, at least initially, unexceptional.

28. Little Sorrel was allegedly born in Connecticut. For more, see "Little Sorrel, Connecticut's Confederate War Horse," Connecticut History.org, n.d., accessed March 31, 2019, https://connecticuthistory.org/little-sorrel-connecticuts-confederate-war-horse/.

29. Karen R. Jones, *Epiphany in the Wilderness: Hunting, Nature, and Performance in the Nineteenth-Century American West* (Boulder: University Press of Colorado, 2015), 244.

30. Faust, "Equine Relics of the Civil War," 395, 396.

31. While Rienzi is immortalized in art and poetry, most famously Thomas Buchanan Read's "Sheridan's Ride," Rienzi's fame is inextricably linked to his sensationalized ride with Sheridan to Middletown, Virginia.

32. "'Old Sorrel' Gone: Death at Soldiers' Home of Stonewall Jackson's War-Horse," *Richmond Dispatch*, March 16, 1886, 1.

33. "Past in Review," *VMI Cadet*, April 15, 1966, 8.

34. Marr, "Years Ago at V.M.I.," 2.

35. "'Old Sorrel' Gone," 1.

36. Marr, "Years Ago at V.M.I.," 2.

37. Mrs. Jackson, "Stonewall Jackson's Horse," *Alexandria (VA) Gazette*, September 1, 1892, 2.

38. "'Old Sorrel' Gone," 1.

39. Tony Horwitz, "'Stonewall' Jackson's 'Little Sorrel' Finally Laid to Rest," *Palm Beach Post*, July 27, 1997, 6.

40. "Local News," *Peninsula Enterprise* (Accomac, VA), September 21, 1882, 3.

41. "Old Sorrel," *Alexandria (VA) Gazette*, June 1, 1887, 1.

42. "'Old Sorrel' Gone," 1.

43. "Stonewall Jackson's Horse, Little Sorrel," Horse and Man, November 11, 2014, http://www.horseandman.com/horse-stories/stonewall-jacksons-horse-little-sorrel/11/11/2014/.

44. This is a point made in James I. Robertson Jr.'s extensive biography, *Stonewall Jackson: The Man, the Soldier, the Legend* (New York: Simon & Schuster, 1997), 290. There is disagreement as to whether Lewis was enslaved. While Robertson notes

"[a] good case can be made that Lewis was a slave whom Jackson hired from his owner," historian Ervin L. Jordan Jr. has described Lewis, in contrast, as "a free black resident of Lexington." See Ervin L. Jordan Jr., *Black Confederates and Afro-Yankees in Civil War Virginia* (Charlottesville: University Press of Virginia, 1995), 194. The National Park Service points to a potential source of uncertainty regarding Lewis's status as an enslaved person: payments made by Jackson to W.C. Lewis for "hire of Jim." See "Jim Lewis," National Park Service, https://www.nps.gov/frsp/learn/historyculture/jim-lewis.htm.

45. Often these accounts quote Boteler from Robertson's biography, 291. See, for instance, Faust, "Equine Relics of the Civil War," 400; Kevin Levin, "Stonewall Jackson's Black Friend," Civil War Memory, March 23, 2013, http://cwmemory.com/2013/03/26/stonewall-jacksons-black-friend/; Kim Mariette, "Little Sorrel and Rienzi: Morgan Mounts of the Civil War," *Breed Research*, August 2012, 49; Richard G. Williams Jr., *Stonewall Jackson: The Black Man's Friend* (Nashville: Cumberland House, 2006), 138–139.

46. Alexander Boteler quoted in Robertson, *Stonewall Jackson*, 291. See Robertson, *Stonewall Jackson*, endnote 20, 841.

47. See, for instance, Williams, *Stonewall Jackson*.

48. Williams, *Stonewall Jackson*, 89.

49. Robertson, *Stonewall Jackson*, 191.

50. Robertson, *Stonewall Jackson*, 191.

51. Williams, *Stonewall Jackson*.

52. John R. Blackmon, "Confederates Honor Black History," *Columbian-Progress* (Columbia, MS), February 26, 1998, 3.

53. On the tenets of the Lost Cause, see Alan T. Nolan, "The Anatomy of the Myth," in *The Myth of the Lost Cause and Civil War History*, ed. Gary W. Gallagher and Alan T. Nolan (Bloomington: Indiana University Press, 2000), 11–34.

54. Williams, *Stonewall Jackson*, 143. This is a detail also included in Jordan, *Black Confederates*, 195. I thank Alison Bell for sharing research from her book, *The Vital Dead* (under contract with University of Tennessee Press) and helping me pull together a number of disparate details.

55. I thank Trina Jones and Karen Goodchild at Wofford College for encouraging me to think about sacred relics in these broader terms.

56. Horwitz, "Finally Laid to Rest," 7A.

57. Donald Gilliand, "'High Art' with Human Skull Goes on Display at Carnegie Museum," TCA Regional News, Trib Live, January 29, 2017, https://archive.triblive.com/news/high-art-with-human-skull-goes-on-display-at-carnegie-museum/.

58. Mariette, "Little Sorrel and Rienzi," 53. For more on the controversy surrounding Rienzi/Winchester, see Faust, "Equine Relics of the Civil War."

59. Pat Jarrett, "A Man and His Horse," *News Leader* (Staunton, VA), October 8, 2008, 3.

60. Martha M. Boltz, "Bones of Warhorse Will Be Interred near Jackson," *Washington Times*, July 19, 1997, 3.

61. See W. Donald Rhinesmith, "Traveller: 'Just the Horse for General Lee,'" *Virginia Cavalcade* 33, no. 1 (1983): 38–47.

62. "'Old Sorrel' Gone," 1.

63. Dave Madden, *The Authentic Animal: Inside the Odd and Obsessive World of Taxidermy* (New York: St. Martin's, 2011), 7.

64. Jones, *Epiphany in the Wilderness*, 229, 230.

65. Gregory J. Dehler, *The Most Defiant Devil: William Temple Hornaday and His Controversial Crusade to Save American Wildlife* (Charlottesville: University of Virginia Press, 2013), 54.

66. Christina M. Colvin, "Freeze-Drying Fido: The Uncanny Aesthetics of Modern Taxidermy," in *Mounting Animals: Rituals and Practices Surrounding Animal Death*, ed. Maro DeMello (East Lansing: Michigan State University Press, 2016), 65.

67. Rachel Poliquin, *The Breathless Zoo: Taxidermy and the Cultures of Longing* (University Park: Pennsylvania State University Press, 2012), 208.

68. Poliquin, *Breathless Zoo*, 211.

69. "Jackson's War Horse: Stonewall's Little Old Sorrel Back in Richmond," *Richmond Dispatch*, November 23, 1887, 1.

70. T. C. Morton, "Little Sorrel' Not Buried in North Carolina," *Lexington (VA) Gazette*, August 20, 1902, 1.

71. Jefferson Davis's funeral performed the same function. See Robert J. Cook, *Civil War Memories: Contesting the Past in the United States since 1865* (Baltimore: Johns Hopkins University Press, 2017), 56–61.

72. The horse's date of death is noted on the panel text accompanying the exhibit.

73. Lisa Fine, "Jackson's Steed Finally Receives Proper Burial; VMI Ceremony Honors Faithful Mount," *Richmond Times-Dispatch*, July 21, 1997, B-1.

74. Sarah Kay Bierle, "Stonewall's Horses," *Emerging Civil War*, January 19, 2017, https://emergingcivilwar.com/2017/01/19/stonewalls-horses/.

75. Fine, "Jackson's Steed," B-1.

76. Fine, "Jackson's Steed," B-1.

77. Fine, "Jackson's Steed," B-1.

78. Boltz, "Bones of Warhorse."

79. Fine, "Jackson's Steed," B-1.

80. Boltz, "Bones of Warhorse."

81. "Southern Anniversaries," *Tampa Bay Times*, April 23, 2000, 7D.

82. Horwitz, "Finally Laid to Rest," 7A.

83. "Horse of Another Color," *Smithsonian Torch*, May 1969, 2.

84. "Museum Endowment Established," *Institute Report*, December 6, 1985, 1.

85. Horwitz, "Finally Laid to Rest," 7A.

86. Mark Hinson, "It's Hard to Beat a Dead Horse (When It's Stuffed)," *Tallahassee Democrat*, April 29, 2007, 2D.

87. Lori Stevens, "Civil War Steed Receives Spa Treatment," *Institute Report*, October 2007, 1.

88. George Degennaro, "Little Sorrel's Ultimate Makeover," *VMI Cadet*, October 5, 2007, 2.

89. "Stonewall's Richmond Likeness Gets a Rinse and a Fresh Wax Job," *News Leader* (Staunton, VA), August 5, 2004, A2.

90. Jay Conley, "General's Prized Horse Gets Makeover," *Richmond Times-Dispatch*, October 10, 2007, B-8.

91. Stevens, "Civil War Steed," 7.

92. See Mark M. Smith, *The Smell of Battle, the Taste of Siege: A Sensory History of the Civil War* (New York: Oxford University Press, 2015).

93. Mike Robertson, "Little Sorrel," *VMI Cadet*, February 20, 2009, 3.

94. Ophelia Johnson, "Putting Civil War Horses on a Pedestal; Statue to Be Unveiled at Historical Society," *Richmond Times-Dispatch*, September 17, 1997, D-1.

95. This is a point made in Faust, "Equine Relics of the Civil War," 405.

96. Bob C. Layton, *Discovering Richmond Monuments: A History of River City Landmarks Beyond the Avenue* (Charleston: The History Press, 2013), 48.

3. Black Confederates and Performances of Living Reconciliation

1. Teresa Roane, tour of the United Daughters of the Confederacy Headquarters, Richmond, Virginia, May 4, 2014. This is a story Roane also shared in a video available on YouTube, "Teresa Roane Speaks on Southern Heritage," June 3, 2014, https://www.youtube.com/watch?v=NWujYlPDJ2U&t=1s.

2. Teresa Roane, tour of the UDC Headquarters.

3. Teresa Roane, presentation at Crowne Plaza Downtown, Richmond, Virginia, May 13, 2014.

4. The literature on slavery is vast, engaging a number of scholarly conversations and debates. As historian Dylan Penningroth notes, "the concept of slave agency [w]as a direct challenge to those earlier schools of thought that had portrayed slaves as either grateful recipients of their masters' benevolence or victims of a 'holocaust,' utterly stripped of their humanity." Dylan Penningroth, "Writing Slavery's History," *OAH Magazine of History* 23, no. 2 (2009): 16. These "earlier schools of thought" are captured by the works of Ulrich B. Phillips, *American Negro Slavery: A Survey of the Supply, Employment and Control of Negro Labor as Determined by the Plantation Regime* (Baton Rouge: Louisiana State Press, 1918, 1994) and Stanley Elkins, *Slavery: A Problem in American Institutional and Intellectual Life* (Chicago: University of Chicago Press, 1998), respectively. Historians such as Herbert Gutman, *The Black Family in Slavery and Freedom, 1750–1925* (New York: Pantheon, 1976) and Lawrence Levine, *Black Culture and Black Consciousness: Afro-American Folk Thought from Slavery to Freedom* (New York: Oxford University Press, 1977) challenged these works in the 1970s by demonstrating the vibrancy of Black culture, emphasizing the strength of families and religion, and in so doing, reiterating the agency of enslaved people.

5. Sgt. Major James Haymes is also referred to as Abdur Ali-Haymes in news articles. See, for instance, Allison Perkins, "Confederate White House Shows Visitors Another Side," *News and Record* (Greensboro, NC), April 5, 2003, https://www.greensboro.com/confederate-white-house-shows-visitors-another-side/article_f853da74-fc6a-5b70-92c4-a7ed15673cdf.html.

6. This restructuring was linked to the 2013 merger of the Museum of the Confederacy and the American Civil War Center at Historic Tredegar. I say "restructuring" here somewhat diplomatically. Haymes is considerably less sanguine about his departure from the Museum and White House of the Confederacy.

7. See Peter Holley, "Why This Black Defender of the Confederate Flag Says Slavery Was 'a Choice,'" *Washington Post*, June 30, 2015, https://www.washingtonpost.com/news/morning-mix/wp/2015/06/30/why-some-black-defenders-of-the

-confederate-flag-believe-slavery-was-a-choice/?utm_term=.f7dbaf11ebe8; Logan Jaffe, "Battle Flag—Karen Cooper," n.d., accessed March 31, 2019, https://vimeo .com/126991396.

8. Joel Burgess, "Flag," *Asheville Citizen-Times*, August 18, 2015, A4.

9. License plates supporting "Confederate Heritage" have been the source of controversy in recent years. In 2006 such a license plate was the subject of debate in Florida. Dara Kam, "Dixie Highway? Group Seeks Plate to Hail Roots," *Palm Beach Post*, April 1, 2006, 1A, 25A. The issue was thrust into the public spotlight in Virginia in 2015, following Dylann Roof's massacre of nine Black congregants at Emanuel AME Church in Charleston, South Carolina.

10. See, for instance, H. K. Edgerton, "Confederate Flag Case at Supreme Court About Liberty," *Asheville Citizen-Times*, March 23, 2015, A7.

11. Bill Alexander, "Ferguson Grand Jury Vindicates a Local Interpretation," *Asheville Citizen-Times*, December 11, 2014, A4.

12. "American Hero H. K. Edgerton Schools the Left on Confederate History," Tea Party.org, August 22, 2018, https://www.teaparty.org/american-hero-h-k-edger ton-schools-left-confederate-history-320609/.

13. "H. K. Edgerton T-Shirt," New CSA Store, n.d., accessed March 31, 2019, https://www.newcsastore.com/products/h-k-edgerton-t-shirt.

14. "Meet H. K. Edgerton," The Lamp, August 25, 2015, https://ladyliber tyslamp.wordpress.com/2015/08/25/meet-h-k-edgerton/.

15. WFAA Staff, "KKK Protests Black Confederate Flag Supporter," May 10, 2016, https://www.wfaa.com/article/news/nation/kkk-protests-black-confederate -flag-supporter/185040598.

16. Derrick Lewis, "Black Confederate Supporter Says Flag, Silent Sam Aren't Race Related," CBS17.com, August 22, 2018, https://www.cbs17.com/news/local -news/orange-county-news/black-confederate-supporter-says-flag-silent-sam-aren-t -race-related/1389352138.

17. Fred McCormick, "Local Responses to Ferguson, Mo. Vary," *Asheville Citizen-Times*, December 4, 2014, A2.

18. Another famous Black Confederate, according to the Southern Poverty Law Center, is J. J. Johnson of Ohio, who has stated that "if you think the Confederate flag is insulting to you [and you are black], you are being used, or as we say it in the hood, you bein' played—for a fool." Quoted in "Black Neo-Confederate H. K. Edgerton Discusses Beliefs," *SPLC Intelligence Report*, September 15, 2000, https:// www.splcenter.org/fighting-hate/intelligence-report/2000/black-neo-confederate -hk-edgerton-discusses-beliefs. Another contemporary Black Confederate is Anthony Hervey, who wrote *Why I Wave the Confederate Flag, Written by a Black Man* (Blooming-ton, IN: Trafford, 2006).

19. Hunglikejesus, Response to "Meet H. K. Edgerton," August 27, 2015, https://ladylibertyslamp.wordpress.com/2015/08/25/meet-h-k-edgerton/.

20. Scott Eric Kaufman, "African-American 'Flagger' Says Confederate Flag Isn't About Race: 'Slavery Was a Choice,'" Salon, June 30, 2015, https://www.salon .com/2015/06/30/african_american_flagger_says_confederate_flag_isnt_about _race_slavery_was_a_choice/.

21. Teresa Roane, email to author, February 9, 2017. Roane made a point of noting the existence of slavery outside the South when speaking before the Dur-

ham City-County Committee on Confederate Monuments and Memorials in August 2018. See https://www.youtube.com/watch?v=eEB_oDevoYo.

22. Laura Browder, *Slippery Characters: Ethnic Impersonators and American Identities* (Chapel Hill: University of North Carolina Press, 2000), 4.

23. This is not a myth subscribed to by the Far Right. As historian Benjamin Alpers has written, members of the Far Right, the likes of whom protested in Charlottesville in mid-August 2017 as part of the white supremacist Unite the Right rally, have resisted the notion of a "Rainbow Confederacy." Benjamin Alpers, "The Myth of Black Confederates," Public Seminar, January 14, 2018, http://www.publicseminar.org/2018/01/the-myth-of-black-confederates/. This point is further elaborated in Allegra Kirkland's "White Nationalists Push Back against Efforts to Honor Black Confederates," Talking Points Memo, January 5, 2018, https://talkingpointsmemo.com/muckraker/historians-white-nationalists-unite-opposition-south-carolina-monument-black-confederates.

24. Bruce Levine, "In Search of a Usable Past: Neo-Confederates and Black Confederates," in *Slavery and Public History: The Tough Stuff of American Memory*, ed. James Oliver Horton and Lois E. Horton (Chapel Hill: University of North Carolina Press, 2006), 189, 190.

25. Lisa A. Flores and Christy-Dale L. Sims, "The Zero-Sum Game of Race and the Familiar Strangeness of President Obama," *Southern Communication Journal* 81, no. 4 (2016): 209.

26. Kevin Levin, "H. K. Edgerton, Neo-Confederates and the Limits of Black Political Action," Civil War Memory, May 1, 2016, http://cwmemory.com/2016/05/01/h-k-edgerton-neo-confederates-the-limits-of-black-political-action/.

27. Sarah Wilson, *Melting Pot Modernism* (Ithaca, NY: Cornell University Press, 2010), 8.

28. Wilson makes this point in *Melting Pot Modernism*, 3. For more on nativism, see John Higham's *Strangers in the Land: Patterns of American Nativism, 1860–1925* (New Brunswick, NJ: Rutgers University Press, 2002).

29. Philip Gleason, "The Melting Pot: Symbol of Fusion or Confusion?" *American Quarterly* 16, no. 1 (1964): 44.

30. Rubén G. Rumbaut, "The Melting and the Pot: Assimilation and Variety in American Life," in *Incorporating Diversity: Rethinking Assimilation in a Multicultural Era*, ed. Peter Kivisto (Boulder, CO: Paradigm, 2005), 4.

31. Israel Zangwill, *The Melting Pot: Drama in Four Acts* (New York: Macmillan, 1923).

32. Rumbaut, "The Melting and the Pot," 2.

33. Barry Isenhour, interview with author, April 27, 2014.

34. This is a point made by Vanessa Agnew, who notes that reenactment "spans diverse history-themed genres—from theatrical and 'living history' performances to museum exhibits, television, film, travelogues, and historiography." For more on this point, see Vanessa Agnew, "Introduction: What Is Reenactment?" *Criticism* 46, no. 3 (2004): 327–339.

35. Elizabeth Carnegie and Scott McCabe, "Re-enactment Events and Tourism: Meaning, Authenticity and Identity," *Current Issues in Tourism* 11, no. 4 (2008): 350.

36. Agnew, "Introduction: What Is Re-enactment?" 327, 328.

37. Agnew, "Introduction: What Is Re-enactment?" 328.

38. Tony Horwitz, *Confederates in the Attic: Dispatches from the Unfinished Civil War* (New York: Pantheon, 1998).

39. Agnew, "Introduction: What Is Re-enactment?" 330.

40. Mike Allen, "Confederacy Museum Provokes Dismay with Period-Costume Ball," *New York Times*, February 11, 1996, https://www.nytimes.com/1996/02/11/us/confederacy-museum-provokes-dismay-with-period-costume-ball.html.

41. Ellen Nakashima, "Richmond in Uproar over Confederate Ball," *Washington Post*, February 24, 1996, https://www.washingtonpost.com/archive/local/1996/02/24/richmond-in-uproar-over-confederate-ball/f08ecbe8-922c-454e-b05c-c7b1b9d54de0/?utm_term=.70d278136e0e.

42. Mike Allen, "Dissent Doesn't Stop Guests at Confederate Ball from Whirling the Night Away," *New York Times*, February 26, 1996, https://www.nytimes.com/1996/02/26/us/dissent-doesn-t-stop-guests-at-confederate-ball-from-whirling-thenight-away.html.

43. Manuel Roig-Franzia, "At Charleston's Secession Ball, Divided Opinions on the Spirit of S.C.," *Washington Post*, December 22, 2010, http://www.washingtonpost.com/wp-dyn/content/article/2010/12/21/AR2010122105341.html.

44. For more on this phenomenon, see John M. Coski, *The Confederate Battle Flag: America's Most Embattled Emblem* (Cambridge, MA: Harvard University Press, 2005), 124–126.

45. The University of Richmond's 1961 yearbook, for instance, includes among the list of the fraternity Kappa Alpha's "social highlights" the "Share Cropper's Stomp" and "Old South Ball." Race & Racism at the University of Richmond, n.d., accessed March 31, 2019, http://memory.richmond.edu/items/show/2851.

46. Agnew, "Introduction: What Is Re-enactment?" 330.

47. Mark Guarino, "Will Civil War Reenactments Die Out?" *Washington Post*, August 25, 2017, https://www.washingtonpost.com/entertainment/museums/will-civil-war-reenactments-die-out/2017/08/25/f43c6bc0-874b-11e7-a50f-e0d4e6eco70a_story.html?utm_term=.c5da1b1d5d9b.

48. Jay Anderson, "Living History: Simulating Everyday Life in Living Museums," *American Quarterly* 34, no. 3 (1982): 291.

49. Stephen J. Hunt, "Acting the Part: 'Living History' as a Serious Leisure Pursuit," *Leisure Studies* 23, no. 4 (2004): 388.

50. Anderson, "Living History," 291.

51. Attfield cited in Carnegie and McCabe, "Re-enactment Events and Tourism," 359.

52. Fred E. H. Schroeder, "Living History: Getting Beyond Nostalgia?" *Journal of Museum Education* 10, no. 3 (1985): 19.

53. H. K. Edgerton is an exception, periodically donning a Confederate uniform in his marches.

54. Browder, *Slippery Characters*, 10.

55. Kam, "Dixie Highway?"

56. Anderson, "Living History," 295.

57. Richard Handler and William Saxton, "Dyssimulation: Reflexivity, Narrative,

and the Quest for Authenticity in 'Living History,'" *Cultural Anthropology* 3, no. 3 (1988): 247.

58. Deetz's claims are summarized in Anderson, "Living History," 298.

59. "'Slave Auction' Divides Crowd in Williamsburg," *Baltimore Sun*, October 11, 1994, http://articles.baltimoresun.com/1994-10-11/news/1994284122_1_colonial-williamsburg-foundation-slave-auction-re-enactment.

60. Chandelis R. Duster, "Meet the Black Woman Reclaiming the Narrative of the Civil War," NBC News, July 12, 2017, https://www.nbcnews.com/news/nbcblk/meet-black-woman-reclaiming-narrative-civil-war-n782006.

61. Schroeder, "Living History," 20.

62. Rumbaut, "The Melting and the Pot," 8.

63. Julia Higgins, "Immigration: The Myth of the Melting Pot," *Newsweek*, December 26, 2015, https://www.newsweek.com/immigration-myth-melting-pot-408705.

64. Teresa Roane, "Confederates of Color," Fredericksburg, Virginia, May 28, 2016.

65. Historian Kevin Levin wrote about Roane's August 2018 presentation. See Kevin Levin, "NC Committee Endorses Neo-Confederate History," Civil War Memory: The Online Home of Kevin M. Levin, August 24, 2018, http://cwmemory.com/2018/08/24/durham-committee-endorses-neo-confederate-history/. For Roane's full presentation before the Committee in Durham, see "City-County Committee on Confederate Monuments & Memorials August 23, 2018," https://www.youtube.com/watch?v=eEB_oDevoYo.

66. Roane, "Confederates of Color." This is a point she also made at a public talk, "Minorities in the Confederate Military," on May 8, 2018. The full talk can be accessed at https://www.youtube.com/watch?v=o5n3jXi8Gso.

67. J. Christopher Holloway, "The Guided Tour: A Sociological Approach," *Annals of Tourism Research* 3 (1981): 384.

68. This is a statement Roane made publicly while speaking before the Durham City-County Committee on Confederate Monuments and Memorials in August 2018. See https://www.youtube.com/watch?v=eEB_oDevoYo.

69. In September 2018 the Museum of the Confederacy at 1201 East Clay Street closed its doors in preparation for the projected 2019 opening of the new American Civil War Museum, to be housed at Historic Tredegar. See Colleen Curran, "After 122 Years on Clay Street in Downtown Richmond, the Museum of the Confederacy Is Closing Its Doors and Moving," *Richmond Times-Dispatch*, September 26, 2018, https://www.richmond.com/entertainment/museums/after-years-on-clay-street-in-downtown-richmond-the-museum/article_8e0a7775-8e71-504f-929b-83a45be4a9ba.html.

70. This is a claim she made during her public talk before the Durham City-County Committee, "City-County Committee on Confederate Monuments & Memorials August 23, 2018," https://www.youtube.com/watch?v=eEB_oDevoYo.

71. Sgt. Maj. James Haymes, interview with author, June 9, 2014.

72. Eduardo Bonilla-Silva, *Racism without Racists: Color-blind Racism and the Persistence of Racial Inequality in America* (Lanham, MD: Rowman & Littlefield, 2014).

73. Haymes interview.

74. Haymes interview.

75. "Remarks by Sgt Major James Haymes, Jr, Confederate Memorial Day, Oakwood Cemetery, Richmond Va," May 12, 2018, https://www.facebook.com /378823865585630/videos/remarks-by-sgt-major-james-haymes-jr-confederate -memorial-dayoakwood-cemetery-ri/1257082821093059/.

76. Haymes interview.

77. Karen Cooper, interview with author, May 2014.

78. Cooper interview.

79. Cooper interview.

80. Cooper interview.

81. Panama Jackson, "Somebody Get Your Confederate Flag Wavin' Cousin Karen Cooper," Very Smart Brothas, June 30, 2015, https://verysmartbrothas.the root.com/somebody-get-your-confederate-flag-wavin-cousin-karen-c-1822521788.

82. Meg Wagner and Kirstie McCrum, "Black Woman Speaks Out on Behalf of Confederate Flag and Says 'Slavery Was a Choice,'" *Mirror,* July 2, 2015, https:// www.mirror.co.uk/news/world-news/black-woman-speaks-out-behalf-5990006.

83. Brooks D. Simpson, "Another Controversy in Lexington, Virginia," Cross-roads, July 20, 2015, https://cwcrossroads.wordpress.com/2015/07/20/another -controversy-in-lexington-virginia/. For more on the story, see Laurence Hammack, "Confederate Battle Flag Polarizes Rockbridge County and Lexington," *Roanoke Times,* July 23, 2015, https://www.roanoke.com/news/virginia/confederate-battle -flag-polarizes-rockbridge-county-and-lexington/article_98929a38-595f-5b6f-815d -cac293dcd000.html?mode=jqm. See also Brooks D. Simpson, "Raymond Agnor 1, Virginia Flaggers 0," Crossroads, July 24, 2015, https://cwcrossroads.wordpress .com/2015/07/24/raymond-agnor-1-virginia-flaggers-0/.

84. Simpson, "Another Controversy in Lexington, Virginia."

85. As Simpson notes on his blog, the Virginia Flaggers' initial post in response to Agnor's ad was removed. http://restoringthehonor.blogspot.com/2015/07/are -black-virginia-flaggers-forbidden.html?m=1. This site is no longer available.

86. Brooks D. Simpson, "More Trouble in Flaggerland: Tripp Lewis versus Karen Cooper," Crossroads, August 27, 2016, https://cwcrossroads.wordpress.com /2016/08/27/more-trouble-in-flaggerland-tripp-lewis-versus-karen-cooper/.

87. Associated Press, "Farrakhan Defends Role of the Confederate Flag," *Deseret News,* July 19, 2000, https://www.deseretnews.com/article/772358/Farrakhan-de fends-role-of-the-Confederate-flag.html.

88. Daryle Lamont Jenkins cited in Brooks D. Simpson, "Karen Cooper and the Virginia Flaggers: Another View," Crossroads, September 3, 2016, https://cw crossroads.wordpress.com/2016/09/03/karen-cooper-and-the-virginia-flaggers -another-view/.

89. One People's Project, https://onepeoplesproject.com/.

90. "Such Is the Way to the Stars: Richmond, Virginia," *Love + Radio,* November 21, 2018, http://loveandradio.org/2018/11/such-is-the-way-to-the-stars/.

91. "Such Is the Way to the Stars," http://loveandradio.org/2018/11/such-is -the-way-to-the-stars/.

92. Associated Press, "Officials Work to Prevent Repeat of Dueling Hate Rallies," *Index-Journal* (Greenwood, SC), June 26, 2016, 3A.

93. Southern Legal Resource Center, https://www.slrc-csa.org/.

94. Jason Sandford, "Edgerton: Photo of Meeting with White Separatists Depicts a Joke," *Asheville Citizen-Times*, March 31, 1998, B1.

95. Bill Smith, "Backers Defend Lee Bust at Council Meeting," *New-Press* (Fort Myers, FL), April 3, 2018, 4A.

96. David Zucchino, "Politician's Atheism Draws a Constitutional Challenge," *Los Angeles Times*, December 20, 2009, A3.

97. "The UDC and a Richmond Block," *Richmond Times-Dispatch*, November 13, 1957, 18.

98. Susan N. Quinn, "The UDC Story: Women, History and Education," *Richmond Times-Dispatch*, November 11, 1957, 18.

99. "New Battle of Richmond Seen as Angry UDC, Solons Tangle," *Fort Lauderdale News*, January 29, 1954, 4.

100. "Memorial Building," United Daughters of the Confederacy, https://www .hqudc.org/memorial-building-2/.

101. Roane, tour of the UDC Headquarters.

102. MacCannell cited in Elizabeth C. Fine and Jean Haskell Speer, "Tour Guide Performances as Sight Sacralization," *Annals of Tourism Research* 12 (1985): 78.

103. Roane, tour of the UDC Headquarters.

104. Quinn, "UDC Story."

105. "City-County Committee on Confederate Monuments & Memorials August 23, 2018," https://www.youtube.com/watch?v-eEB_oDevoYo.

106. Brendan Wolfe, "United Daughters of the Confederacy and White Supremacy," *Project Blog: Encyclopedia Virginia*, August 30, 2018, https://www.evblog.virginia humanities.org/2018/08/united-daughters-of-the-confederacy-white-supremacy/.

107. "City-County Committee on Confederate Monuments & Memorials August 23, 2018," https://www.youtube.com/watch?v=eEB_oDevoYo.

108. Maude Waddell, "South's Treasures Kept Safe in Richmond, VA," *Asheville Citizen-Times*, March 14, 1929, 26.

109. "White House of the Confederacy, Now the Confederate Museum, and Its Relics of the War between the States," *Richmond Times-Dispatch*, February 12, 1922, 48–49.

110. Waddell, "South's Treasures Kept Safe."

111. Jim Wamsley, "Relics of War House in Former White House of the Confederacy," *Daily Press* (Newport News, VA), April 10, 1960, 37.

112. "The White House of the Confederacy," American Civil War Museum, https://acwm.org/visit-us/exhibits/museum-and-white-house-exhibits.

113. Haymes interview. Italics represent Haymes's spoken emphasis.

114. Barry Isenhour, tour of the United Daughters of the Confederacy Headquarters, Richmond, Virginia, May 4, 2014.

115. On Jewish assimilation and becoming white, see Michael Rogin, "Blackface, White Noise: The Jewish Jazz Singer Finds His Voice," *Critical Inquiry* 18, no. 3 (1992): 417–453; Matthew Frye Jacobson, *Whiteness of a Different Color: European Immigrants and the Alchemy of Race* (Cambridge, MA: Harvard University Press, 1999).

116. "Ku Klux Klan Parade in Richmond" (1925), *Encyclopedia Virginia*, n.d., accessed March 31, 2019, https://www.encyclopediavirginia.org/media_player?mets _filename=evr6330mets.xml; Angela Helm, "Virginia Newspaper Runs KKK Flyer on Its Front Page. Who Thought This Was a Good Idea?" The Root, April 28, 2018, https://www.theroot.com/virginia-newspaper-runs-kkk-flyer-on-its-front-page

-ang-1825621912; KKK Rally Broadside, 1966, http://edu.lva.virginia.gov/dbva /items/show/73.

117. For instance, Matthew Gottlieb, "The Lost Causation of William Flegen-heimer," unpublished paper.

118. Haymes interview. My colleague Brie Swenson Arnold shared the experience of taking a tour with Sgt. Maj. Haymes at the White House of the Confederacy on May 23, 2015, where she observed him using the language of "servants," underplaying the oppressiveness of slavery as an institution. She was accompanied by her colleague, Patrick Naick, and twelve students from Coe College enrolled in their course "Slavery, Civil War, Civil Rights: Race, Place, and Memory across the US."

119. Roane, "Confederates of Color."

120. Midori Takagi, *"Rearing Wolves to Our Own Destruction": Slavery in Richmond, Virginia, 1782–1865* (Charlottesville: University Press of Virginia, 1999).

121. Roane, "Confederates of Color."

122. Tagaki, *"Rearing Wolves to Our Own Destruction,"* 147.

123. Holley, "This Black Defender."

124. As historian Jarret Ruminski notes, there is an extensive literature on the resistance of enslaved people. See Jarret Ruminski, *The Limits of Loyalty: Ordinary People in Civil War Mississippi* (Jackson: University Press of Mississippi, 2017), 246–247 n15.

125. Walter Johnson, "Agency: A Ghost Story" in *Slavery's Ghost: The Problem of Freedom in the Age of Emancipation* by Richard Follett, Eric Foner, and Walter Johnson (Baltimore: Johns Hopkins University Press, 2011), 28, quoted in Ruminski, *Limits of Loyalty,* 149.

126. Walter Johnson, "On Agency," *Journal of Social History* 37, no. 1 (2003): 114.

127. Teresa Roane during interview with Sgt. Maj. James Haymes and author, June 9, 2014. This is a point she also made in a public lecture, "Teresa Roane Speaks on Southern Heritage," June 3, 2014, https://www.youtube.com/watch?v= NWujYlPDJ2U&t=1s.

128. Roane would resist the arguments made, for instance, in Ta-Nahesi Coates, "The Case for Reparations," *Atlantic,* June 2014, https://www.theatlantic.com/mag azine/archive/2014/06/the-case-for-reparations/361631/.

129. Roane, "Confederates of Color."

130. Roane, "Confederates of Color."

131. Memorial Service for Real Daughter of the Confederacy," *Times Examiner,* October 29, 2014, https://timesexaminer.com/historical/2024-memorial-service -for-real-daughter-of-the-confederacy.

132. "Memorial Service for Real Daughter of the Confederacy."

133. Roane, "Confederates of Color."

134. OPP HQ, "H. K. Edgerton," One People's Project, October 18, 2017, http://onepeoplesproject.com/2017/10/18/h-k-edgerton/.

4. Cooking Confederate and Nostalgic Reenactment

1. Bill Lohmann, "Southern Cooking Is Simple, Unpretentious and Delicious," *St. Petersburg Times,* August 20, 1987, 20-D.

2. Lohmann, "Southern Cooking Is Simple," 20-D.

3. Barbara Sullivan, "Home-Style Southern Food Satisfies," *Orlando Sentinel*, October 15, 1987, G-15.

4. Dupree was dubbed "the only woman since Julia Child to capture the airwaves with more than 100 public television shows airing concurrently on PBS and The Learning Channel." Janet Harrison English, "Thanks for the Memories," *Clarion-Ledger*, October 6, 1993, E-1.

5. Ree Drummond, from Pawhuska, Oklahoma, introduces herself to readers as a "desperate housewife" who "live[s] in the country." For more on her empire, see https://thepioneerwoman.com/.

6. Richard L. Eldredge, "Her 'Home Cooking' Travels Well," *Atlanta Constitution*, July 12, 2002, E-2.

7. Jana Hoops, "Classes Set for July 15 in Jackson," *Clarion-Ledger* (Jackson, MS), May 31, 2006, 5-A; Amy Culbertson, "Deen of Cuisine Shares Recipe for Life," *Detroit Free Press*, May 6, 2007, 8J.

8. Judith Schoolman, "Buying Martha Stewart: Maven of Style, Gracious Living Is Taking Her Company Public," *New York Daily News*, October 18, 1999, 35.

9. Richard L. Eldredge, "Busy Savannah Chef Whips Up Movie Role," *Atlanta Constitution*, August 20, 2004, B-2.

10. "About Paula," Paula Deen, n.d., accessed March 31, 2019, https://www.pauladeen.com/about-paula/.

11. Kristen Wiig first played Paula Deen in a March 2012 episode of *Saturday Night Live*.

12. Richard Fausset, "Former Deen Employee Alleges Racism," *Los Angeles Times*, March 6, 2012, A8.

13. Rod Dreher, "A Reluctant Defense of Paula Deen," *Press and Sun-Bulletin* (Binghamton, NY), July 7, 2013, 4C.

14. Amy Maclin, "Why I Feel Bad About Paula Deen," Oprah.com, May 2017, http://www.oprah.com/inspiration/paula-deen-racist-remarks-spawn-embarassment.

15. Jessica Chasmar, "Paula Deen Cookbooks Surge to Top Spots on Amazon Best Sellers," *Washington Times*, June 27, 2013, https://www.washingtontimes.com/news/2013/jun/27/paula-deen-cookbooks-surge-top-spots-amazon-best-s; Koa Beck, "Disturbing Wedding Trend: Getting Married at a Plantation," Salon.com, January 5, 2014, https://www.salon.com/2014/01/05/disturbing_wedding_trend_getting_married_at_a_plantation/. Plantation weddings are the subject of a project on which I am working tentatively titled "Southern Charm: Plantation Weddings, History, and Forgetting."

16. Marcie Cohen Ferris, *The Edible South: The Power of Food and the Making of an American Region* (Chapel Hill: University of North Carolina Press, 2014), 1.

17. Janet Theophano, *Eat My Words: Reading Women's Lives through the Cookbooks They Wrote* (New York: Palgrave, 2002), 6.

18. Amy Heyse, "Women's Rhetorical Authority and Collective Memory: The United Daughters of the Confederacy Remember the South," *Women and Language* 33, no. 2 (2010): 32. On the role of white women as arbiters of collective memory of the Confederacy, see also W. Fitzhugh Brundage, *The Southern Past: A Clash of Race and Memory* (Cambridge, MA: Harvard University Press, 2008), chap. 3; Karen L. Cox, *Dixie's Daughters: The United Daughters of the Confederacy and the Preservation of*

Confederate Culture (Tallahassee: University Press of Florida, 2003); Caroline E. Janney, *Burying the Dead but Not the Past: Ladies' Memorial Associations and the Lost Cause* (Chapel Hill: University of North Carolina Press, 2008).

19. Patricia G. Davis, "The *Other* Southern Belles: Civil War Reenactment, African American Women, and the Performance of Idealized Femininity," *Text and Performance Quarterly* 32, no. 4 (2012): 310–311.

20. Megan J. Elias has argued that engaging with southern cooking entails "a little historical reenactment." See Megan J. Elias, *Food on the Page: Cookbooks and American Culture* (Philadelphia: University of Pennsylvania Press, 2017), 41.

21. Scott Magelssen, "Living History Museums and the Construction of the Real Through Performance," *Theatre Survey* 45, no. 1 (2004): quoted in Elizabeth Carnegie and Scott McCabe, "Re-enactment Events and Tourism: Meaning, Authenticity and Identity," *Current Issues in Tourism* 11, no. 4 (2008): 363.

22. Alexander Cook, "The Use and Abuse of Historical Reenactment: Thoughts on Recent Trends in Public History," *Criticism* 46, no. 3 (2004): 487.

23. Cook, "Use and Abuse of Historical Reenactment," 490.

24. Elias, *Food on the Page*, 2. One popular example is culinary historian Michael W. Twitty's *The Cooking Gene: A Journey through African-American Culinary History in the Old South* (New York: HarperCollins, 2017), which received the 2018 James Beard Award for Best Food Writing and Book of the Year.

25. Elias, *Food on the Page*, 2.

26. See Part III, "Consuming the South: Foodways and Performance of Southern Culture," in Anthony J. Stanonis, ed., *Dixie Emporium: Tourism, Foodways, and Consumer Culture in the American South* (Athens: University of Georgia Press, 2008) for case studies considering food and foodways in southern culture.

27. Sydney Beveridge, "Freedom Fries, Liberty Cabbage, and Other Product Renamings," *Mental Floss*, July 14, 2008, http://mentalfloss.com/article/19061/get-your-country-out-my-happy-meal-liberty-cabbage-freedom-fries-and-other-product.

28. Thomas Germain, "A Racist Little Hat: The MSG Debate and American Culture," *Columbia Undergraduate Research Journal* 2, no. 1 (2017), https://curj.columbia.edu/article/a-racist-little-hat-the-msg-debate-and-american-culture/.

29. Irma and Marion Rombauer, "Mohrenkoepfe or Moors' Heads," in *Joy of Cooking* (Indianapolis: Bobbs-Merrill, 1964), 640.

30. Jen Chung, "Baker Now Apologizes for 'Drunken Negro Face' Cookies," *Gothamist*, January 24, 2009, http://gothamist.com/2009/01/24/baker_now_apologizes_for_drunken_ne.php.

31. Wilbur W. Caldwell, *Searching for the Dixie Barbecue: Journeys into the Southern Psyche* (Sarasota, FL: Pineapple Press, 2005), x.

32. Mark Spivak, *Moonshine Nation: The Art of Creating Cornbread in a Bottle* (Guilford, CT: Lyons Press, 2014).

33. Helen Worth, *Damnyankee in a Southern Kitchen* (Richmond, VA: Westover, 1971), vii.

34. Theophano, *Eat My Words*, 8.

35. Alyssa Rosenberg, "Why We Should Keep Reading 'Gone with the Wind,'" *Washington Post*, July 1, 2015, https://www.washingtonpost.com/news/act-four/wp/2015/07/01/why-we-should-keep-reading-gone-with-the-wind/?utm_term=.48ab13bcea5e.

36. Anne Carter Zimmer, *The Robert E. Lee Family Cooking and Housekeeping Book* (Chapel Hill: University of North Carolina Press, 2002); Stephen A. McLeod, ed., *Dining with the Washingtons: Historic Recipes, Entertainment, and Hospitality from Mount Vernon* (Chapel Hill: University of North Carolina Press, 2011); Damon Lee Fowler, *Dining at Monticello: In Good Taste and Abundance* (Charlottesville, VA: Thomas Jefferson Foundation, 2005).

37. "Punch Up Your Holiday," *Tennessean*, December 15, 1997, D1.

38. Bill Daily, "Mount Vernon's Life Wasn't Always a Party," *Chicago Tribune*, February 15, 2012, 3N.

39. Janie Nelson, "Native Son Has a Place in History: Stephen McLeod's Work at Mount Vernon Leads to Elegant Cookbook," *Tallahassee Democrat*, February 15, 2012, 21.

40. Jane Ammeson, "What Would Washington Eat? A Look at the Favorite Meals of Founding Fathers," *Times* (Munster, IN), July 5, 2014, C1.

41. Janie Nelson, "Try Recipes from 'Dining with the Washingtons,'" *Tallahassee Democrat*, February 15, 2012, 21.

42. Mrs. George Lyman, *Recipes from the Time of Washington until the Second World War* (Boston, 1942), 68.

43. For more on Jim Crow and the ways it permeated popular and material culture, see "What Was Jim Crow" and the accompanying Image Gallery, https://www.ferris.edu/jimcrow/what.htm.

44. Elias, *Food on the Page*, 41.

45. Daily, "Mount Vernon's Life."

46. Staff Reports, "DAR to Hold Washington Birthday Lunch," *Atlanta Constitution*, February 7, 2012, B5.

47. This was the premise of Julie Powell's *Julie and Julia: 365 Days, 524 Recipes, 1 Tiny Apartment Kitchen* (Boston: Little, Brown, 2005). The book was ultimately adapted into a film featuring Meryl Streep and Amy Adams, titled *Julie and Julia* (2009).

48. Zimmer, *Robert E. Lee Family Cooking*, 4.

49. Theophano, *Eat My Words*, 86.

50. William C. Davis, *The Civil War Cookbook* (Philadelphia: Courage Books, 2003), 10.

51. Andrew F. Smith, *Starving the South: How the North Won the Civil War* (New York: St. Martin's, 2011), 12–13, summarized in Ferris, *Edible South*, 50.

52. Some say the numbers grew into the thousands. Mary DeCredico, "Richmond Bread Riot," *Encyclopedia Virginia*, February 10, 2012, https://www.encyclopediavirginia.org/Bread_Riot_Richmond.

53. "Bread Riot in Richmond: Three Thousand Hungry Women Raging in the Streets. Government and Private Stores Broken Open," *New York Times*, April 8, 1863, https://www.nytimes.com/1863/04/08/archives/bread-riot-in-richmond-three-thousand-hungry-women-raging-in-the.html.

54. Heyse, "Women's Rhetorical Authority," 38.

55. "IX—The Confederate Receipt Book," *Semi-Weekly Standard (NC)*, August 4, 1863, 2.

56. Anne L. Bower, "Our Sisters' Recipes: Exploring 'Community' in a Community Cookbook," *Journal of Popular Culture* 31, no. 3 (1997): 137.

57. Chris Wohlwend, "Whether Slick or Stapled, Community Cookbooks Preserve Tasty Traditions while Raising a Lot of Dough for Some Worthy Causes," *Atlanta Constitution*, April 16, 1992, W1.

58. H. M. Price, "Heard on the Street Corners," *Marshall (TX) News Messenger*, December 13, 1942, 1.

59. "Yesteryear: Marshall in the Years Past," *Marshall (TX) News Messenger*, December 12, 1952, A4.

60. Gabriel is often referred to as Gabriel Prosser, bearing the last name of his enslaver. However, following historian Douglas Egerton, I include only Gabriel's first name here since "no contemporary document" uses the name Gabriel Prosser. Douglas R. Egerton, *Gabriel's Rebellion: The Virginia Slave Conspiracies of 1800 and 1802* (Chapel Hill: University of North Carolina Press, 1993), 189.

61. "Mary Randolph: First Burial at the Arlington Estate," n.d., accessed March 31, 2019, http://www.arlingtoncemetery.net/maryrand.htm.

62. "Meet 19th-Century Cookbook Author Mary Randolph," *Chesterfield Observer*, July 15, 2015, https://www.chesterfieldobserver.com/articles/meet-19th-century -cookbook-author-mary-randolph/.

63. "Ante Bellum Advice," *Tampa Tribune*, November 7, 1952, 36.

64. Ann McDuffie, "Bread Puddings Have Rich American Heritage," *Tampa Tribune*, November 3, 1964, 8-B.

65. Fred Arthur Bailey, "E. Merton Coulter," *New Georgia Encyclopedia*, April 1, 2003, http://www.georgiaencyclopedia.org/articles/history-archaeology/e-merton-coulter-1890-1981.

66. E. Merton Coulter, "Introduction," *Confederate Receipt Book: A Compilation of Over One Hundred Receipts, Adapted to the Times* (Athens: University of Georgia Press, 1960), 7.

67. For more on the relationship between consumption and power, see Ted Ownby, *American Dreams in Mississippi: Consumers, Poverty, and Culture, 1830–1998* (Chapel Hill: University of North Carolina Press, 1999).

68. "A Splendid Cup of Coffee with Acorns and Eggs," *Montgomery Advertiser*, August 13, 1961, 12.

69. See, for example, Jeanne Lesem, "Don't Try These Recipes," *Republic* (Columbus, IN), June 21, 1960, 7; "Views of Others: Recipes, 1863," *News-Press*, July 3, 1960, 7 (drawn from *LaGrange [GA] Daily News*).

70. "Reports Given UDC Chapter," *Statesville (AR) Record and Landmark*, November 22, 1971, 10. The *Danville (VA) Bee* also reported, "1863 Recipes Served UDC Chapter Members," November 3, 1971, 31.

71. Ritz Crackers "debuted" in 1934. Lisa Abraham, "No Apples? No Problem: You Can Make Pie If You Have a Box of Ritz Crackers," *Herald and Review* (Decatur, IL), December 31, 2009, D2.

72. Abraham, "No Apples?"

73. Coulter, "Introduction," 9.

74. "Splendid Cup of Coffee."

75. Heyse, "Women's Rhetorical Authority," 40.

76. B. Franklin Cooling, "Simmering South: From Antebellum Era to the Sunbelt" *Jackson (TN) Sun*, May 8, 1983, 18.

77. "1863 Recipes," *Danville Bee*, November 3, 1971, 31.

78. Patricia B. Mitchell, *Confederate Camp Cooking* (Chatham, VA: P. B. Mitchell, 1991).

79. Mitchell, *Confederate Camp Cooking*, 6.

80. Patricia B. Mitchell, *Mrs. Billy Yank's Receipt Book: Cooking on the Home Front* (Chatham, VA: P. B. Mitchell, 1993).

81. Heyse, "Women's Rhetorical Authority," 43.

82. Louis Szathmary, "Fried Catfish, Fritters Vied with New Elegance," *Akron Beacon Journal*, October 30, 1974, 81.

83. Karen Hess, "A Chronicle of Cookery," *New York Times*, July 28, 1974, https://www.nytimes.com/1974/07/28/archives/a-chronicle-of-cookery.html.

84. Elias, *Food on the Page*, 25.

85. "I Wish They Still Made Cookbooks Like This," *Honolulu Star-Bulletin*, April 13, 1969, 13.

86. Elias, *Food on the Page*, 26.

87. Charles Culbertson, "Cook Like It's 1877: Take a Page from an Old Recipe Book," *News Leader* (Staunton, VA), February 24, 2007, B9.

88. "I Wish They Still Made Cookbooks Like This."

89. Myra Waldo, "Our Gourmet President," *Honolulu Star-Bulletin*, April 13, 1969, 10.

90. Carol Botwin, "Young World," *Honolulu Star-Bulletin*, April 13, 1969, 14.

91. "Why in the World Would Any Woman Want a Cookbook That's 100 Years behind the Times?" *Times Standard* (Eureka, CA), January 10, 1971, 43.

92. Tara McPherson, *Reconstructing Dixie: Race, Gender, and Nostalgia in the Imagined South* (Durham, NC: Duke University Press, 2003), 53.

93. "The Tom Caricature," Jim Crow Museum of Racist Memorabilia, n.d., accessed March 31, 2019, https://ferris.edu/HTMLS/news/jimcrow/tom/homepage.htm.

94. John Egerton, "Foreword: A Gallery of Great Cooks," in *The Jemima Code: Two Centuries of African American Cookbooks*, ed. Toni Tipton-Martin (Austin: University of Texas Press, 2015), xi.

95. Joan Marie Johnson, "'Ye Gave Them a Stone': African American Women's Clubs, the Frederick Douglass Home, and the Black Mammy Monument," *Journal of Women's History* 17, no. 1 (2005): 63.

96. "Mrs. B. E. Moncure Writes Cook Book," *Daily Press* (Newport News, VA), July 4, 1937, 10.

97. For more on the effort to erect a Mammy monument in Washington, DC, see Johnson, "'Ye Gave Them a Stone,'" 62–86.

98. "'Emma Jane' Rites Sunday," *Daily Press* (Newport News, VA), May 23, 1953, 13.

99. "Mrs. B. E. Moncure Writes Cook Book."

100. "'Emma Jane' Rites Sunday," 13.

101. See Kelley Fanno Deetz, *Bound to the Fire: How Virginia's Enslaved Cooks Helped Invent American Cuisine* (Lexington, KY: University Press of Kentucky, 2017) for more on the history and legacies of enslaved cooks.

102. Theophano, *Eat My Words*, 8.

103. Elias, *Food on the Page*, 41.

104. Bower, "Our Sisters' Recipes," 143.

105. Kennan Ferguson, "Intensifying Taste, Intensifying Identity: Collectivity through Community Cookbooks," *Signs: Journal of Women in Culture* 37, no. 3 (2012): 704.

106. Sonja Gleaton, "Cookbook Gives a Taste of History," *Times and Democrat* (Orangeburg, SC), November 10, 2004, 17.

107. "Pelican's History," Pelican Publishing Company, n.d., accessed March 31, 2019, http://pelicanpub.com/about.php.

108. Ferguson, "Intensifying Taste," 698.

109. "Acknowledgements," in Lynda Moreau, ed., *The Confederate Cookbook: Family Favorites from the Sons of Confederate Veterans* (Gretna, LA: Pelican, 2000), 11.

110. "Confederate Cookbook: Family Favorites from the Sons of Confederate Veterans," *Times and Democrat* (Orangeburg, SC), October 4, 2000, 17.

111. Heyse, "Women's Rhetorical Authority," 32.

112. Dennis Abrams, "Pelican Expands the Meaning of 'Regional,'" *Publisher's Weekly*, November 17, 2017, https://www.publishersweekly.com/pw/by-topic/industry-news/publisher-news/article/75427-pelican-expands-the-meaning-of-regional.html.

113. Patrick J. Griffin, "Foreword," in Moreau, *Confederate Cookbook*, 9.

114. Laura Tutor, "Roadside Dining Attractions," *Anniston (AL) Star*, May 16, 2001, 1E.

115. Tutor, "Roadside: Culinary Inspiration from the Curb," *Anniston (AL) Star*, May 16, 2001, 5E.

116. It was not seen as a compromise to many. See Becky Little, "Why the Confederate Flag Made a 20th Century Comeback," *National Geographic*, June 6, 2015, https://news.nationalgeographic.com/2015/06/150626-confederate-flag-civil-rights-movement-war-history/.

117. Charles Kelly Barrow, "Sons of Confederate Veterans: A Century of Service, Heritage, and Honor," in Lynda Moreau, ed., *Sweetly Southern: Delicious Desserts from the Sons of Confederate Veterans* (Gretna, LA: Pelican, 2004), 13–14. Subsequent references to *The Confederate Cookbook* and *Sweetly Southern* are given parenthetically within the text.

118. Heyse, "Women's Rhetorical Authority," 39.

119. Kathleen Purvis, "Paula Deen Kicks Off Her $75M Comeback Campaign," *Arizona Daily Star*, September 27, 2014, Class 5.

5. Historical Diorama and Protecting the Confederate Habitat

1. "Barber Paints Richmond Scene," *Rappahannock (VA) Record*, October 30, 1997, 5.

2. "Barber Paints Richmond Scene"; "Biography," John Barber Art, n.d., accessed September 23, 2018, http://www.johnbarberart.com/about/.

3. "Barber Paints Richmond Scene."

4. "John Morton Barber," John Barber Art, n.d., accessed September 23, 2018, http://www.johnbarberart.com/.

5. "Barber's Maritime Art on Display at RW-C," *Rappahannock (VA) Record*, October 6, 1988, 3.

6. "Mercié Talks About Lee: The Model of the Statue as First Proposed European Option," *Richmond Dispatch*, May 25, 1890, 1.

7. For more on the power of equestrian statues, see Maurie D. McInnis, "To Strike 'Terror,'" in *Civil War in Art and Memory*, ed. Kirk Savage (New Haven, CT: Yale University Press, 2016), 125–146.

8. Monique Calello, "As Richmond's Confederate Statues Go, So Might the South's," *USA Today*, February 13, 2018, https://www.usatoday.com/story/news/nation-now/2018/02/11/black-history-month-richmond-confederate-statues/1001960001/.

9. Gary Robertson, "War's Lost, but the Fight Endures; Sons of Confederate Veterans Pushes Hard for the Things It Wants," *Richmond Times-Dispatch*, September 29, 1997, A-1.

10. Charles Reagan Wilson, *Baptized in Blood: The Religion of the Lost Cause, 1865–1920* (Athens: University of Georgia Press, 2009), 29.

11. Parke Rouse, "Richmond Keeps 'Cult of Confederacy' Alive," *Daily Press* (Newport News, VA), June 3, 1990, J3.

12. As of May 15, 2019, "Monument Avenue" has received 882 reviews on TripAdvisor and is ranked #13 of 156 things to do. See https://www.tripadvisor.com/Attraction_Review-g60893-d278375-Reviews-Monument_Avenue-Richmond_Virginia.html.

13. "Monument Avenue," Visit Richmond, VA, n.d., accessed March 31, 2019, https://www.visitrichmondva.com/listings/monument-avenue/913/. TripAdvisor has Monument Avenue ranked at #13, but the Visit Richmond site has not updated that ranking.

14. For more on the Art 180 mural controversy, see Richmond.com staff, "Monument Ave. Art 180 Staying Put," *Richmond Times-Dispatch*, March 26, 2012, https://www.richmond.com/arts-entertainment/monument-ave-art-staying-put/article_c23872b0-9d68-5375-8123-928b87652925.html; "Art 180 Ordered to Remove Portraits from Monument Avenue," Fan of the Fan, http://fanofthefan.com/2012/03/art-180-ordered-to-remove-portraits-from-monument-avenue/ (website no longer available); Vernal Coleman, "Political Permits," *Style Weekly*, April 10, 2012, https://www.styleweekly.com/richmond/political-permits/Content?oid=1696691; Vernal Coleman and Melissa Scott Sinclair, "Art 180 Murals Move across Monument," *Style Weekly*, April 17, 2012, https://www.styleweekly.com/richmond/art-180-murals-move-across-monument/Content?oid=1699046.

15. "Our Platform," CSA II: The New Confederate States of America, n.d., accessed March 31, 2019, http://www.newcsa.com/ourplatform.

16. "Ex-Confederate Capital Eyes Statues' Removal," *Lancaster (Ohio) Eagle-Gazette*, September 9, 2017, A2.

17. On the diorama, see Elizabeth Barlow Rogers, "Representing Nature: The Dioramas of the American Museum of Natural History," *SiteLINES: A Journal of Place* 8, no. 2 (2013): 10.

18. Donna Harraway, "Teddy Bear Patriarchy: Taxidermy in the Garden of Eden, New York City, 1908–1936," *Social Text* 11 (1984–1985): 24.

19. Chris Gatewood, "Sons of Confederate Veterans Mark 100th Anniversary," *News Leader (Staunton, VA)*, August 5, 1996, A3.

20. Carrie Johnson, "200 See Confederate Parade: Group Contends It's Devoted to Heritage, Not Hate," *Richmond Times-Dispatch*, August 5, 1996, B-1.

21. "Heritage Group Marks Civil War with Parade," *Daily Press* (Newport News, VA), February 26, 2012, A11.

22. "Annual Tour Showcases Virginia's Rich Natural and Cultural Heritage," *Rappahannock (VA) Record*, January 23, 2003, A8.

23. "Virginia Civil War Centennial" (advertisement), *Boston Globe*, June 4, 1961, 8-B.

24. Hank Kurz Jr., "Capital Hosting Worlds," *Daily Press* (Newport News, VA), September 15, 2015, Capital/B4.

25. "Richmond 2015 Bike Route Sparks Outrage: 'Horrific Embarrassment,'" NBC12, September 17, 2015, http://www.nbc12.com/story/30060142/richmond -2015-bike-route-sparks-outrage-horrific-embarrassment.

26. "Barber Paints Shockoe Slip," *Rappahannock (VA) Record*, April 16, 1998, B5.

27. "Along the Avenue," *Rappahannock (VA) Record*, June 8, 2000, A8.

28. "Barber Releases Monument Ave. Print," *Rappahannock (VA) Record*, June 29, 2000, C20.

29. "Gala Art Sale Is Successful for John Barber," *Rappahannock (VA) Record*, December 5, 2002, B8.

30. "Timeline," Lumpkin's Slave Jail Site/Devil's Half Acre Project, n.d., accessed March 31, 2019, http://www.lumpkinsjail.org/about/timeline/.

31. Larry O'Dell, "Virginia Apologizes for Role in Slavery," *Washington Post*, February 25, 2007, http://www.washingtonpost.com/wp-dyn/content/article/2007 /02/25/AR2007022500470.html.

32. "Graffiti Almost Gone," *Richmond Times-Dispatch*, February 21, 1998, B-3.

33. Chris Burritt, "Richmond in Tug of War over History," *Atlanta Journal-Constitution*, March 9, 2000, 4. For more on the burning of the mural at the floodwall and heritage tourism in Richmond, see Marie Tyler-McGraw, "Southern Comfort Levels: Race, Heritage Tourism, and the Civil War in Richmond," in *Slavery and Public History: The Tough Stuff of American Memory*, ed. James Oliver Horton and Lois E. Horton (Chapel Hill: University of North Carolina Press, 2006), 151–167.

34. "Sons Want Mural Burning Treated as Hate Crime," *Daily Press* (Newport News, VA), January 19, 2000, C3.

35. "Conservative Citizens Group Calls for 4-Months Boycott of Richmond," *Rappahannock (VA) Record*, February 24, 2000, A4.

36. Marc Fisher, "Still Binding Up a Nation's Wounds: Southerners Upset over Plan to Erect Statue of Lincoln in Richmond," *Daily Press* (Newport News, VA), February 16, 2003, Statue/K5.

37. Fisher, "Still Binding Up a Nation's Wounds"; Hamilton Lombard, "Richmond's Quiet Transformation," StatCh@t: From the Demographics Research Group at UVA, April 7, 2015, http://statchatva.org/2015/04/07/richmonds-quiet-trans formation/.

38. "Latest Effort to Honor Ashe Stirs Debate," *News Leader* (Staunton, VA), September 22, 2003, 2. In February 2019 Richmond city council voted to rename the Boulevard after Arthur Ashe. Mark Robinson, "Richmond City Council Renames Boulevard for Arthur Ashe," *Richmond Times-Dispatch*, February 11, 2019, https://

www.richmond.com/news/local/city-of-richmond/richmond-city-council-renames
-boulevard-for-arthur-ashe/article_7b8cb974-0ecb-55d4-a320-2f53ae2cf8d9.html.

39. Will Jones, "City's Mayoral Hopefuls Cautious on Davis Statue; They Avoid a Direct Stance on Offer by a Confederate Group," *Richmond Times-Dispatch*, July 1, 2008, B-3.

40. Steve Szkotak, "Is Davis Statue Just 'Tit-for-Tat'?" *Daily Press* (Newport News, VA), June 18, 2008, A9.

41. "Robert E. Lee Statue Vandalized," *News Leader*, January 18, 2004, 3.

42. "Stonewall's Richmond Likeness Gets a Rinse and a Fresh Wax Job," *News Leader* (Staunton, VA), August 5, 2004, 2.

43. Helene Cooper, "Virginia, a State in Flux, Is Also a State in Play," *New York Times*, May 4, 2012, https://www.nytimes.com/2012/05/05/us/politics/virginia-a -state-in-flux-is-also-a-state-in-play.html.

44. "Future of Richmond's Past," *Richmond's Journey*, n.d., accessed March 31, 2019, https://acwm.org/richmonds-journey/future.

45. Michael Paul Williams and Karin Kapsidelis, "Reconciling Our Past; Seeing Our Future," *Richmond Times-Dispatch*, January 24, 2010, A-1. I use the phrase "Slave Trail" as the official reference to the seventeen-marker path developed by the Richmond Slave Trail Commission in April 2011. The preferred name of the path by many, however, is the Trail of Enslaved People, which is more attentive to the role historical actors played in shaping this history.

46. Alan Suderman, "Richmond Confederate Monument Vandalized," *Daily Press* (Newport News, VA), June 26, 2015, A8.

47. Michael Paul Williams, "It's Time for Confederate Monuments to Come Down," *Richmond Times-Dispatch*, June 26, 2015, 1B.

48. Graham Moomaw and Brandon Shulleeta, "Jefferson Davis Statue on Monument Avenue Vandalized," *Richmond Times-Dispatch*, June 25, 2015, http://www .richmond.com/news/local/city-of-richmond/jefferson-davis-statue-on-monu ment-avenue-vandalized/article_251992bb-cf9a-58e6-9bcd-ec4d50dede87.html.

49. John Ramsey, "McAuliffe Orders Confederate Flag Off Virginia License Plates," *Richmond Times-Dispatch*, June 23, 2015, https://www.richmond.com/news /local/mcauliffe-orders-confederate-flag-off-virginia-license-plates/article _24731074-9400-5766-9dfb-56c92e310923.html.

50. For more on the tarring of the Stuart monument, see Nicole Maurantonio, "Tarred by History: Memory, Materiality, and Protest," *de arte* 53, nos. 2–3 (2018): 51–69.

51. Mark Robinson, "Richmond Has Spent $16,000 Cleaning Monuments in Last Two Years," *Richmond Times-Dispatch*, October 18, 2017, https://www.richmond .com/news/local/city-of-richmond/richmond-has-spent-cleaning-monuments-in -last-two-years/article_cf953ed0-e4fd-578e-a31a-a082ed6009b4.html.

52. On imaginings of the "frontier," see Joy S. Kasson, *Buffalo Bill's Wild West: Celebrity, Memory, and Popular History* (New York: Hill & Wang, 2000), 114–120.

53. Katherine Calos, "The Civil War 150th: From 'Behind the Lines,'" *Richmond Times-Dispatch*, February 16, 2012, A2.

54. Karen Wonders, "Habitat Dioramas as Ecological Theatre," *European Review* 1, no. 3 (1993): 285.

55. "Diorama Cutouts," *Highland Recorder* (Monterey, VA), May 21, 1937, 1.

56. Wonders, "Habitat Dioramas," 285.

57. Harraway, "Teddy Bear Patriarchy," 25.

58. Wonders, "Habitat Dioramas."

59. Karen A. Rader and Victoria E. M. Cain, *Life on Display: Revolutionizing U.S. Museums of Science and Natural History in the Twentieth Century* (Chicago: University of Chicago Press, 2014), 67, 69.

60. Rader and Cain, *Life on Display*, 63.

61. "Wrestling Leopards, Felling Apes: A Life in Taxidermy," *All Things Considered*, December 4, 2010, https://www.npr.org/2010/12/04/131107085/wrestling -leopards-felling-apes-a-life-in-taxidermy.

62. Mark Alvey, "The Cinema as Taxidermy: Carl Akeley and the Preservative Obsession," *Journal of Cinema and Media* 48, no. 1 (2007): 25.

63. Karen R. Jones, *Epiphany in the Wilderness: Hunting, Nature, and Performance in the Nineteenth-Century American West* (Boulder: University Press of Colorado, 2015), 230.

64. Among Akeley's colleagues was Frederick Webster, Little Sorrel's taxidermist, who had been known for "stereographic photographs of his taxidermy mounts." See "Chapter 7: Francis Lee Jaques and the American Museum of Natural History Bird Halls," n.d., accessed March 31, 2019, http://peabody.yale.edu/james-perry -wilson/chapter-7-francis-lee-jaques-and-the-bird-halls.

65. Rader and Cain, *Life on Display*, 58.

66. Rader and Cain, *Life on Display*, 78.

67. Rob Owen, "The City of Richmond through the Eyes of 'Homeland' Cast," *Richmond Times-Dispatch*, February 8, 2018, https://www.richmond.com/enter tainment/television/the-city-of-richmond-through-the-eyes-of-homeland-cast /article_3e4461c6-dcaa-5603-91c4-c1a9230a8542.html.

68. Frederick Jackson Turner, *The Frontier in American History* (New York: Henry Holt, 1921), http://www.gutenberg.org/files/22994/22994-h/22994-h.htm.

69. Rebecca M, "Wanted to visit in case they may be removed," TripAdvisor, August 6, 2018, https://www.tripadvisor.com/Attraction_Review-g60893-d278375 -Reviews-or40-Monument_Avenue-Richmond_Virginia.html.

70. "The Sale of the Season," *Richmond Dispatch*, May 3, 1873, 4.

71. "Restrictions," *Times Dispatch*, April 17, 1913, 11.

72. "Wednesday, April 21, 1897," *Richmond Dispatch*, April 8, 1897, 8.

73. "Wednesday, June 29, 1898," *Richmond Dispatch*, June 18, 1898, 8.

74. For more on the design competition for the Lee monument, see Kirk Savage, *Standing Soldiers, Kneeling Slaves: Race, War, and Monument in Nineteenth-Century America* (Princeton, NJ: Princeton University Press, 1997), 139–148.

75. "The Memory of Lee: Ceremonies Proposed at the Unveiling of Mercie's Statue," *Richmond Dispatch*, February 9, 1890, 8.

76. "The Souvenir 'Dispatch,'" *Richmond Dispatch*, May 28, 1890, 1.

77. Robert J. Cook, *Civil War Memories: Contesting the Past in the United States since 1865* (Baltimore: Johns Hopkins University Press, 2017), 61.

78. Whether or not this piece of rope has historical provenance, the mythology surrounding the rope signals significance unto itself. Lee Monument rope, Prints and Photographs, Library of Virginia.

79. "The Lee Monument Unveiling," *Richmond Planet*, May 31, 1890, 1. For additional documentation, see Claire Johnson, "Complicated History: The Memorial to Robert E. Lee in Richmond," Fit to Print, July 27, 2017, http://www.virginia memory.com/blogs/fit-to-print/2017/07/27/complicated-history-the-memorial -to-robert-e-lee-in-richmond/.

80. "The Lee Monument: History and Description of the Recumbent Figure of Gen. R. E. Lee," *Staunton (VA) Spectator*, July 3, 1883, 2.

81. "Mercié Talks About Lee."

82. Savage, *Standing Soldiers, Kneeling Slaves*, 135.

83. "Mercié Talks About Lee."

84. Edwin Slipek, "When Dali Met Sally," Style Weekly, May 27, 2014, https:// www.styleweekly.com/richmond/when-dali-met-sally/Content?oid=2079679; Kevin Concannon, "Dali in Virginia," *SECAC Review* 15, no. 5 (2010): 598–607.

85. Andrew Cain, "Virginia Women's Monument Will Include a New Confederate Statue to 'the Angel of the Lost Cause,'" *Richmond Times-Dispatch*, December 15, 2017, https://www.richmond.com/news/virginia/government-politics/virginia -s-women-s-monument-will-include-a-new-confederate/article_4cf6a6fa-7fa2-5725 -b533-0492ad52aabd.html.

86. Emily Spivack, "The Story of Elizabeth Keckley, Former-Slave-Turned-Mrs. Lincoln's Dressmaker," *Smithsonian*, April 24, 2013, https://www.smithsonianmag .com/arts-culture/the-story-of-elizabeth-keckley-former-slave-turned-mrs-lincolns -dressmaker-41112782/.

87. See, for instance, a letter from Mary J. Wood, "Confederate on Virginia Women's Monument 'Will Diminish' It," *Richmond Free Press*, February 9, 2018, http:// richmondfreepress.com/news/2018/feb/09/confederate-virginia-womens-monu ment-will-diminish/.

88. For more on Monument Avenue, see Matthew Mace Barbee, *Race and Masculinity in Southern Memory: History of Richmond, Virginia's Monument Avenue, 1948–1996* (Lanham, MD: Lexington Books, 2014). On the controversy surrounding the placement of the Arthur Ashe monument, see Leib, "Separate Times, Shared Spaces."

89. Michael Paul Williams, "'An Avenue for All': At Least Some of the City's Ghosts Are Exorcised at Ceremony," *Richmond Times-Dispatch*, July 11, 1996, A-1.

90. Gordon Hickey, "Statue' Path Wasn't Smooth: Debates Focused on Symbolism, Heroes, Justice, Site, Sculptor," *Richmond Times-Dispatch*, July 8, 1996, A-1.

91. "Message by Former Klan Leader Fuels Controversy over Lee Banner," *Daily Press* (Newport News, VA), July 16, 1999, 34.

92. Annette Pritchard and Nigel Morgan, "Mythic Geographies of Representation and Identity: Contemporary Postcards of Wales," *Journal of Tourism and Cultural Change* 1, no. 2 (2003): 111.

93. Gordon Waitt and Lesley Head, "Postcards and Frontier Mythologies: Sustaining Views of Kimberley as Timeless," *Environ Plan D* 20, no. 3 (2016): 319.

94. Elizabeth Edwards, "Postcards: Greetings from Another World," in *The Tourist Image: Myths and Myth Making in Tourism*, ed. T. Selwyn (London: Wiley, 1996), 201, quoted in Marion Markwick, "Postcards from Malta: Image, Consumption, Context," *Annals of Tourism Research* 28, no. 2 (2001): 422.

95. Atila Yüksel and Olcay Akgül, "Postcards as Affective Image Makers: An Idle Agent in Destination Marketing," *Tourism Management* 28, no. 3 (2007): 717.

96. Patricia C. Albers and William R. James, "Travel Photography: A Methodological Approach," *Annals of Tourism Research* 15, no. 1 (1988): 138–139.

97. Waitt and Head, "Postcards and Frontier Mythologies," 320.

98. Waitt and Head, "Postcards and Frontier Mythologies," 323.

99. Markwick, "Postcards from Malta," 420.

100. Albers and James, "Travel Photography," 136.

101. This quote is drawn from the back of a postcard representing the monument to Robert E. Lee.

102. I received assistance in dating the historic postcards from Bill Gilliam. For more on the early history of picture postcards in the United States, see George and Dorothy Miller, *Picture Postcards in the United States, 1893–1918* (New York: Clarkson N. Potter, 1976).

103. Markwick, "Postcards from Malta," 427.

104. Harry Kollatz, "The Story of Vindicatrix," *Richmond Magazine*, September 29, 2017, https://richmondmagazine.com/news/richmond-history/the-story-of -vindicatrix/.

105. This postcard is included among the collection within the Library of Virginia.

106. McInnis, "To Strike 'Terror.'"

107. Transcripts from the Monument Avenue Commission Public Forum held at Virginia Historical Society on August 9, 2017.

6. Heroes, Villains, and the Digital Confederacy

1. Megan Garber, "Why Charlottesville?" *Atlantic*, August 12, 2017, https://www .theatlantic.com/national/archive/2017/08/why-charlottesville/536700/.

2. "Jason Kessler," Southern Poverty Law Center (SPLC), n.d., accessed March 31, 2019, https://www.splcenter.org/fighting-hate/extremist-files/individual /jason-kessler.

3. Charles P. Pierce, "There's Blood on the Streets of Mr. Jefferson's Town," *Esquire*, August 10, 2018, https://www.esquire.com/news-politics/politics/a227 00465/charlottesville-anniversary-race-america/.

4. Kathryn Blackhurst, "Left Conflates Southern Heritage with Hate in Wake of Charlottesville," LifeZette, August 15, 2017, https://www.lifezette.com/2017/08 /left-conflates-southern-heritage-with-hate-in-wake-of-charlottesville/.

5. Carly Sitrin, "Read: President Trump's Remarks Condemning Violence 'on Many Sides' in Charlottesville," Vox, August 12, 2017, https://www.vox.com /2017/8/12/16138906/president-trump-remarks-condemning-violence-on-many -sides-charlottesville-rally.

6. Blackhurst, "Left Conflates Southern Heritage."

7. Libby Nelson, "'Why We Voted for Donald Trump': David Duke Explains the White Supremacist Charlottesville Protests," Vox, August 12, 2017, https://www .vox.com/2017/8/12/16138358/charlottesville-protests-david-duke-kkk.

8. According to the SPLC, the alternative right or "alt-right" "is a set of far-right ideologies, groups, and individuals whose core belief is that 'white identity' is under attack by multicultural forces using 'political correctness' and 'social justice'

to undermine white people and 'their civilization.'" For more on this definition, see "Alt-Right," SPLC, n.d., accessed March 31, 2019, https://www.splcenter.org /fighting-hate/extremist-files/ideology/alt-right.

9. Jonah Engel Bromwich, "White Nationalists Wield Torches at Confederate Statue Rally," *New York Times*, May 14, 2017, https://www.nytimes.com/2017/05/14 /us/confederate-statue-protests-virginia.html?module=inline.

10. Hawes Spencer and Matt Stevens, "23 Arrested and Tear Gas Deployed After a K.K.K. Rally in Virginia," *New York Times*, July 8, 2017, https://www.ny times.com/2017/07/08/us/kkk-rally-charlottesville-robert-e-lee-statue.html ?module=inline.

11. "Message from Past Commander-In-Chief Michael Given [*sic*]," Virginia Flaggers, June 22, 2015, http://vaflaggers.blogspot.com/2015/06/message-from -past-commander-in-chief.html. This message was also posted to the Virginia Flaggers Facebook group.

12. "Message from Past Commander-In-Chief."

13. This is a stance that was articulated also by Joshua Zeitz, "What Happened in Charlottesville Is All Too American," Politico, August 13, 2017, https://www .politico.com/magazine/story/2017/08/13/what-happened-in-charlottesville-is -all-too-american-215482.

14. Benjamin Wallace-Wells, "Corey Stewart's Virginia Restoration," *New Yorker*, June 13, 2018, https://www.newyorker.com/news/benjamin-wallace-wells/corey -stewarts-virginia-restoration.

15. Susan Du, "Duluth's Corey Stewart Turns Confederate Poster Boy in Virginia Governor Race," City Pages, April 27, 2017, http://www.citypages.com/news /duluths-corey-stewart-turns-confederate-poster-boy-in-virginia-governor-race /420512894.

16. Jane Coaston, "Virginia Republicans Just Nominated an Alt-Right Hero to Run for Senate," Vox, August 8, 2018, https://www.vox.com/2018/6/13/17458452 /alt-right-corey-stewart-virginia-gop.

17. Virginia Flaggers (@thevaflaggers), "Virginia Flaggers on the ground this afternoon, forwarding the colors at the #vmfa Virginia Museum of Fine Arts . . . ," Twitter, August 12, 2017, https://twitter.com/thevaflaggers/status/89648173 4136614922.

18. David Theo Goldberg, *The Threat of Race: Reflections on Racial Neoliberalism* (Malden, MA: Blackwell, 2009), 22.

19. For more on this cultural shift, see Angela Chan, *Kill All Normies: The Online Culture Wars from Tumblr and 4chan to the Alt-Right and Trump* (Winchester, UK: Zero Books, 2017). On alt-right memes, see Adrienne L. Massanari and Shira Chess, "Attack of the 50-Foot Social Justice Warrior: The Discursive Construction of SJW Memes as the Monstrous Feminine," *Feminist Media Studies* 18, no. 4 (2018): 525–542.

20. Chaim Noy, "Participatory Media and Discourse in Heritage Museums: Co-constructing the Public Sphere?" *Communication, Culture and Critique* 10, no. 2 (2016): 280, 282, 295.

21. Massanari and Chess, "Attack of the 50-Foot Social Justice Warrior," 538.

22. In her examination of Dixie-net, the Confederate Network, and the Heritage Preservation Association, media studies scholar Tara McPherson refers to the

"cyber-Confederacy." In this chapter, however, I refer to the "digital Confederacy" in an effort to underscore the ways in which the social media platforms I examine forge connections between individuals and groups of people. Tara McPherson, "I'll Take My Stand in Dixie-Net: White Guys, the South, and Cyberspace," in *Race in Cyberspace*, ed. Beth E. Kolko, Lisa Nakamura, and Gilbert B. Rodman (New York: Routledge, 2000), 117–131.

23. "Who Are the VA Flaggers?" The Virginia Flaggers, n.d., accessed March 31, 2019, https://vaflaggers.blogspot.com/.

24. McPherson, "I'll Take My Stand in Dixie-Net," 119. This work is also cited in Tara McPherson, *Reconstructing Dixie: Race, Gender, and Nostalgia in the Imagined South* (Durham, NC: Duke University Press, 2003), 105–115.

25. In mid-July 2018 the Charlottesville city council voted 4–1 to yet again rename the parks. Emancipation Park, formerly Lee Park, was renamed Market Street Park. Justice Park, formerly Jackson Park, was renamed Court Square Park. Councilor Wes Bellamy represented the lone vote against the resolution. "Charlottesville City Council changes the names of two renamed parks," *Daily Progress*, July 16, 2018, https://www.dailyprogress.com/news/local/city/charlottesville-city-coun cil-changes-the-names-of-two-renamed-parks/article_9ac64d52-8963-11e8-853a -a3864982745e.html.

26. Virginia Flaggers, Facebook, February 16, 2018, 10:51 p.m. References to Facebook are preserved in screenshots in the author's possession.

27. Virginia Flaggers, "Now playing #TarpWars #BoycottCVille #Southern Avenger," Facebook, February 25, 2018, 12:14 p.m.

28. Andrew Gordon, "Star Wars: A Myth of Our Time," *Literature/Film Quarterly* 6, no. 4 (1978): 314.

29. Emma Cott, "How Our Reporter Uncovered a Lie That Propelled an Alt-Right Extremist's Rise," *New York Times*, February 5, 2018, https://www.nytimes .com/2018/02/05/insider/confronting-a-white-nationalist-eli-mosley.html.

30. Paul Scanlon, "George Lucas: The Man Who Brought Back Fantasy," *Democrat and Chronicle* (Rochester, NY), August 29, 1977, G1, 6.

31. Scanlon, "George Lucas," G1.

32. Gordon, "Star Wars," 314.

33. Gordon, "Star Wars," 314.

34. Michael Wood, "The Ethics of 'Star Wars,'" *Honolulu Star-Bulletin*, August 24, 1980, B4.

35. Gordon, "Star Wars," 324, 315.

36. Aljean Harmetz, "The Stars of 'Star Wars': Artoo_detoo, See Threepio—Objects of Our Affection," *Detroit Free Press*, June 12, 1977, C1.

37. Bruce Schulman, *The Seventies: The Great Shift in American Culture, Society, and Politics* (Cambridge, MA: DaCapo Press, 2001), xv.

38. Harmetz, "The Stars of 'Star Wars,'" C1.

39. Dan Caffrey, "The 10 Best Star Wars Parodies," Consequences of Sound, May 21, 2018, https://consequenceofsound.net/2018/05/the-10-best-long-form -star-wars-parodies/full-post/.

40. Editorial Board, "Statue Tarps Fail to Address Real Issue," *Cavalier Daily*, February 8, 2018, http://www.cavalierdaily.com/article/2018/02/statue-tarps-fail -to-address-real-issue.

41. Alexis Gravely, "White Nationalists Gather for Another Torchlit Rally at Lee Statue," *Cavalier Daily*, October 7, 2017, http://www.cavalierdaily.com/article/2017/10/white-nationalists-gather-for-another-torchlit-rally-at-lee-statue.

42. Amy B. Wang, "Holocaust Denier Is Unopposed in GOP Primary in Illinois," *St. Louis Post-Dispatch*, February 6, 2018, A9.

43. Nathaniel Cary, "Templeton Tours Confederate Roots," *Greenville (SC) News*, February 3, 2018, AA1.

44. Rachel Ohm, "White Nationalist Heimbach Plans to Speak at UT," *Tennessean*, February 4, 2018, 13A.

45. Gordon, "Star Wars," 316, 318.

46. Gordon, "Star Wars," 319.

47. Amy Heyse, "Women's Rhetorical Authority and Collective Memory: The United Daughters of the Confederacy Remember the South," *Women and Language* 33, no. 2 (2010): 38.

48. Joseph Campbell, *The Hero with a Thousand Faces*, (Princeton: Princeton University Press, 1973), summarized in Gordon, "Star Wars," 320. For more on the "monomyth," see Campbell, *Hero with a Thousand Faces*, part 1, chapters 1–3.

49. Gordon, "Star Wars," 320.

50. "Who Are the VA Flaggers?"

51. Gordon, "Star Wars," 321.

52. Jason Bainbridge, "Beyond the Law: What Is So 'Super' about Superheroes and Supervillains?" *International Journal for the Semiotic of Law* 30, no. 3 (2017): 369.

53. Federico Pagello, "The 'Origin Story' Is the Only Story'": Seriality and Temporality in Superhero Fiction from Comics to Post-Television," *Quarterly Review of Film and Video* 34, no. 8 (2017): 732.

54. "Now playing #TarpWars #BoycottCVille #SouthernAvenger."

55. Virginia Flaggers, Facebook, July 21, 2018, 3:51 p.m.

56. Virginia Flaggers, "A Young Man Traveled to Charlottesville Today to Stand Guard at the LEE Monument in LEE Park . . ." Facebook, August 15, 2017.

57. My claim here aligns with what McPherson writes of the "cyber-Confederacy": it "reconfigure[s] white Southern masculinity by borrowing from the language of the civil rights struggle." McPherson, "I'll Take My Stand in Dixie-Net," 120.

58. Thomas J. Sugrue, "Restoring King," *Jacobin*, January 18, 2016, https://www.jacobinmag.com/2014/01/restoring-king/.

59. Blackhurst, "Left Conflates Southern Heritage."

60. Virginia Flaggers, "Pretty much . . ." Facebook, August 19, 2017.

61. Jennifer Hyland Wang, "'A Struggle of Contending Stories': Race, Gender, and Political Memory in *Forrest Gump*," *Cinema Journal* 39, no. 2 (2000): 93.

62. HR Thau Comment on Virginia Flaggers, "Pretty much . . ." Facebook, August 19, 2017.

63. Jack Lule, *Daily News, Eternal Stories: The Mythological Role of Journalism* (New York: Guilford, 2001), 57.

64. Campbell, *Hero with a Thousand Faces*, summarized in Gordon, "Star Wars," 324.

65. G. Thomas Goodnight, "Ronald Reagan's Re-formulation of the Rhetoric of War: Analysis of the 'Zero Option,' 'Evil Empire,' and 'Star Wars' Addresses," *Quarterly Journal of Speech* 72 (1986): 391.

66. Goodnight, "Ronald Reagan's Re-formulation," 400.

67. Virginia Flaggers, "Enough time has passed for municipalities around the country . . ." Facebook, February 24, 2018, 11:30 p.m.

68. Between 1986 and 1988 and again from 1991 to 1992, writer William Shetterly and artist Vince Stone published the comic *Captain Confederacy*. Unlike the "Southern Avenger" I discuss in this chapter, *Captain Confederacy* explores a future South in which the Confederacy succeeded—yielding a racially segregated Jim Crow South. McPherson writes, "*Captain Confederacy* is not anti-South; from within its frames emerges a fondness for the region and many of its rhythms, but there is also a recognition of the complexities of place and the responsibilities born of historical memory. Neither is southernness naturalized as whiteness." McPherson, *Reconstructing Dixie*, 144.

69. Rebecca Wanzo, "The Superhero: Meditations on Surveillance, Salvation, and Desire," *Communication and Critical/Cultural Studies* 6, no. 1 (2009): 93.

70. One exception has been Ryan Coogler's *Black Panther*, which premiered during the same month the Tarp Wars meme was at its height. Annabel Rackham, "Why Marvel's Black Panther Is No Ordinary Superhero Movie," *BBC News*, February 9, 2018, https://www.bbc.com/news/entertainment-arts-42992914; Tre Johnson, "Black Superheroes Matter: Why a 'Black Panther' Movie Is Revolutionary," *Rolling Stone*, February 16, 2018, https://www.rollingstone.com/movies/movie-news/black-superheroes-matter-why-a-black-panther-movie-is-revolutionary-198678/.

71. Wanzo, "Superhero," 93.

72. Pagello, "'Origin Story,'" 729, italics in original.

73. Umberto Eco, "The Myth of Superman: The Amazing Adventures of Superman," *Diacritic* 2, no. 1 (1972): 15.

74. Pagello, "'Origin Story,'" 728, 732.

75. "Richmond Man Charged in Connection to Justice Park Incident," NBC29.com, February 23, 2018, http://www.nbc29.com/story/37578058/christopher-james-wayne-arrest-02-23-2018. The Virginia Flaggers posted an interview conducted by Rob Schilling with Chris Wayne, https://www.facebook.com/watch/?v=1200415270093148.

76. "Richmond Man Arrested for Third Time on Charges Related to Confederate Statues," *Daily Progress*, February 23, 2018, https://www.dailyprogress.com/news/crime/richmond-man-arrested-for-third-time-on-charges-related-to/article_4eeb6e74-18d1-11e8-abe1-b759ec4a8cb8.html.

77. Virginia Flaggers, "#BreakingNews Southern Avenger arrested late last night in Jackson Park in Charlottesville after tarps covering both the Lee and Jackson monuments were removed six times over the past two weeks . . ." Facebook, February 23, 2018, 3:18 a.m.

78. Virginia Flaggers, "#BREAKINGNEWS Lee rides again! On the eve of the scheduled ruling tomorrow regarding the illegal tarps in Charlottesville . . ." Facebook, February 27, 2018, 1:30 a.m.

79. Virginia Flaggers (@thevaflaggers), "#winning #TarpWars," Twitter, February 27, 2018, https://twitter.com/thevaflaggers/status/968654422371897345.

80. Nick Carbone, "Top 10 Memes of 2011, 4. #winning by Charlie Sheen," *Time*, December 7, 2011, http://content.time.com/time/specials/packages/article/0,28804,2101344_2100875_2100912,00.html.

81. David Weigel, "The Avenger without a Mask," *Slate*, August 5, 2014, http://www.slate.com/articles/news_and_politics/politics/2014/08/jack_hunter_the_former_southern_avenger_rand_paul_s_ex_aide_makes_a_comeback.html.

82. Jack Hunter, "The 'Southern Avenger' Repents: I Was Wrong about the Confederate Flag," *Daily Beast*, June 22, 2015, https://www.thedailybeast.com/the-southern-avenger-repents-i-was-wrong-about-the-confederate-flag.

83. Milo Yiannopolous, "Jack Hunter: Anatomy of a Cuckening," *Breitbart*, May 6, 2016, http://www.breitbart.com/milo/2016/05/06/anatomy-of-a-cuckening/.

84. Jim Ehlen (@jpe33180), "So the #SouthernAvenger has turned over a new leaf but leaves me wondering what he was avenging in the first place," Twitter, June 25, 2015, https://twitter.com/jpe33180/status/613958951302893568.

85. Virginia Flaggers (@thevaflaggers), "WCSC: 'If I were KKK would I hold you like this?, widespread picture shows peace in Virginia," Twitter, August 19, 2017, https://twitter.com/thevaflaggers/status/899069056761966593.

86. Kevin Fuller, "What a bunch of uneducated dumbasses . . ." Virginia Flaggers, Facebook, August 15, 2017.

87. Shaun Smith, "They act the way they do bc . . ." Virginia Flaggers, Facebook, August 15, 2017.

88. "1960 Sugar Bowl LSU vs Ole Miss," Virginia Flaggers, Facebook, July 28, 2018.

89. Virginia Flaggers (@thevaflaggers), "Why do Italian soccer fans and other foreigners fly the Confederate flag?" Twitter, July 12, 2018, https://twitter.com/thevaflaggers/status/1017491209462472704.

90. Virginia Flaggers (@thevaflaggers), "Gods and Generals: Bob Dylan 'Cross the Green Mountain' Music Video," Twitter, July 4, 2018, https://twitter.com/thevaflaggers/status/1014650993160663040.

91. Gary W. Gallagher, *Causes Won, Lost, and Forgotten: How Hollywood and Popular Art Shape What We Know about the Civil War* (Chapel Hill: University of North Carolina Press, 2008), 147, 143.

92. Virginia Flaggers (@thevaflaggers), "Are You Southern Enough to Finish ALL These Southern Phrases? Bet Not!" Twitter, July 28, 2018, https://twitter.com/thevaflaggers/status/1023199048357081088.

93. Virginia Flaggers (@thevaflaggers), "20 quotes that'll make you fall in love with being Southern all over again," Twitter, July 9, 2018, https://twitter.com/thevaflaggers/status/1016370237724389377.

94. Virginia Flaggers (@thevaflaggers), "Well . . . duh!" Twitter, July 26, 2018, https://twitter.com/thevaflaggers/status/1022316689688592384.

95. Virginia Flaggers (@thevaflaggers), "Here's why southerners refer to all soft drinks as 'coke,'" Twitter, July 19, 2018, https://twitter.com/thevaflaggers/status/1020136573936066560.

96. McPherson observes this as well in the so-called "cyber-Confederacy," noting that "almost all of the sites decry any racism, hate-mongering, or Klan or neo-Nazi activity." She summarizes, "Often, the pages express dismay (some seemingly genuine, others less so) over the continued perceptions that protecting Southern heritage means one must be racist." McPherson, "I'll Take My Stand in Dixie-Net," 124.

Conclusion: The Future of the Neo-Confederate Museum

1. Virginia Historical Society (VHS) was renamed the Virginia Museum of History and Culture in February 2018.

2. This quote is drawn from the transcripts of the Monument Avenue Commission Public Forum on August 9, 2017. I thank Kelley Libby for providing me with the audio.

3. Sara McCloskey, "New Monument Highlighting Historic African Americans Coming to Richmond," WAVY.com, July 10, 2018, https://www.wavy.com/news /local-news/new-monument-highlighting-historic-african-americans-coming-to -richmond/1294625126. More on the Emancipation Proclamation and Freedom Monument can be seen on the website of the Virginia Martin Luther King, Jr. Memorial Commission, http://mlkcommission.dls.virginia.gov/lincoln/monument .html.

4. In addition to the monuments mentioned, several of the statues included as part of the Virginia Women's Monument, scheduled to be dedicated on October 14, 2019, will increase the number of Black women commemorated in statue form. For the list of the twelve women chosen to be depicted as part of the Virginia Women's Monument, see http://womensmonumentcom.virginia.gov/thetwelve.html.

5. Nancy Sorrells, "Va. Historical Society a valuable keeper of history," *News Leader* (Staunton, VA), November 5, 2001, A3.

6. Charles Stafford, "Embers in Memory of Civil War Still Alive," *Daily Press* (Newport News, VA), April 23, 1961, 12-D.

7. The first part was built in 1913. As the "History of the Battle Abbey" notes, the structure was "built in seven stages between 1912 and 2014." Virginia Museum of History and Culture, accessed March 31, 2019, http://68.169.55.4/collections -and-resources/virginia-history-explorer/history-battle-abbey.

8. "Virginia Museum of History and Culture," The History List, accessed March 31, 2019, https://www.thehistorylist.com/venues/virginia-museum-of-history-cul ture-richmond-virginia.

9. Associated Press, "A Piece of History Unearthed at Virginia Historical Society," *News Leader* (Staunton, VA), May 28, 2012, 3.

10. Marc Cheatham, "Monument Avenue Commission's Goal Did Not Motivate Me to Leave My House," WTVR, August 11, 2017, https://wtvr.com/2017/08/11 /marc-cheatham-monument-avenue-1/.

11. Cristela Guerra, "Deconstructing the Confederate Flag," *Boston Globe*, February 26, 2018, B2.

12. This quotation is drawn from the transcripts of the Monument Avenue Commission Public Forum on August 9, 2017.

13. This quotation is drawn from the transcripts of the Monument Avenue Commission Public Forum on August 9, 2017.

14. Mark Robinson, "'It's Theater of the Absurd': Monument Avenue Commission's First Public Hearing Borders on Chaotic," *Richmond Times-Dispatch*, August 9, 2017, http://www.richmond.com/news/local/city-of-richmond/it-s-theater-of -the-absurd-monument-avenue-commission-s/article_48b3cf9d-9d87-5bd9-9405 -ce20b4111dbf.html.

15. RVA Mag (@RVAmag), "Tensions flare at first Monument Avenue Commission #rva #confederate @LevarStoney," Twitter, August 10, 2017, https://twitter.com/RVAmag/status/895713438239825921.

16. Loveless Brad (@Bcox42), "Dear @Levar Stoney & Monument Avenue Commission, here are my proposed changes to add 'context' to Richmond's Confederate monuments," Twitter, August 11, 2017, https://twitter.com/Bcox42/status/895970079103475717.

17. Patrick Wilson (@patrickmwilson), "@RTDMPW: Stoney's Monument Avenue panel is veering toward dead end," Twitter, August 11, 2017, https://twitter.com/patrickmwilson/status/895993210622947329.

18. Shawn Cox (@ShawnCoxRTD), "Column from @RTDMPW: Stoney tried to straddle fence on Monument Avenue, but the fence is now on fire #RVAmonuments," Twitter, August 10, 2017, https://twitter.com/ShawnCoxRTD/status/895840085651980288.

19. Flyer collected on August 9, 2017, at the Monument Avenue Commission, in the author's possession.

20. Michael Paul Williams, "Stop Pitting Statues Against Richmond's Schools," *Richmond Times-Dispatch*, August 31, 2017, https://www.richmond.com/news/local/michael-paul-williams/williams-stop-pitting-statues-against-richmond-s-schools/article_83fb7c2e-0a26-5ae9-913b-5939a1c3d878.html.

21. Flyer collected on August 9, 2017, at the Monument Avenue Commission, in the author's possession.

22. Susan Du, "Duluth's Corey Stewart Turns Confederate Poster Boy in Virginia Governor Race," *City Pages*, April 27, 2017, http://www.citypages.com/news/duluths-corey-stewart-turns-confederate-poster-boy-in-virginia-governor-race/420512894. For a video of Stewart's public speech at the "Old South" ball in Danville, Virginia, see https://www.youtube.com/watch?v=t4rk6a1za4Y.

23. For more on Stewart, see Kevin Robillard, "Corey Stewart's Lost Cause," Politico, May 15, 2017, https://www.politico.com/magazine/story/2017/05/15/why-corey-stewart-thinks-the-lost-cause-is-a-winning-strategy-215138.

24. Andrew Kaczynski and Nathan McDermott, "Corey Stewart Praised Southern Secession in 2017 Campaign Appearance," CNN Politics, August 8, 2018, https://www.cnn.com/2018/08/08/politics/kfile-corey-stewart-southern-secession/index.html.

25. Laura Vozzella, "As Va. GOP Seeks New Course, Corey Stewart Says He's Finished with Statewide Politics," *Washington Post*, December 15, 2018, https://www.washingtonpost.com/local/virginia-politics/as-va-gop-seeks-a-new-course-corey-stewart-says-hes-done-statewide/2018/12/15/f7b7c706-fe35-11e8-83c0-b06139e540e5_story.html?utm_term=.158b4203a144.

26. "'Politics Sucks': GOP's Corey Stewart Quits Field Altogether," AP News, January 8, 2019, https://www.apnews.com/ff3142b056d940688956019cc4db8fb4.

27. These quotations are drawn from the transcripts of the Monument Avenue Commission Public Forum on August 9, 2017.

28. This quotation is drawn from the transcripts of the Monument Avenue Commission Public Forum on August 9, 2017.

29. See Peter Holley, "Why This Black Defender of the Confederate Flag Says

Slavery Was 'a Choice,'" *Washington Post,* June 30, 2015, https://www.washington post.com/news/morning-mix/wp/2015/06/30/why-some-black-defenders-of-the -confederate-flag-believe-slavery-was-a-choice/?utm_term=.4d479cf1a923.

30. Karen Cooper, interview with author, May 2014.

31. Goad was previously referred to as Goad Gatsby. Goad KC is a name he uses in public materials as well. David Streever, "Crowd Assembled to Yell at Lee Statue, While Drinking Out of Brown Bags," *RVAMag,* October 23, 2017, https://rvamag .com/news/crowd-assembles-to-yell-at-lee-statue-while-drinking-out-of-brown-bags .html.

32. Austin Walker, "Facebook Protests—Serious or Not—Get People Moving," Medium, December 5, 2017, https://medium.com/@AWalk3r/facebook-protests -serious-or-not-get-people-moving-9a7523d272c2.

33. Logan Jaffe and Zachary Sigelko, "One Hipster's Battle against the Confederate Flaggers," *Atlantic,* June 23, 2015, https://www.theatlantic.com/video /index/396503/hipsters-battle-against-confederate-flaggers/.

34. I purchased one such book while at Washington and Lee. See Margaret Samdahl, *"My Colt": The Story of Traveller,* illustrated by Carol Blair (2018), which tells the story of General Robert E. Lee's warhorse.

35. Susan A. Crane, "Memory, Distortion, and History in the Museum," *History and Theory* 36, no. (1997): 46.

36. These quotes are drawn from the plaques visible within the Jefferson Davis Memorial Chapel on the seventeenth floor of the West Hospital at the Virginia Commonwealth University Medical Center.

37. "For the Glory of God and to the memory of Jefferson Davis," MCV Chapel.

38. The petition can be accessed at https://petitions.moveon.org/sign/rename -the-jefferson (accessed March 31, 2019).

39. Laura Vozzella, "Poll Shows 'Trump Effect' on Face for Va. Governor," *News Leader,* September 27, 2017, 5A.

40. Monument Avenue Commission Report (2018), Prepared for the Office of the Mayor and City Council, City of Richmond, Virginia, July 2, 2018, https://blox images.newyork1.vip.townnews.com/richmond.com/content/tncms/assets/v3 /editorial/9/8d/98dfbab1-3a10-52d4-ab47-f4a2d9550084/5b3a9346537e5.pdf.

41. Jeff E. Schapiro, "Kings Dominion Renaming Iconic Rebel Yell Roller Coaster," *Richmond Times-Dispatch,* February 3, 2018, https://www.richmond.com /business/local/kings-dominion-renaming-iconic-rebel-yell-roller-coaster /article_5c754b18-61de-51ec-8590-a0a118b5378a.html.

42. Reflecting on the one-year anniversary of the deadly Unite the Right rally in Charlottesville, Virginia, the *New York Times* published an op-art, "Monuments for a New Era," *New York Times,* August 10, 2018, https://www.nytimes.com/2018/08/10 /opinion/charlottesville-confederate-monuments.html.

43. Emily Elizabeth Goodman, "Unraveling the Complicated Confederacy Legacy, One Strand at a Time," Hyperallergic, October 22, 2017, https://hyperallergic .com/406577/sonya-clark-unraveling-speed-museum-of-art-2017/.

44. The book was sent in response to my quote in Christopher Torchia, "Remove or Keep a Statue? South Africa Debates Painful Legacy," December 16, 2018, https://www.dailyherald.com/article/20181216/news/312169903.

45. H. V. Traywick Jr., *The Monumental Truth: Five Essays on Confederate Monuments in the Age of Progressive Identity Politics* (Manakin-Sabot, VA: Dementi Milestone, 2018), iv.

46. Traywick, *Monumental Truth*, 3.

47. Traywick, *Monumental Truth*, 4.

48. Andrew M. Davenport, "A New Civil War Museum Speaks Truths in the Former Capital of the Confederacy," *Smithsonian*, May 2, 2019, https://www.smithsonianmag.com/history/civil-war-museum-speaks-truths-former-capital-of-confederacy-180972085/?utm_source=twitter.com&utm_medium=socialmedia.

49. Gregory S. Schneider, "Richmond's New Civil War Museum Aims to Shatter Conventional Views of the Conflict," *Washington Post*, April 26, 2019, https://www.washingtonpost.com/local/virginia-politics/richmonds-new-civil-war-museum-aims-to-shatter-conventional-views-of-the-conflict/2019/04/26/f0b7e7ce-6785-11e9-a1b6-b29b9oefa879_story.html?utm_term=.d46d996e7283.

50. Schneider, "New Civil War Museum."

Index